TOTAL QUA
LEADERSHI
A TRAINING
APPROACH

JOSEPH LOUIS PICOGNA

International Information Associates, Inc.
Morrisville, Pennsylvania U.S.A.

Library of Cong[illegible]: 93-77639

Picogna, Joseph L.

Total Quality Leadership: A Training Approach

ISBN 0-945510-15-2

International Information Associates, Inc.
P.O. Box 773, Morrisville, PA 19067 U.S.A.

Current Printing [last digit]:

10 9 8 7 6 5 4 3 2 1

Printed in the United States of America

"Only mediocre people are always at their best"
- Somerset Maugham-

DEDICATION

To Joan Katz,
In Memory Of The Blessings
That You Shared With Us!

Table of Contents

Appendices
.... The "Microlabs"

FOREWORD

This is a unique work, a first in many respects because it represents a comprehensive reference manual which links three critical aspects of the training enterprise, determining priorities, planning and producing interventions, and implementing programs, the key aspects of any organization development effort. In addition, these topics are linked to the total quality efforts that should be paramount in any contemporary organization, are presented in an easy to read format and offer a wealth of practical examples. The author is an experienced program development expert and accomplished trainer, and his anecdotes present a very refreshing sense of realism to the subject matter. The material is timely, applies to organizations in both the private and public sectors, and is a valuable teaching tool. It is a must for those employed as or aspiring to be, organization and management development specialists. As an educator, I can recall what now seems to be a rather short-lived yet halcyon attempt from the 1960's to the 1970's, to improve the quality of instruction in classrooms. Joseph Picogna has captured the essence of that time and translated the essentials of development into a book that should be important to those who work in a boardroom or classroom, those interested in moving their organizations forward and making their people more productive.

D. Barry MacGibney, Haddon Township, New Jersey

ACKNOWLEDGMENTS

We learn in a variety of ways, by doing, by observing, and, by coming under the influence of others. My career has been blessed by the presence of individuals who were effective role models not only because they cared enough to impart knowledge, but because they possessed the skills to do so. It is to the Temple University community that I seem to turn when searching for new learning techniques, new ways of nurturing others, of building relationships. Ted Amidon, a distinguished professor, who embodies what some might call "presence," the ability to invite others to be comfortable and participate with him. Ted introduced me to program design and demonstrated a standard for professionalism that I have attempted, unsuccessfully, to match over the last twenty years.

My current chairperson, Stuart Schimdt, is a true behavioral scientist with an uncanny knack for influencing others and building strong interpersonal relationships. His support for my experimentation into new arenas and his capacity to see clearly the essence of an issue, have proven invaluable to my own self-improvement efforts. Naomi Decter and Sonia Voynow, two dynamic individuals who demonstrate, on a daily basis, the skill capacities illustrated in Part I of this book. They have led many clients to a realization of program needs and provided me with ample opportunities to validate the techniques contained herein. Dorothy Seegers, the first support staff person who for me exemplified the role of the executive behind the scenes. It was she who taught me the importance of manager as developer and the value of providing training for those who make organizations successful, the secretaries, clerks, and others like them who carry the burden of achieving total quality. My students, who over these many years, have constantly challenged me to increase my standards to meet their growing abilities.

My life-long friend, John Flynn, whose ability to keep things in perspective is a priceless asset. Earl Johnson, who taught me the value of modeling expectations and constantly training each individual to be able to assume responsibility for the whole, regardless of the size of the organization. My managing editor and publisher, Richard Bradley, and foremost, my loving wife Marie, who performed the monumental task of copy-editing the manuscript and, who, as a third grade teacher, constantly reminds me of the joy of influencing others.

Finally, to the thousands of trainees that I have encountered, may you share my appreciation for the time that we spent together.

CONTRIBUTORS

The following graduate students were all human resource practitioners when they completed the MBA concentration in training at Temple University. They are the developers of the practicum models that are presented throughout the text:

Kristen Braughler	Mary Anne Kowalick
Susan Carrochi	Pamela Lieb
Brian Holt	John Matlaga
Jennifer Johnson	Wendy McKeon
Pamel Kennedy	Patricia Robson

PREFACE

We live in an age in which organizations in both the private and public sectors face the challenge of constantly upgrading the capacity of their work force. Companies now proclaiming their everlasting dedication to quality, are, in effect, confirming the notion that their people are the means by which they will become more productive and that effective leadership is the means to this end. Developing an appropriate organizational culture and establishing climates by which work teams learn to use their collective strengths to mitigate individual weaknesses are functions of the supervisory process. For example, a popular notion reflected in most management texts these days is that staff need to be "brought on board" through a participatory process rather than be coopted into performing key tasks. Yet such skills are beyond the experience base of most managers. An effective program of training can help managers recognize their responsibility to act in a developmental manner toward staff, an important first step on the road to quality. There are no simple solutions to this dilemma. One rather basic and viable tool for addressing this type of problem is training. More than $30 billion will be spent on training this year. Yet much of what transpires under the rubric of training can be characterized as extremely counterproductive in meeting the real needs of an organization. Recently a so-called "training officer" of a large public domain organization contacted me for the purpose of determining my interest in providing workshops for "her staff". She referred to my reputation as a trainer as a factor which would enhance the credibility of her efforts. Her specific interest was in the area of "...training people in sexual harassment." After stifling the temptation to ask her if she was looking for a how-to manual, I informed her that I had several programs which focused on managing diversity but that I needed some specific information to customize a training scenario that would best meet her needs. Her response, unfortunately, was of a type that I have encountered all too frequently in my career. She had no real assessment of program needs. She was interested in a price and was motivated primarily by a requirement passed down from on high to provide each staff member in the organization with "training" in sexual harassment. She was also very proud of her "model," that is, the means by which she would save money and meet the mandate. This involved training almost 1500 people in one day, meeting 250 an hour, allowing 10 minutes for each group to migrate into the training center. I told her that I had no interest in helping her complete a checklist at the expense of all hope of achieving behavioral change and that she should negotiate for a better resource base if the topic was at all important to the organization. Her response was also rather typical. She stated that all training was delivered in this manner because the staff was expected to return promptly to their jobs and further that she was routinely given charges and expected to complete them in a cost-effective manner. I was also told that she anticipated having no difficulty hiring someone who would be more cooperative. I am sure she was correct concerning that item!

The story is true and the scene is being repeated daily throughout the country. Much of what is termed training is actually unplanned and lacks effectiveness. Indeed, to many disaffected employees, attempts to train them to acquire new skills all too often have the impact of an additional control mechanism, a rigid management response that will require even more work to be performed. This book involves different ways of tackling this problem. It is designed to provide those charged with organizing the learning process with the skills necessary to build a viable training climate, develop a constituency for growth, deliver successful programs, and measure the recurring impact of training in the workplace.

PART I: ASSESSING THE NEED: A SYSTEM APPROACH

INTRODUCTION

What is training? Why is it important to the process of total quality management? The former question can be answered in a variety of ways, depending on the perspective of the respondent. Most frequently, I am told that training is a management function necessary to effect change, and moreover, that such change is reflected in the areas of knowledge, skills, and abilities. If we accept this position as being valid, how can we articulate the importance of training to the TQM enterprise? One key variable is the function of "management" in our definition of training. If we define management as the art and science of getting things done, with and through people, then the role of training in any systematic organization development becomes clear. Training is a dynamic process, it is a natural artifact and consequence of becoming more productive in whatever endeavor an organization engages in, from manufacturing truck tires, to providing service, to building a constituency in a local municipality. *Quality means doing things right the first time and every time, and training is our most valuable tool in accomplishing this end.*

Building teams, empowering staff, mitigating resistance to change, these worthy initiatives are the kinds of objectives that are often identified as corporate critical success factors and which then become priorities for those individuals called trainers. Training then is a means to an end, a capacity for meeting ever changing organizational needs, priorities, and values. Its role should be viewed as central among the strategic and operational planning, controlling, and staffing functions of an organization and its posture must always reflect credibility, i.e., the worth of training must be obvious to those who plan it, provide it, experience it, and profit by it.

This book is designed as a reader for those who must assess the worth as well as potential of their training establishment. It is also designed as a template against which senior staff of any organization may become proficient in sensing strengths and weakness and using the former to mitigate the latter. Those who would become practitioners will profit also from reading this book. It contains a "how-to" manual to enable those charged with the program development function to produce quality initiatives, programs that will be successful in both the short and long term. Finally, it teaches the art of stand-up presentation skills, from Openers to Closers, and provides tips on becoming an effective consumer of external training consultants and prepackaged instructional programs.

1

THE ROLE OF TRAINING IN CONTEMPORARY ORGANIZATION MANAGEMENT

Why Train?

Many theorists have answered this question in similar ways by saying different things. Caffarella (1987) probably captures the trend of a generic response by listing three reasons why training occurs: to prepare people to do their jobs, to improve performance of people already at work, and to assist the organization as a whole to grow and develop. These reasons are rather basic and unarguable. However, most assignments seem to develop because of three quite diverse reasons: some senior executive has targeted a staff member for remediation, a company is looking for a panacea to reverse a negative performance trend, or a requirement is imposed from some external source. These situations are challenging because the circumstances around the training will be offered are not "ideal" and the population may be hostile or at least indifferent. The experienced trainer reading this is probably thinking, "So what's new?", and, they are correct. The ideal assignment is very rare, probably only public seminars qualify because the population is unknown and motivated by a need to improve or at least by paying the fee, the material is geared to some mean set of expectations, and long term impact is not really a concern. This type of situation will not be dealt with in any detail in this section because the number of such assignments which occur is relatively small and those which can have some type of impact on the organization are almost non-existent. There are exceptions, as always, to this set of assumptions and it is necessary for us to pause and consider a few of them. US HealthCare, a leading HMO type provider, always seems to have staff, including support personnel, at the public seminars I offer for Temple University. Their representatives are sharp, highly motivated and are pursuing a definitive improvement plan, of which the particular seminar topic is a tangible component. When you interact with these folks, they seem to know exactly why they are participating in a certain seminar and where the skills they are to learn will take them. One is left with the impression that this organization has the foresight to develop career ladders that are scaled on the basis of skill mastery, and that each plateau reached provides its own reward structure.

For years, management theorists have preached the necessity of paying people more because they had more to offer, i.e., skills attainment, not because they had achieved the title of manager. This approach becomes even more critical as an information based society becomes a reality, with enlarging spans of control, and far fewer "management" type positions available. If you believe in this outcome, if you wish you organization to behave like a symphony orchestra, then you must become an advocate of effective training as the vehicle to achieve it. Consider the case in which an organization seeks to provide bonuses, but is intrinsically motivated by a long term improvement goal. My advice would be to pay a bonus for engaging in an effective decision making process, not necessarily on the basis of the outcomes of that process. How do we get people top behave this way? Create the appropriate culture, build an effective rewards model, and *train them to appreciate the value of their circumstances and the means to preserve them!*

Independence Blue Cross and Blue Shield is another firm which makes a sizable investment in providing their staff with access to the skills which the company feels are necessary to progress to a higher plateau of value to the organization. They ascribe a notion of "professionalism" to all positions in the organization and support staff who demonstrate the aptitude are encouraged to participate in an MBA program. The enthusiasm, commitment, and potential of such students seems unlimited and it is a joy to experience. Peter Senge, in his book, *The Fifth Discipline*, writes of "learning organizations", a scenario in which people excel and develop because they want to. There is a vision of shared excellence in which rework is recognized as the enemy of even mediocrity. Surely such an organization is ahead in the race for total quality management. If you have not encountered any such animal, read on, because I have come to know one quite well. It is not an auto assembly plant, it does not produce sophisticated electronic parts, it is not a member of the defense industry, it will never qualify for the Baldrige Award or satisfy Dr. Deming. It is one of the largest public domain bureaucracies in the world, the General Services Administration.

My particular piece of GSA is Region Three, located in Philadelphia, Pennsylvania, and, my particular hero is Thurman M. Davis, the Assistant Regional Administrator for the Public Buildings Service. The Region Three office itself is large, larger than most private sector clients which I serve, and operates in a climate affected by all of the variables which could and can destroy productivity in many organizations: a confused and constantly changing set of priorities, uncertain funding, too few of the right kind of staff, too many personnel problems to be addressed via the civil service mechanism, and a dearth of tangible rewards which are truly available to the majority of staff. Despite these conditions, Region Three is a winner in my book. The enthusiasm, dedication to excellence, the focus on a common set of critical success factors, the desire to be cooperative, are only exceeded by the capacity exhibited by most staff with which I am familiar, to pursue objectives to a successful conclusion and accept new challenges willingly.

I believe that Mr. Davis would be a key player in this success story even if he did not hold such a lofty position. He nurtures his employees by leading them to new horizons, by training them in the skills necessary to enhance the embodiment of their technical capacity, and he values their efforts and shows it. If quality depends on leadership, GSA Region Three strives for it by training for it.

My initial assignment for this agency was to help prepare them for the major annual evolution in their professional lives, the funding presentation before the Planning and Project Review Board in Washington, D.C. Mr. Davis was my contact and the major presenter. He just didn't want something different from the traditional slide-tape "achievements" portfolios that most regions depended on to win funding in the never ending battle for soft money that dominates public servants of every jurisdiction. Mr. Davis wanted to create a style of presentation that would highlight the capacity and potential of his people. His objectives were multivariate in nature. Building a comprehensive picture of what Region Three could be expected to deliver would cement short term funding, build an expectation for future priority funding, and most importantly, convey to the staff the message that they were considered an elite force that deserved special recognition for the jobs they routinely performed so well.

The presentation was a success and the very next assignment involved training senior managers in the philosophy and mechanics of critique, coaching and encouragement of the Region Three team. The first program was entitled, "Managing for Excellence" and there were two goals established: provide an in-depth analysis of effective human resources management through enhanced interpersonal relationships; and build a collaborative, achievement-oriented work force and enhance performance through organization, employee, and self-development. The primary skills areas taught were effective organizational communication and conflict management.

Thus, one person had a vision of quality for his staff, communicated it quite convincingly, and provided the circumstances and resources to achieve it. Quality through training. That is why we should train, and on a continuous basis.

Training and Quality

For almost five decades, the United States faced a menace which possessed a vastly superior numerical force and an untried yet imposing technological base with the redundant capacity to incinerate our every dream. The relative burden on the U.S. military establishment was eased because it was able to function in a centrally focused, well funded, and highly motivated environment. Now, the threat may still be present, and it is complicated by the uncertainty of possibly unknown competitors and the resource base represents comparative 1938 spending levels. The business community in this country faces such uncertainty and menace as a routine matter, and while the consequences are not as severe, the competition is just as deadly.

One way to deal effectively with this situation is to build a shared vision of critical success factors and keep people aligned toward achieving and modifying them. Senge (1990) writes that organizations which excel are those that discover how to tap the potential of their people to commit to a goal, and further, how to build their capacity to learn at all levels of the organization. We learn from experience but we often cannot optimize our problem solving potential, the "learning horizon" according to Senge, because our experience base is so limited. Organizations can correct this deficiency by building design teams that engage in process integration, the systematic response to identifying and meeting challenges.

Many companies will be quick to tell you of their efforts to increase knowledge, skills, and abilities in their workforce, but seem puzzled when they are asked to what end these delivery vehicles, i.e., training programs, are directed. This problem is especially acute if you continue to press them once they respond by saying they are improving quality. Eliminating rework and reducing customer complaints are worthy ambitions but building a culture of commitment and then providing the right skills needed to excel are what training is all about.

Consider the case of the Gateway Arch, our national monument to the Great Westward Expansion made possible by Thomas Jefferson and his purchase of the Louisiana Territory. In 1804, Meriwether Lewis had a vision, which he was able to communicate to William Clark and others like him. The result was an 8500 mile expedition which lent credibility to a struggling nation.

In 1963, work was begun on an equally ambitious quest, from the same site from which Lewis launched his expedition. The contemporary challenge was building an arch top commemorate those early pioneers and yet the men and women who built the arch were just as truly pioneers. Each of the triangular-shaped 54 ton sections were virtually hand made. The hundreds of engineers, steel and iron workers, architects, and just plain laborers worked from a vision of quality, based on the knowledge that as much as 1/64th inch discrepancy in the entire 630 foot high edifice would exceed the tolerable safety margin!

Two years later the vision was fulfilled, the arch was completed, and it is still standing tall. How could such craftsmanship be possible? Very simple...this project was managed from a cultural base which invited the staff to become part of a common heritage, the recreation of the spirit of Lewis and Clark. They were trained in the difficulties of the challenge they faced, the consequences of error, and the intrinsic rewards that would accompany success. They were told that computer generated models had predicted thirteen deaths would be suffered during the construction. There were no deaths and few injuries. The work force was aligned, they were kept focused, and they were magnificently successful. Has the last 27 years which has witnessed the growth of the entitlement mentality stripped us of our potential to duplicate this feat? I think not, particularly among companies that have learned to empower staff and manage diversity. In the sober 1990's, companies will achieve quality if they learn how to change limiting factors not reinforce them.

Motivation, Leverage and Quality

One firm that has had to come to this realization is the Hughes Aircraft Company. Hughes has built a reputation for quality, both from a product as well as from a service perspective. Unfortunately, its major customer, the US Department of Defense is no longer buying as many as three hundred radar sets a year ! Hughes has taken some interesting steps to maintaining its profitability and its primary niche, serving the defense industry. Their professed goal is to increase value to customers and there are two objectives which they hope will lead them to the fulfillment of that goal.

The most visible strategic move that Hughes has made is to expand its market share. Examples of this initiative may been seen in the purchase of the former business lines of General Dynamics in Pomona and San Diego California, the folks that brought you the Tomahawk missile. Of far greater importance are the internal steps that have operationalized this strategy of increasing market share, the internal objective of developing an orientation of continuous improvement. This objective is based on a carefully conceptualized and designed training program based on continuous measures of improvement. The CEO learned the mechanics of this concept from an external consultant, trained his immediate subordinates, and then had each of them replicate the program all the way through the organization.

A practical approach to the problem of having a vision, establishing a focus and bringing the workforce along with you! My money is on Hughes.

We Need Some Training Around Here!

While the number of training programs which just seem to be thrown together is fortunately small, the majority of even the best organized programs may not have primary outcomes defined or be directed toward specific organizational needs, hence they are useless in building a quality impetus. Caffarella (1988) has a very effective presentation concerning the categorization of learning outcomes into knowledge acquisition, skills building, and attitudinal change. A global depiction you might say, but an effective template by which not only training programs, but also institutional commitment may be developed.

The utility of defining learning needs by such categories and then delivering training which is geared to observable behavior modification among the participants in these same areas may be viewed as multivariate in nature. First, such an approach is simplistic enough to be understood at every level of the organization so at the very least, every one should be speaking the same language and pointing to the same tangible "benefits. Second, the approach is totally consistent, thereby insuring a very easy transition between the process of needs identification and program development. Third, even the most skeptical of middle managers would be concerned about being viewed as obstructionist were they to deny their staff access to a program that has been advertised as one which will enhance a particular skills array. You will look like a genius!

Mitchell (1987) builds on this theme from a perspective which examines resistance to change normally encountered by anyone trying to mount a comprehensive in-house training program. His approach resembles the major tenets of the situational leadership model, particularly in determining "readiness", i.e., some composite scale of ability and willingness, and is probably much more realistic than the more traditional categorization approaches to defining training benefits. The simple truth of the matter is that even people in trouble in their organization are not going to warmly embrace your efforts to upset their routine and remove their staff for what they feel may be inordinate amounts of time. The situation is analogous to the problem of trying to transition a typing pool from their precious typewriters to some infernal contraption called a word processor. How many tutorial manuals have sat in their little plastic wrappers, unused for decades, because their worth as a time saver has never been communicated properly. Setting the stage, or as Mitchell defines it, overcoming self-interest, lack of trust, and mistaken impressions, is a necessary precursor before any trainer takes the stage.

As a young Naval Officer many, many years ago in Newport, Rhode Island, I had the opportunity to go on board an British destroyer which was making a port visit to the Naval Base. While there, I observed a major training evolution, non-rated enlisted personnel were being taught how to swim. The rational for the training was communicated effectively by the senior petty officer present who bellowed, "If you fall overboard you will drown unless you know how to swim". The technique employed was equally straightforward. All the trainees were simply marched off the fantail into the water while an instructor stood above on the ship illustrating various "strokes" which could used in such situations. To my knowledge, no one drowned and everybody seemed to have a good time in the end. There was an Olympic sized, indoor pool located on the base in which US sailors spent six weeks being taught how to swim. I have often wondered about the comparative effectiveness of the two training styles and the role of the British petty officer's "needs identification" in the success of his approach.

A sense of practicality must also be maintained, especially when you, as the budding trainer, are attempting to respond to some need articulated by a senior member of the organization. I once delivered a six day training program for a manufacturing firm located in an urban war zone that resembled the now all too familiar street scenes of Beirut. The CEO had shopped for the "perfect program by examining numerous brochures and requested that I combine several of my programs into a smorgasbord of training. It took several contacts to the plant to properly define his rational for the training and to develop some notion of the skills needed to fulfill his expectations. "We have got to get some training here!" seemed to his motto as well as the extent to which he could relate to what he was after, and what he was after was not based on any inputs or feedback from the target population. This was a real interesting case and we will return to it in later chapters which are devoted to needs sensing and technique.

Another of my experiences is applicable to this topic. I was conducting an intense three-day program in leadership for a large public domain organization. The assignment was very typical, in that the senior administrator had turned to training as a panacea for a fairly sick operation. Also, it was one of my first experiences in which a "target" was nominated in advance. This individual was described to me as the middle manager form hell. Tenure made him invulnerable to most forms of discipline and he seemed to relish his role as a difficult person. He also appeared to have an answer for every negative characteristic of his division. For example, his boss described his reaction to having an inordinate number of requests for lateral transfers as a condemnation of the other managers who didn't supervise their staff properly.

I met this individual on my second visit in which I was "examined" by the most senior group of managers who were prospective trainees in the program. He cornered me after the meeting to let me know that "he" was responsible for the assignment and that he knew "...I wouldn't let him down". The senior administrator, in reviewing my proposed content for the seminar, had predicted an explosion by our target, because I was going to focus on an accountability model for managers. Sure enough, by the middle of the second day it happened. He rose from the table, unable to contain himself any longer, and while almost frothing from the mouth exclaimed: "I am tired of hearing you talk about things we need to do to improve. My problem is bad workers. For 23 years I have had nothing but bad workers."

The silence was almost as dramatic as in the climax of Herman Wouck's the *Caine Mutiny*, in which Captain Queeg is shown to be a leader who ill-used those in his charge. It is not often that one has such a practicum example in a workshop, but this was a perfect illustration of the attitudes I was attempting to overcome. The next hour was spent revicwing our real life scenario in terms of the concepts which we had been practicing. The senior administrator knew that he needed some training and he got his desired results.

Some Necessary Preconditions

All training initiatives have to be established with some degree of credibility, especially if they are to contribute significantly to any kind of TQM or TQL effort. The needs analysis is probably best developed by knowledgeable individuals who work close to the level of the target population. However, the support of the program, the allocation of resources, and the mandate of expected outcomes has to come from a power base, i.e., a key executive who at least can create the impression that they can influence the course of events in the corporation. Once during the period of my life which my wife describes as my having had a real job, I had to "transition" someone in a supervisory position. Her job was to develop staff and program development initiatives and I insisted that the needs sensing mechanism be based on a participatory approach.

Well, she did maintain a heavy meeting schedule, in which all sorts of inputs were collected which she immediately proceeded to ignore. The result was that each package she developed sat on a shelf because no one could see the relevance of her efforts. She had failed to develop a sense of ownership for the programs. When pressed for a reason why the staff inputs were disregarded, she responded that she had been at her job for a lot longer than I had been at mine and she knew that process was important for appearance sake but she ultimately knew what was best for the staff. I never replaced that person in that job. Instead, we built a cadre of trainers and facilitators from the very staff that my failed executive chose to ignore. Not only did we increase the quality of our programs, the trainees felt some responsibility for their efforts and we were subsequently able to use the existing structure to begin a quality circle for the organization. All this happened over twenty years ago.

In a contemporary situation, I offer the following as preconditions for success:

- Key decision makers are committed to developing their human resource assets as a means of increasing profitability.

- The process of program development is understood by shareholders in the organization and a resource base is available to support training.

- There is a comprehensive and continuous program of sensing threats and opportunities, strengths and weaknesses.

- Some component of the organization is charged with building solutions to meet the identified needs and to relate these to the critical success factors that are the focus of the organization.

Sounds pretty simple, eh? Well read on...

2

THE ORGANIZATION AUDIT

A Strategic Perspective

Knowing what to do before beginning any venture seems like good advice to follow in whatever undertaking we may pursue. Unfortunately, the training enterprise in most firms does not have the ability to take advantage of such reasoning. At the end of chapter one, several preconditions were listed as being necessary to create an environment which supports the development of quality improvement programs. It never ceases to amaze me how many organizations still operate as if no one on staff ever took an undergraduate course in business policy. School districts take on a life of their own which mirrors the degree of confrontation that exists between the boards of education and the teacher association. Public domain entities often operate in a state of inertia brought on by what I refer to as a civil service stupor, a kind of resignation that not much will happen because so little is expected. Private sector firms may even survive with such a mentality yet it is doubtful that they could prosper.

Consider the case of two of my clients. Both firms were begun between 1950 and 1960, each was founded as a family business, and both engage in light manufacturing involving leisure products. Today, one is a $50 million firm, while the other is in excess of $900 million. The latter organization is a text book study of dynamic leadership in which family members have long been replaced where more capable people could be found. The CEO works approximately 60 hours a week, a total which he reports is almost invisible because of the diversity and enjoyment he derives from each day. Weekends are his own except for the occasional inspiration that any successful entrepreneur must pursue when the moment is right. This person is a leader, he knows few buzz words yet his firm espouses a true participatory management approach in which management values people because they provide production. Empowerment is seen not spoken. Decision making is forced as low as possible in the organization. Each manager is required to maintain a log of his or her attempts to delegate responsibility and the results of such efforts, and enhancements to products and operations are routinely solicited from the rank and file, who work in an expectancy based motivation model.

I am often called in to discuss new seminars or nuances of existing programs, but never to engage in a needs assessment! Why? This firm maintains a truly strategic outlook concerning its business needs, its competition, and its internal capacity. These indices are quantitatively based and are used in a qualitative sense. For example, every employee knows what their job is and what the impact is if that job is not done properly, and, the definition of "properly" is known, modified as circumstances may change, and is accompanied by appropriate technical training. Quality is defined as doing things right, the first time, and every time. Moreover, that definition of quality is operational because employees know what is expected of them and how they are to get there.

This company is successful because it is organized to pursue seven principles of quality. There is a clear consistent communication of goals throughout all levels and senior executives are aligned toward the fulfillment of no more than six critical success factors. A work ethic has been identified and is based on a realization that staff want to do a good job and expect appropriate training to enable them to be successful. The company is expected to provide leadership which maintains a developmental orientation toward staff, assumes responsibility, and rewards performance. Quality is mathematically measured. For example, there is a performance threshold for major evolution in the process of doing business every day. Items such as late deliveries are measured in terms of their impact on customer satisfaction. Settling for less than the best is considered dangerous and contrary to the corporate culture. Finally, employees at every level have been taught to define quality from the perspective of the client or customer and to continuously track performance and record the results. By the way, slippage or performance deficits are considered to be problems confronting the organization, not failures to be assigned individually via a policy of assigned liability.

It should be obvious by now why I need only to describe what's new, not help define needs for the CEO. He already has certain skill enhancements in mind before I am contacted and is always prepared with an answer when I ask him why he chooses certain programs. His answers are always directed at solving problems he anticipates but seldom realizes. Some of the topics which I have trained his managers in include: effective organization communication, negotiation, leadership, conflict management, power and influence, and developing support staff.

Our first company is not blessed with this sort of leadership. The seventy year old CEO works over 100 hours a week, the time, not the substance of effort, controls when he ceases his labors, and his spouse still works right beside him. He arrives before 6:00 AM and leaves after 7:00 PM and is not beyond expecting salaried employees to follow suit. Saturday is just another work day and on Sunday he writes notes. Every son has worked for the company all their lives and the wife has now advanced to the position of senior bookkeeper. The chief executive once described her role to me as the person he can most trust to watch things.

Managers whom I have gotten to know in my programs often complain of receiving twenty or more notes on a Monday morning, most on topics which they consider trivial and disruptive to their daily efforts. Turnover among the rank and file averages 150% annually. This CEO considers staff to be redundant and points with pride to his ability to stay in business despite the turnover and apparent dissatisfaction among his work force. This individual is interested only in controlling expenditures. I once saw a series of memos which told an interesting tale. Apparently, on one of his inventory inspections, he could not account for a three-hole punch, an item that costs less than $5.00 in most office supply houses. His Director of Operations, the recipient of several increasingly threatening notes, had first been ordered to find the missing item, and then, when it was learned that the punch, which was over a decade old, was broken, had been told to return it to the vendor for credit. I bet you have already guessed that the ops boss had his salary docked because he had ordered this useless piece of equipment to be disposed.

This CEO is equally interested in training as is the first executive described in this section. His interest, however well intentioned, is limited to whatever is "hot" in management training. While I might argue for such topics as safety, delegation, performance based compensation, and employee development, he argues for "quality", "empowerment", and "worker loyalty", and none of the training assignments which he books is ever supported with sufficient resources. For example, programs could only be run for a three hour period at a time. Had I not insisted that this was the minimum experience needed to teach a skills module, the program would have been run in one to one and one-half hour components, on site in the factory, with participants expected to answer their page.

The staff themselves put up partitions in as small section of the cafeteria and disconnected the page. The HR director, who really put herself at risk to try and accomplish something in this organization, provided coffee and other refreshments and a fan which at least created the impression that we were combating the July heat and humidity. Moving off site, arranging a full day experience, the most basic of considerations were beyond our ability to arrange. Of the original dozen middle managers which I encountered in my first training session, all where gone from the company by the third seminar, which occurred just eighteen months later. How unfortunate! Each of these staff members had impressed me with their enthusiasm for doing a credible job, their ability to work well with little or no supervision, and for their attitudes considering the leadership challenges which they faced in dealing with a neglected work force. Although they had much to give, they had no where to give it, they were not aligned, they were not even respected. I never knew what the CEO expected as a consequence of training. To him it seemed to be the thing to do because everybody else was doing it.

For example, in opening my workshop on total quality management for this group, none of the participants could give a definition or list a single characteristic in support of the corporate quality goal, which was, "Quality Requires Superior Performance." No one knew what "superior" meant and all were frustrated even considering the notion of TQM because the CEO had a zero defects mentality. All this effort, all those hours, on the part of the senior leadership of the organization, appeared to me to be nothing more than a gigantic exercise in running in place.

The leadership of an organization has to define expectations in terms of performance and relate rewards to performance. The culture, values, and norms of the firm must reflect this philosophy. A company that lacks such distinguished leadership cannot master the art of change, cannot empower staff to bring about reduced costs and increased quality. My departure from this organization was occasioned by a summative report which noted how ironic it was for me to have been retained to improve the skills base of managers who were going off to work for the competition.

David Packard, an Assistant Secretary of Defense in the Reagan Administration, once wrote: "Excellence requires responsibility and authority being placed formally in the hands of those at the working level who have the knowledge and enthusiasm for the tasks at hand". These are the individuals who must be considered as the primary locus of control for our development efforts. Total quality leadership is dependent on many variables, the most basic of which is this realization. Without the audit, without champions for change, without being aligned, training dollars are not being spent profitably.

Being aligned, having effective leadership, and, building a skills repertoire among the staff. These are indeed essential ingredients in strategically managing an organization. Long term considerations cannot be stressed enough when we are considering the causal relationship among the following variables:

- ☐ Total quality management =
  a strong strategic perspective X an effective training initiative.

Notice that the training component variable has a multiplying effect which geometrically increases the impact of strategic planning on TQM. We shall see the basis of this relationship in the remaining sections of this chapter.

The example discussed in chapter one in which a client had correctly identified the behavior of his "target" problem employee may have seemed to be a success. In the short run I would concur. My observations after the seminar program indicated that the participants were not only cognizant of the skills which had been presented in the program, they were also making a proactive attempt to display these in their day to day interactions with colleagues and staff. Even the "target" now knew enough to be careful, at least in a cosmetic sense. After several more seminars and numerous additional observation experiences, I completed the assignment convinced that I had only minimal impact in meeting the real challenge facing that organization, blatant racial and sexual discrimination, and I could not get anyone in authority there to even discuss these topics with me! All of the skill areas which I had presented should have been part of a larger effort in managing diversity training, with specific cathartic experiences among the participants as a major component of the training.

Assessing Priorities

Relating total quality management to training is difficult to discuss in detail because the program development enterprise should be tailored to the specific needs of the client. In completing organizational audits for clients, I have worked primarily according to the following paradigm:

- Define organization culture and mission
- Bring the client to a decision point
- Gain commitment among those who deal with policy
- Prepare an intervention contract
- Contract for change
- Plan the intervention package
- Implement the intervention

- Communicate and institutionalize the results

- Monitor conceptual and practical application

Assessing the culture of the organization is an important first step in identifying discrepancies between the sense of mission, from the client perspective, and the circumstances extant which will help or hinder completing that mission. It is amazing how many senior executives of a firm cannot even agree on a limited number of criteria of success for their company. The second step, bringing the client to a decision point, involves identifying the particular niche for the organization and those critical factors which will enable the shareholders of that organization to know when they have been successful. I once was told the story of a newly appointed bus driver on a city transit system. His eagerness was seen daily as he attempted to assist passengers, answer their questions regarding transfers and directions, and always waited until everyone was seated before resuming his route.

These were the ingredients of performance which were important to him. Unfortunately, these activities took time and time was crucial to our driver's immediate supervisor, the dispatcher. When other buses began piling up behind our hero, the dispatcher monitored his route and criticized him severely for "...not doing his job". The driver had his definition of performance changed for him, to the extent that he now realized that his sole commitment was in keeping the schedule, and thus keeping his job.

His solution was unique. He removed all barriers to completing the route ahead of schedule by limiting not only his time at each stop but also the number of stops! One presumes that someone would have forecasted the revenue from fares which should have been collected, but, perhaps we should not attribute too much to that public domain bureaucracy. I imagine that the driver and dispatcher were pleased and the comptroller unaware, which for some is as satisfactory as being pleased. What was important to the survival of the organization was never even within the realm of discussion. Companies interested in total quality management must learn to specify performance in terms of anticipated outcomes and to focus on the basic conceptual process to plan, deliver, and institutionalize an improvement effort.

Gaining commitment from the top is a necessary ingredient for any training initiative to be successful, especially with respect to resource allocation. This sets the stage for everything that is to follow such as planning the intervention contract. This is the process by which all of the program components are deliberated. Items such as time lines, costs, personnel, follow up, form the basis of these discussions. Chapters three and four will present some specific suggestions to accomplishing all of this in a parsimonious manner.

The next step involves specifying the desired outcomes of staff development as skill development areas, behavioral modifications, and/or changes in the command structure, organization, or compensation packages. This is an area in which the organization development (O.D.) specialist must contribute significantly. The intervention package is the means by which the desired ends are achieved. The O.D. specialist and the training professional must combine to insure accuracy, utility, and synergy for any training that is to be attempted. More on this topic in Part II.

Implementing the intervention, communicating the results, and monitoring the application of things learned on the job are inter-related aspects of the process. Accomplishing only one of these variables without the other two in the proper sequence will mitigate significantly the impact of your financial and emotional investments. While a training professional may be the solution for the actual delivery of the program, institutionalizing the results and monitoring their subsequent application must be an accountable assignment of some in-house staff person with the skills and experience to do the job and the clout to recommend necessary actions. We will talk more about this in chapter five.

The common ingredient in most of my assignments has been to begin with an O.D. intervention. This technique serves both to focus the client on key areas which require attention as well as an introduction to the basic conceptual process of planning, delivering and institutionalizing an improvement effort. Several distinguished faculty members from the Temple University School of Business and Management recently spent many months with ITT in Lancaster, Pennsylvania, getting the organization "ready" to profit from a training program. ITT was not only committed to the concept of total quality management, they were committed to maximizing the resources and opportunities available to them to develop and empower staff to be more productive. By the time I arrived at ITT to actually conduct a three day training program entitled, "Managing for Excellence", I found an extraordinary level of readiness, i.e., both the capacity and willingness to participate in the program.

The topics which I presented were fairly typical for such an initiative and included: assessing and defining quality in terms of performance and building a profile of the culture and climate which existed in the organization. Specific areas of skill development included: influence, leadership, conflict management, and communication. What differentiated this program from some others was the commitment from the parent organization felt by the participants and the knowledge of how each skill they were learning would profit them in their respective jobs. Relating needs to skills is the key to transitioning the organization to be ready to profit by any training. It is here that the senior leadership of ITT really took some calculated risks and made significant commitments but it was necessary to their success.

More organizations should be moving to another piece of

the TQM puzzle, the development of career ladders based on knowledge, skills, and abilities. Without such programs, the company cannot hire with a view to future promotion capacity, and this hinders their efforts to qualify current employees in a support staff role for subsequent use in more technically oriented positions. This illustrates both the complexity of the issue as well as the requirement to consider the whole package, i.e., audit, commitment, contract, and training, from a strategic perspective.

There are many organizations which subscribe to this template. Interestingly enough, two of my most recent assignments involved highly productive organizations which operated in the public domain. Both are quite focused on improving the "quality" of their efforts, which they see as more service than production oriented, yet each approaches this mission orientation from quite different perspectives .

The Aviation Supply Office, ASO, is the sole inventory control point for all of Naval Aviation, both domestic and international. This is a huge establishment which manufactures nothing, yet is responsible for millions of dollars of product, incredible complex safety requirements, a distribution system that is world wide, suffocating oversight (since they operate in governmental service) and timelines which are always due or past due.

This giant could easily resemble the bureaucracy that countless graduate theses have castigated. Jobs are protected, incentives are few, and the entitlement mentality is strong enough to create a true comfort zone. However, even the casual observer can detect a strong sense of mission and commitment at most levels of this organization. The senior leadership has insured that members of the staff know what their jobs are, in terms of duties and performance expectations, and, more importantly, what the impact on the organization and the individual will be if a particular job is not done well.

Standards of quality were developed from the bottom up

via groups known as "process action teams". In addition to defining excellence, the teams monitor performance and strengths which are identified are used to mitigate weaknesses. There also exists a capacity to support weaker members of the staff. Cross training is prevalent, employee recognition is both conspicuous and welcomed, and the rewards which are available include intrinsic motivational factors which are truly valued by the employees. Like many successful organizations, the Aviation Supply Office has answered the question, "What happens when the money is no longer enough?", by building a comprehensive reward base, primarily based on recognizing effort and tying resource allocation to top achievers.

They have also defined "total quality" from a leadership perspective by equipping individuals to function at greater capacities. Their emphasis is in preparing for the next crisis not managing it once it occurs. They have mastered what J. Daniel Howard (1992) would refer to as the essence of TQL, staff are focused, they think strategically, and they are not hampered by rigid, inefficient processes. ASO has also made a very significant investment in training. Their human resources department is staffed by very contemporary thinkers who have worked with key decision makers throughout the organization to identify needed skills and then have provided the training to enhance these skills across the board. Their work in statistical process control is a model effort worthy of dissemination to even the private sector. While the needs identification, skill specification, and administrative processing are all in-house evolutions, each seminar has been brokered with contingency employees and consultants providing the training. More about this important concept later. Such training has become the key to charting and staying their course to total quality.

The Defense Personnel Support Center, DPSC, is another case in point of an organization that is aligned in its pursuit of total quality. DPSC procures and produces items that are in common use throughout the uniformed services of the United States. Everything from ketchup to underwear which is not situation specific to a particular service is under the cognizance of DPSC. This organization is about the size of ASO, is also highly regarded in its peculiar areas of specialization. It also has pursued a different yet equally successful path toward quality. The leadership of DPSC realized some years ago that building a “readiness” capacity, the willingness and ability among staff to excel, was a time consuming and rather expensive process, one that dealt with preparing to deal with a crisis not just simply managing one. DPSC was faced with an assignment that confronts many private sector organizations, ever increasing productivity goals, shrinking procurement and R&D budgets, managing an ever more complex set of acquisition regulations, and coordinating a world wide distribution network. All of this takes place in an environment in which initiative would not normally be rewarded or even welcomed.

DPSC staff kept their edge because they had a clear sense of their mission as well as the importance of that mission. Quality circles were begun and these had an immense impact on improving productivity. Training was an essential part of this process, both procedurally and with regard to the skills related to the dynamics of groups. Literacy problems were targeted with an extensive resource base, especially through inhouse staff. Junior level supervisors were taught leadership via mentoring associations established with highly successful senior executives. Skill enhancement also occurred as a consequence of one of the most extensive programs of extension courses that I have ever encountered.

The Training Division of the Human Resources Department maintained a strong effort in recruiting candidates for various courses offered by major universities in the Philadelphia area. Regular faculty were brought on-site to teach credit granting courses in areas such as communications, personnel management, labor relations, and conflict management. The participants were all highly motivated and for a variety of reasons. The credits were funded by the Federal Government as long as the course was completed successfully.

Each staff member knew the role of the particular course in terms of the skill areas involved and their value in qualifying the individual for performance bonuses and managerial positions. Particular emphasis was placed on the completion of various specialty components by the organization. For example, concentrations in labor relations, human resources management, and leadership were established with each area requiring several courses. Students completing each concentration were widely recognized for their achievement, given enhanced areas of responsibility on the job, used in training other staff in their specialty areas, and employed also as counselors for those just beginning each concentration. Another example of a well focused organization profiting from an investment in a training model as the vehicle to achieve total quality!

In the winter of 1991, this dedication to excellence was sorely tested and DPSC met the challenge, winning the equivalent of the Baldrige award from the Defense Logistics Agency.

Sensing Objectives

I once visited the central office of a client school district and found the following slogan emblazoned over the employee entrance:

ALL MY EFFORTS ARE FOCUSED ON THE BOARD OF EDUCATION. ANYTHING THAT I DO THAT DOES NOT BENEFIT THE BOARD OF EDUCATION IS A WASTE OF MY TIME!!!

On the surface this statement, while not innocuous, does

not seem all that much of a threat in an organization. However, once I had spent enough time with the client, I learned how debilitating this slogan had become.

The superintendent believed that he had a moral responsibility to mirror John Calvin in his behavior. His ideas could be considered noble, but he failed to bring anyone along with him. For example, he stood by the employee entrance each morning at exactly 8:00 AM and looked at his watch as each staff member arrived late. It was a badge of honor for him to be able to report to his constituents that, in over 20 years on the job, he hadn't missed a morning in "...setting an example for the staff". While it was incredible to me, and just about every member of the rank and file, that he would waste time to focus such energy on this aspect of his job, his view involved maintaining a sacred trust with respect to the resources placed at his disposal by the public. Holding down salaries, except his own, and maintaining a threadbare facility as an administrative headquarters were examples of the public profile he represented. I never heard this individual talk of instruction or staff development, just the confrontational nature of the teachers union and the poor skills and lack of initiative which he found in the support staff. His leadership style could be characterized as one of co-opting staff rather than giving them the motivation necessary to buy into the priorities of the organization.

The staff perspective, which was of little concern to the superintendent, would seem all too familiar to anyone who works as an organizational behaviorist. The staff attitude was directed toward coping with, rather than cooperating with, the administration. In beginning any workshop on quality, I endeavor to have the participants define the culture of their organization and itemize other items such as the leadership style to which they are exposed as well as situations which lead to conflict in the workplace. One of the consequences of such exercises is that the participants have a listing of rather specific items which frustrate them on the job. In those situations which come to be characterized as "negative" by the remaining work of the seminar, the participants normally list "being unheard" as one of the major causes of frustration. So too did the staff of this school district. The teachers took pride in developing curriculum improvements but where taken serious only when they took their case directly to the spokespersons which they had cultivated among the parents. The support staff were concerned only with getting through the day and avoiding the influence pattern of sanction which seemed to predominate.

The senior staff believed that the superintendent's actions and philosophy were to be expected in a public domain entity and that the lack of concern for staff development and quality was due to the peculiar nature of working in public education and having to "fight the union every step of the way." They seemed to be preoccupied with "looking good", i.e., not inviting criticism. Of course this removed any potential of engaging in the taking of risks which is so necessary to advancing the organization. This school district had no sense of mission, no realization of cultivating a "shareholder" concept among staff, constituents, and their directors, and, absolutely no idea of what attitudes existed among their employees.

I once visited a records store to purchase a "hot" CD of unintelligible music for my teenage daughter. I noticed that the clerk wore a plastic tag that gave his first name and the legend, "I Am Committed To Serving You With Quality". Seeing the word "quality" immediately peaked my attention, and, despite the protests of my wife, who urged me not to create a scene, I asked the young clerk about what that tag meant to him.

"Nothin," was the reply. "I beg your pardon," said I, "but I teach people about quality and am always interested in bringing examples to them." The clerk seemed both confused and annoyed and stated, "Look they told me to wear the tag and I did. Are you some sort of inspector?" Feeling grateful that I was allowed to make my intended purchase, I beat a hasty retreat. I will always remember that the clerk had not been trained to define quality in his performance, only to be concerned with snap inspections.

I once provided a workshop in team building for a large food manufacturing firm that specialized in breakfast cereals. This particular plant was located in Western Pennsylvania and functioned for years in the absence of a union and in the presence of a strong "family" tradition of cooperation and getting the best possible product out the warehouse door. All things change and the workforce of our cereal plant who were used to jobs being handed down from one generation to the next, suddenly found itself being scrutinized by a new corporate structure. One of the inevitable changes was a transformation of the quality control division into something which I came to call the "quality police". I later learned that the new plant manager had determined that the relationship between the people in manufacturing and quality testing had become too "cozy". He apparently was also very proud of the fact that in restructuring this unit with his own people, he was already beginning the transformation of this plant into a "business oriented" organization. All of this in three weeks! Aren't MBA's grand?!

This cognitively dissonant attitude was replicated in numerous ways until the same spirit among the work force which had made the company profitable was now channeled into a union. After a strike and the "transition" of the plant manager things still were not comfortable and I was called in for two three-day workshops for first line supervisors in team building. I heard quite a lot about the quality police. Perhaps our plant manager would have been successful in managing a record store. The supervisors I trained had a lot to offer and I said so in my report. A quality circle would have been appropriate as a vehicle to begin building trust but the new leadership wanted the all too pervasive "quick fix". Another instance of organizational ineptitude, a concentration on form rather than substance.

What these organizations failed to grasp is that they are working from an assumptions base that disregards the key element in any equation of total quality, the work force. Any organization which wishes to assess its priorities in order to define its commitment to quality, must ascertain those benchmarks which exist among staff. These attitudes have a significant mitigation potential in establishing and enhancing organizational capacity for improvement. This type of census will often lead to the identification of items of concern which represent the unseen portion of the organizational iceberg, the intangibles of status, power, influence, conflict, and communication. Such intangibles need to be identified as strengths or weaknesses before they can be used as building blocks of productivity or addressed as challenges as part of a training initiative.

Any sample of employee attitudes should include the items listed in table one.

TABLE 1
SAMPLING EMPLOYEE ATTITUDES

- ✓ The means by which work is organized and assigned
- ✓ The structure for staff development
- ✓ Techniques for solving problems
- ✓ Conflict management potential
- ✓ Means by which creativity is fostered
- ✓ Rewards for exceptional performance; perceived value of such rewards
- ✓ The presence of career ladders
- ✓ The dissemination of information; quality /timeliness of data received
- ✓ Climate/culture descriptions
- ✓ Definitions of mission
- ✓ Descriptions of quality in particular jobs
- ✓ The existence of meaningful two-way communication

This is an imposing list of items and challenges for any organization. Compiling attitudes about such areas could provide a plethora of benefits. Not only does such an activity provide a meaningful needs sensing mechanism, it provides the means by which quality solutions may be collected from the very individuals who do the actual work.

The role of leadership in maintaining a credible approach to sensing needs cannot be emphasized too strongly. I have often found it useful to conduct awareness training for senior staff to acquaint them with a working knowledge of the interrelationships which exist among their operational duties, personal characteristics, and interpersonal skills profile. The purpose of such training is to have the participants realize and define the case and effect pathways that encompass all they are and do on the job, and the relationship between such dimensions of leadership and the concept of total quality management. These relationships are presented in Figure 1.

Figure 1

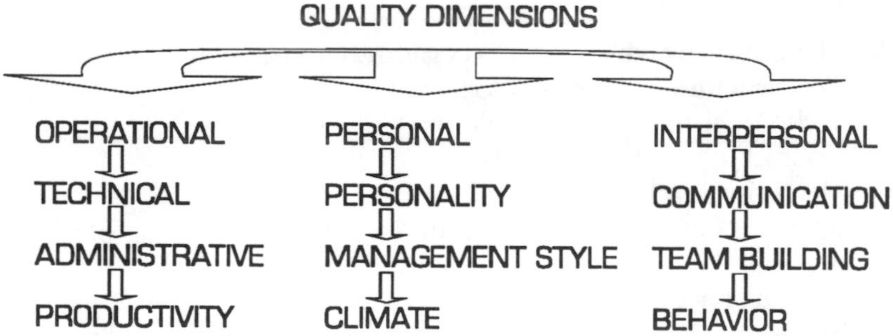

Patricia Galagan (1992), the editor of *Training and Development*, once spun a wonderful tale about an almost beatific company, Alpine Chemical, which struggled mightily to retain its corporate essence as its new parent, Big Brother, sought to impose its culture on a recalcitrant child. Galagan wrote of the maneuvering and dialogue which was part of the strategy each side used to prevail and had her heroine write of teamwork, climate, reward systems, flexibility, delegation, empowerment, and valuing employees as the keys to Alpine's success, all of which were in danger of extinction. "When you evolve to where we are, we'll be happy to join you, but don't kill us in the meantime", this was the battle cry by which Alpine won the right to retain its essence.

While Big Brother is cast as a kind of villain in this article, the leadership of this corporate giant at least was able to appreciate the quality of the argument. They were brought to an understanding of the interrelationships described in figure one.

In preparing the way for staff to embark on a quest for quality, please don't forget the bottom of the iceberg, the intangibles which are management skills that successful leaders must master, much as they do the management functions of planning, directing, organizing, and control. Staffing issues cannot remain the sole concern of the human resources specialists.

A Valid Approach

In 1965, the Elementary and Secondary Education Act was enacted. This singular piece of legislation was to have an unquestioned impact on public education. For the first time, a significant block of funds was earmarked not only for research and development, but also for the dissemination of promising practices. This was a true program development effort because the research had to be a grass roots initiative, i.e., the key players were educators working for local education agencies, and because the work had to have an empirical basis, standards for success had to be identified initially, and then valid and reliable measurement instruments had to be obtained and applied. No program was qualified unless it passed a comprehensive validation panel at both the state and federal levels. During these halcyon days of resource abundance, I was fortunate enough to direct the program for the State of New Jersey. Our team, and it was surely a team effort, was recognized for superior achievement by the National Institute of Education and the National Diffusion Network. In just over five years, we developed and had validated, 121 programs. Our success was due to the following variables.

First, we depended on people with the appropriate experience to develop "good ideas". Second, we provided the necessary consultative expertise in areas such as needs assessment and measurement. Third, milestones were developed with performance expectations established for each. Funding was suspended whenever a milestone could not be surpassed and no project was taken to the development phase unless the needs assessment indicated a substantive market for the product. Fourth, successful outcomes were stated in performance terms so that the quality of our efforts would be readily apparent. Finally, we established a comprehensive training network as the vehicle by which the entire program was administered.

Participants were trained in program development procedures, various skills essential to the specific programs were the topics for still more training, and awareness and commitment training sequences were provided for those who felt some sort of need and were trying to identify solutions to close discrepancies.

The notion of discrepancy analysis was the keystone of that program development experience. The major player in this field at that time was Malcolm Provus (1971). His model was based on a generic planning template with a few wrinkles. The key was the identification of a meaningful standard as a point of departure against which gaps in performance would be identified. Today, that same concept has become a focal point in the drive toward quality. According to Provus, there are five major considerations to be determined in defining this standard of excellence or point of departure. These are presented in Table 2.

Table 2 Provus and Program Evaluation

- ✓ The judgment of authorities about a program
- ✓ The opinions of staff
- ✓ The opinions of those affected by a program
- ✓ A comparison of present outcomes with desired outcomes
- ✓ A comparison of an executed program with its design

If we accept this template, and the literature suggests that the approach is quite valid, then it becomes a *sine quo non* that organizations which refuse, or are unable, to establish appropriate channels of communication, are unable to fulfill the prime ingredients for even defining total quality. Provus also offers a consideration which we shall discuss in coming chapters, the monitoring of an intervention, i.e., comparing the total quality program with its design. Here again is a role for the contingency employee, an expert in program development who can establish the appropriate milestones and statistical techniques for determining whether the planned intervention is achieving its purpose. And what is the planned purpose of an organizational intervention? The answer must be viewed in three parts, which should be considered as a whole: (1) to ensure the quality of the program; (2) to ensure the cost effectiveness of the program; and (3) to enhance the capacity of the organization to make effective decisions.

Provus (1971) considered the program development effort with a great deal of insight and suggested that evaluation efforts, particularly those which are of interest to us, i.e., that which are directed toward mitigating discrepancies, are of limited utility when their purpose is directed to collecting information dealing primarily with the success or failure of a program. A decision maker in a contemporary business environment needs data from a much broader spectrum in order to commit limited resources with a greater probability of efficiency and effectiveness. Those responsible for strategy, organization development, and resource allocation should consider the following conceptual areas:

1. What is the real need we have to address?

Once you can identify a problem not just a symptom, you are on your way to defining a goal. For example, our bus driver should have been trained in all of the aspects of a public transit experience that would keep riders riding, i.e., courtesy, timeliness, and safety. These three variables can be specified as objectives; can be isolated as skills for training experiences; can be stipulated as outcomes for measurement purposes; and can be monitored so that the system can be renewed if necessary.

2. How do we get to where we need to be?

Having a road map is essential if your are lost or navigating strange highways for the first time. So do corporations, school districts, universities, and public service agencies need a plan of attack if they hope to accomplish anything. In order to help direct our path to quality, this component should include both planning and control functions as the concept of operational analysis. The operational analysis concept should include getting the organization ready to move as well as a step by step protocol for that movement. The awareness and commitment training which we used so successfully with the New Jersey Department of Education is an example of operational analysis. Every step along the program development path was specified as a milestone and the process itself provided "readiness" quotients before it was initialized.

3. What support systems to I need?

How much time, money, personnel, administrative support and oversight will have to be expended in order to achieve the desired outcomes? Big business has often been criticized, and quite fairly, for depending on cost analyses as the major factor in making many decisions that impact on the public. Achieving total quality may involve processes similar to those involved in producing Ford Pintos, but costing out the process is not a commonweal issue. The real minefield for our TQM corporate sponsor is the challenge involved not only in estimating costs, but also in identifying the hidden costs of the project. Can an already tight budget deal with unanticipated resistance to change that may treble the cost of training? Will I have to train trainers in order to institutionalize my product? Will assessment instruments have to be constructed in order to gauge the extent to which target skills have been mastered? These are the kinds of issues both TQM champions and those who broker the training programs need to identify and project accurately.

4. How do we monitor the success of our efforts and provide for renewal?

Any student of management is familiar with generic planning models that demand both feedback and the opportunity to use such feedback in order to reconstruct processes which may not be as effective in reality as they seemed on the drawing board. Remember, mere exposure to training does not necessarily guarantee behavior modification. We will discuss this concept in much more detail in Part II.

Shaun McCormack (1992), offered what he called "eight strategic steps" designed to lead organizations to TQM heaven. They are presented in table three as a contemporary version of Provus' work.

Table 3 Building a Strategic Framework

- ✓ Specify current performance standards
- ✓ Identify where outputs are at variance with standards
- ✓ Determine the cause of the variance
- ✓ Identify and Initiate actions to correct the cause of the variance
- ✓ Specify desired performance
- ✓ Compare the desired standards to current standards and identify gaps
- ✓ Develop alternatives to close the gaps
- ✓ Institutionalize new standards

This represents nothing more than that generic planning model which we discussed earlier, but essential to the philosophy of achieving quality by building staff capacity. Why do so many organizations ignore these processes? Stupidity would be a false characterization yet the behavior is so unsound as to border on stupidity. Being farsighted, using the proper tools, knowing how to deal with these issues, are now important skills which any organization interested in survival must cultivate among its managers.

Now that we have some idea of what to do, what topics may be considered "hot" in the world of management development. The Spring, 1992 , issue of the "Management Development Report", of the American Society for Training and Development listed the following as among the top current management development topics: communication, leadership, performance management, problem solving, goal setting, coaching, delegation, and decision making. The same issue reported that 91 percent of the companies in their sample use classroom instruction when training mid-level managers and 95 percent use it for supervisors. *Voila L'essence!* Future chapters will discuss how to use such topics as these as the tools to achieve total quality.

The Function of Training

The word "function" may be defined commonly as the proper action for which a mechanism is employed. Thus is shaped the relationship between the goal of survival, total quality, and the vehicle by which the goal may be attained-training. We have discussed, in general, the use of training as a tool by which various organizational objectives may be achieved. The reality of training is that it is pervasive as much as it is integral to the way in which an organization behaves. Ponder for a moment all of the training experiences to which you have been a part in your current work situation. Your orientation to the firm was a form of training. The means by which you learned how things "worked" represented training as did the measure of latitude from various control mechanism which you learned to exercise. Every behavior which you now exhibit on the job was a learning experience, something in which you were trained. Unfortunately, many of these training experiences were either misguided or misapplied. In addition, many formal training experiences are devoted to what someone in authority thinks needs to be done rather than what may be meaningful to the trainee or truly valuable to the company. Training could have been the means by which you discovered the nature of change or the motivation to excel. You could have been trained to ascertain your behavior modification needs or to apprise your leadership potential. You could even have been trained to see the dangers in perpetuating an entitlement mentality in the workplace.

Training represents power because it is the means by which others can be influenced. How much sooner would you have reached your professional maturation level had your organization realized the potential of training. We will never know much equity has been wasted or never been built because of the lack of proper training, and thankfully, we cannot even estimate the cost of such waste. The serious student of total quality now has the tools to examine their own situation, apply a needs assessment template, and identify the key issues. In the coming chapters we shall discuss strategies by which the correct processes may be utilized and the appropriate people involved to develop them.

3

A COMMUNICATIONS APPROACH

Entitlement and the New Cynicism

One of the most successful companies in the extremely competitive world of computer program development is Microsoft. Their prices are competitive, their programs work well, and the company makes money, lots of it. What I most admire about this company, what I actually enjoy in my contacts with them, is the quality of customer responsiveness. I attribute the success of Microsoft primarily to the quality which is represented by their people. Their technical skills appear to be excellent but their demeanor is superb and that is what makes or breaks a customer contact opportunity. Anyone interested in quality service should call Microsoft to learn how it is done, even if you do not need product assistance. The introductory telecom menus are easy to comprehend and the wait never seems long because of distractions such as music and product updates. Every caller is treated as if only they matter. The representatives are not only extremely patient in working through problems, they take the initiative to teach, i.e., they offer suggestions on how to embellish certain applications. Best of all, they seem to be truly empathetic. When an expert will take the trouble to kibitz and tell you how many times they screwed up a software package, your self-esteem tends to recover rather quickly.

The customers are not only always right, their satisfaction matters. I once called to order a printer driver library disk, something that another manufacturer was supposed to install. The Microsoft analyst walked me through a layperson description of what I needed to get done, told me that the appropriate software was not as yet available and took the trouble to give me several suggestions of how to solve the problem. When I mentioned that someone I knew had been able to procure the same driver I was seeking from Microsoft, the analyst told me to hold while she double-checked. A few minutes later she returned to the call, apologized for mis-reading her document availability library, and told me that she was shipping the needed software free of charge! Our only disagreement in this entire transaction occurred when I tried to insist that she send an invoice with the disk. I actually felt that I owed them that, given the manner in which I had resolved my problem. True story!

There is a lot for an organizational behaviorist to be excited about here. After many years of auditing organizations, one gets a "feel" for the quality of an entity within a few moments after sampling the level to which initiative and responsiveness exist within the staff. No staff could universally and consistently deliver the performance which I have encountered within Microsoft unless they shared a sense of vision with the senior leadership of the organization. The Microsoft analysts and representatives create the appearance that they have been trained to recognize what is important to their business, the role they play in accomplishing this important work, and the impact on the entire company if that work is not done well. You could not fabricate a better role model for a graduate level case study. We spend a great deal of time teaching MBA candidates about the value of intrinsic motivation. The folks at Microsoft exhibit a spirit that could never be co-opted, and money cannot possibly be the primary reason. Microsoft is productive and profitable because their people are empowered and have been trained to increase their capacity to define quality performance.

Another company which exhibits these characteristics is the United States Automobile Association, or USAA as it is more commonly known. USAA sells insurance to officers of the active or reserve armed forces of the United States. That is their business but the secret to their success is that they provide service to their clients. During the last year I had occasion to exchange one leased auto for another. The deal involved different financing entities, different dealers and makes of cars, and a very short window of opportunity because our previous car seemed to be on the verge of expiring. From the time we chose our vehicle to the moment we picked up the new car required less than 48 hours. I made several phone calls and spoke to a lot of different departments but never felt any frustration and avoided haggling with a salesperson. USAA took care of the turn-in, negotiations on the financing and purchase price, wrote new insurance coverage, arranged for title and transfers, and all attending contracts. They even notified me that I could refinance my other vehicle because their interest rates were now more favorable.

A lot of companies proclaim to offer one stop shopping, but how many have employees who will work an hour or two beyond their normal quitting time to cement a deal because you have expressed a sense of urgency? I particularly enjoy the manner in which USAA representatives embrace your problems as their own and follow through when you need a solution that has not been programmed into their control mechanisms. They personalize their service, feel no need to defend themselves when their organization screws up, and avoid the tendency to abuse computer generated form letters and faxes. The staff members value being recognized as "blue ribbon" employees, a distinction that sets them above an already high standard of performance.

These are quite laudable scenarios. Unfortunately, these success stories are few and far between. I once had a few pages of an original manuscript destroyed by a copying company that prides itself on customer satisfaction. Their policy was never to charge a client for a job if the client was not satisfied. This company, however, never seemed to create an awareness in their employees of the value of this approach. Such offers were made matter of factly, and on the occasion which I described above, the individual displayed such nonchalance that his offer actually exacerbated rather than mitigated my dissatisfaction. When I complained to the manager, I was informed that it was his store, that originals were often destroyed, that my average annual 50,000 impressions was a "small" account, and he would prefer that I took my business elsewhere since they had failed to satisfy me on several occasions. If I were that manager, I would have striven to create the impression that the store belonged to our clients and their problems would be mine and that a copy business is built from one $.08 impression to the next. By the way, the last time I took the trouble to check, I estimated that all the people to whom I had told this story and who moved their business, averaged close to 5.5 million impressions annually which no longer went to that copying chain!

What differentiates the doers from the reactors? I believe that if you could identify and categorize a reasonable number of companies based on a dichotomy of customer responsiveness, you would probably not find significant differences in their control mechanisms, financial goals, or even mission statements. What are the mitigating factors that enable a corporation to be categorized into one or the other aspects of our dichotomy? My experience indicates that an entitlement mentality is a major factor behind those that are less than successful in satisfying the consumer and that this attitude may be attributed to a new cynicism in the workplace.

What is this entitlement mentality that we have heard so much of recently? Bardwick (1991) describes this condition as a crippling factor that has become an insidious disease. Consider the labor unions in public education who refuse to consider performance as a variable in either retaining a job or winning an increment or their members who believe that they deserve a raise just because they are alive the following September. We are no longer in an age of economic boom and demographic bust. Every reasonably intelligent person who has not been lost at sea for the last five years knows this, so why do so many organizations tolerate nonperformance?

Batten (1989) offers some interesting insights by stating that the majority of managers today still manage by directive. People become pigeonholed as to their skill base and they plateau , i.e., they reach the upper limit of their promotibility potential or that promotibility threshold has been lowered for them. These staff can be counted on to lose their confidence, become angry, and avoid taking any risks. They certainly will never be accused of being creative. Today, more than ever, organizations must employ people who are not afraid of using and developing their strengths and possess courage and confidence. Instead, the entitlement society provides us with people who are often so cautious they constantly fear for their own survival and deny their ability to compete.

Managers who do not lead by expectation use only one aspect of the situational leadership model, they primarily tell, although push and drive are usually characterizations that fit this approach. Companies can no longer afford nonproductive staff, they are the seeds of failure. Managers who lack courage and vision, who do not possess the discipline to preserve, who lack the skills to get people involved and make a commitment to goals, they are the gateways to disaster. They often establish "safety zones", control mechanisms which insure conformity and destroy initiative. Just think of yourself as a consumer who has a problem and is received by a customer service representative who quotes delimiting procedures which only exacerbate your distress levels instead of finding unique opportunities to satisfy. Staff do not like working in such circumstances and tend to retreat to the lowest level of effort by which they can get by. Clients will tend to look elsewhere when confronted by such behavior.

Stress, paralysis, and fear, these conditions are the legacy of entitlement. To what do we owe this cynicism? Each must look unto themselves. Kanter and Mirvis (1989) have examined the truly American phenomenon of living and working in an age of discontent and disillusionment and they hypothesize that the majority of our workforce is composed of outright cynics who have become rather clever in putting their own self-interest ahead of the common good, at least as it may be defined by management.

Organizations today are very much capable of preying on a number of variables which mitigate against employee comfort levels. These may include: a perceived glut of available labor, the low mobility of some females and minorities, the overqualification status possessed by managers who have been "transitioned", and the despair felt by those long without gainful employment. I have worked with a school district that was noted far and wide for its poor employment practices. The Board of Education created the impression that they knowingly preyed on those encumbered by the situations described above and then they squeezed them some more, winning concessions whenever an opening presented itself, all in the best interests of the taxpayer of course. I once observed a labor relations negotiation session in which management argued all night over an obscure benefit that would have cost less to concede than the fees being paid to their solicitor and negotiator over the course of that long night! Everyone who worked there felt abused and put-upon. Their working conditions were abysmal and their pay left each without a sense of self-fulfillment. Constantly searching for work and keeping a part-time job was a preoccupation of many. The most common feeling reported to me was that management seemed intent on stripping each employee of their self-respect. Many staff actually felt embarrassed to work in the district and some never discussed their job with friends and family. From the perspective of the Board of Education, all of whom worked in what they liked to refer to as the real world, productivity was paramount and privilege could be earned only through performance. Neither side sought to facilitate problem solving, neither side sought to communicate the impact of the other's position on them. Instead, confrontation and mistrust abounded with both management and labor frankly admitting that their struggle had become one to determine who would control the organization. When people's aspirations are ignored, when their expectations are mismanaged, when promises are abrogated, then cynicism finds a fertile environment.

How do organizations become cynical? Failing to meet job expectations is a good place to start. Promises of a fast track to success, an inability to delegate, an over-dependence on control mechanisms which stifle creativity, poor communication habits, unfocused culture, work team climates based on coercive influence systems, each of these are ingredients which normally are found in an environment dominated by cynicism. Many companies simply are out of step with the changing aspirations and outlooks of blue collar workers with respect to the culture they develop for the workplace.

Kanter and Mirvis found that people learn to shield their dignity through cynicism. Indeed, self-interest, despair, disillusionment are all learned behaviors. How ridiculous must it seem to a burned out employee to be forced to attend training programs on productivity or quality when their only ambition is to get through the day. We are caught in a deadly transition of woe. My generation feels betrayed because all that they anticipated was never available. At best, we aspire to survive, run in place instead of advancing. Yet this affliction seems minor as we view those who are to follow, the first generation in our history which cannot aspire to a higher standard of living their parents. An entire generation with more to offer than any which preceded it, yet whose skills are not being matched by job opportunities or even challenges.

Breaking this cycle involves creating an environment with realistic opportunities to achieve, realistic requiring to do so, and realistic probabilities of reward. Perhaps the public school teacher unions would be less intransigent toward change if administrators possessed courage and boards of education were willing to fund an expectancy based motivational model. Braddock recommends establishing a psychology of learning in which requirements are matched with abilities and winners are rewarded. Making challenges achievable, creating a desire to be your most severe critic, teaching people what is truly important about their job, these are essential ingredients in any accountability model. Those who have faced significant commitments, those who have experienced being right, those who have been made responsible, those who have been commended for the manner in which they think, these are the true winners today. These are people who have learned to earn, to be productive, who hold themselves to task. That is the objective and training is the vehicle to reach this objective.

Overcoming Discontent

Organizations develop a type of socialization process which ultimately will determine the norms of behavior, the culture, which will exist. Unfortunately, this process often evolves in a non-structured manner so that culture is not determined purposively and fails to develop as a tool for the leadership of the organization. The leadership process requires that positive climates be established within each work team so that each may contribute to a culture that defines quality. Batten suggests that those in authority can fulfill this leadership model by helping their staff remain focused, i.e., getting their people involved so that they can make a commitment and thus a contribution to the goals of the organization. When employee expectations are downplayed, they will eventually develop a cynical attitude as a defense mechanism.

Competition, distrust, a very passive work ethic, and dysfunctional conflict will dominate the work place. Service organizations, particularly in the public sector, often succumb to such tribulations. When staff do not see any advantage in caring about client needs, when they see "nothing for themselves" in taking initiative and working hard, then the job fails to offer people a chance to become winners. In contrast, when the majority of people in an organization can visualize a causal relationship between their welfare and the fulfillment of company goals, then a motivational climate exists which practically guarantees results.

Much is being written today about "empowerment". It is frustrating to someone in my profession to see such concepts being reduced to buzzwords and bantered about until they no longer are trendy. Empowerment represents a cultural orientation, it represents people and leadership and trust. When these things come together empowerment can equal a higher level of competitive standing in the readily changing economic environment which confronts most "organizations. In addition to being a vehicle to enhanced productivity, empowerment can provide for increased employee morale, an improved labor relations environment, and a climate in which the development and growth of employees is nurtured. These are secondary level benefits of entitlement which have more strategic implications for the organization. Managers must be a particular target for a corporate entity which wishes to creater an empowered work force. Managers routinely and universally adopt decision making as their primary role and this attitude is the enemy of empowerment. Indeed, it is the ally of entitlement.

The objective of an organization based empowerment initiative should be the self-directed team, the smallest unit of the cost center which can assume responsibility for productivity and influence other strategic business units. Awards and incentives often work best when they are directed at this operational level. Of course, training is again the key to achieving this scenario. People need to be trained to understand empowerment, to empower, and be empowered. Work will be done differently in organizations that have learned to empower their employees and training simulations are the best means to present new procedures, technologies, and control mechanisms. For example, many corporations have adopted the concept of quality circles as a means of sharing job knowledge and equity, improving communication, and improving decision making. Despite the number of organizations that have installed the Q-circle, the number of success stories is relatively few in number. Why? Such techniques depend on a leap of faith that most companies have not engendered in their employees. Credibility must exist before an organization may focus on increasing quality. Managers can be trained to act in a manner that creates the impression that they are committed to excellence and a participatory approach to problem solving. This type of work climate creates the potential for an energetic and enthusiastic work force to develop. Building a sense of self-esteem and converting complacency to ambition are learned leadership skills.

In companies that are successful, management is often described as open and honest (Kanter and Mirivis, 1989). The corporate culture appeared to be high-minded, and workers displayed an interest in areas such as: attaining an occupational identity, maintaining ties with colleagues, and further developing their talents, in addition to the very tangible motivation of money. These companies can afford to give people more influence over their work which means they can reap the full measure of talent that each can bring to task fulfillment because there exists an up-beat work ethic. Loyalty can no longer be bought with a paycheck. Greater self-expression and participation in controlling the fate of their organization are basic expectations for the contemporary worker, at least the ones who still have something to offer.

What can empowered employees do for an organization? They think better, they are creative, they assume responsibility and make decisions, and they are more intrinsically motivated. They also seem to have more fun at work and that is something I always look for in an organization.

Empowered individuals are now helping some firms begin benchmarking, a sort of type casting of rival firms noted for excellence in some area of operation, and then institutionalizing the best aspects of the rival, while challenging the not so excellent performance areas. Theoretically, the firm which is adopting these changes should be stronger by a geometric quotient, and so on with each succeeding benchmarking adoption. The process itself is fairly simple, with components of the model resembling a generic planning and problem solving process. The people whom you assign to this task should include those who will be charged with implementing whatever improvements are identified and judged suitable for installation. Project specialists trained in needs analysis, qualitative analysis, and planning are certainly useful but an absolute requirement is a training component for the model. Staff need to have an awareness created which will orient them to the benefits as well as the realities of the process. They also need to be trained in those process skills related to benchmarking as well as program development and adoption. AT&T has developed a large organization protocol for benchmarking which involves support of a team of specialists who staff the effort for each division which begins the process. AT&T also supports this effort with training in the process of both managing and creating a climate of readiness for benchmarking.

Getting it Done

Brinkerhoff and Gill (1992) criticize the majority of contemporary corporate training efforts as being politically distanced from the business of the organization with the result that management often treats training with a great deal of skepticism. Training must play a part in any initiative by which a firm rededicates its efforts to total quality. Trainers can maintain a proper perspective for their work by striving to deliver training programs that are dedicated to quality as a consequence of their design. The highest quality training is that which is designed to consistently produce results that add value to the organization. This value should be measured in people terms, i.e., the skills needed to deliver an ever increasing capacity to improve the quality of work which is the business of the organization.

Batten echoes this challenge and offers a vehicle to achieve the capacity to pursue excellence, it is called leadership. While emphasizing tough-mindedness, Batten recommends getting there by improving your communication, learning to compete with yourself, preaching and living synergistically in the workplace, building on strengths and being proactive.

Leaders build productivity by strengthening the skills of their staff, better decision making, more effective goal setting, and a concentrated effort in developing interpersonal relationships. These are the keys to improving the traditional management skills of planning, control, organizing, staffing, and directing. Leaders recognize improvement, no matter how small. They communicate well, they define policies and they use performance appraisal systems as staff development tools. Leaders make their staff feel significant and listened to. They build value in people and their challenging expectations stir others to increased performance. Leaders encourage their staff to work smarter not harder and instill quite old fashioned values of pride in accomplishments. Leaders are often hard on issues which must be addressed but they are not hard on the people who must deal with them. They focus on using strengths to overcome weaknesses and they recognize the role of manager as a resource rather than as an authority figure. When managers dwell on weaknesses they inhibit growth, stifle creativity, and hamper performance. Individuals will stop caring when management stops providing sufficient purpose, meaning, and support.

Organizations which intend to achieve total quality must first focus on renewal. Achieving value-added results requires joint human effort. Getting members involved in a team, i.e., establishing a strong expectation-oriented approach depends in no small measure on the quality of communications within the organization, the benchmark of its culture and climate setting initiatives.

Bardwick (1991) has identified three conditions which are found normally when organizations are revitalized. They are: challenge, empowerment, and significance. This list has been derived from Dr. Bardwick's research as to the nature of the most productive staff motivators, what she describes as "...earning the status of being a winner". Challenge, empowerment, and significance are three conditions which are needed in order for employees to feel enriched, i.e., to satisfy the need for job satisfaction, that which is now held commonly as the "new" motivator. Niehouse (1986) has also studied changing trends in effective motivational techniques and offers a low-cost mechanism which focuses on leadership. Being fair, being flexible, communicating what needs to be done, portraying a strong productivity based work ethic, these are Niehouse's keys to providing inspiration and motivation.

Operationalizing such motivational characteristics are fairly easy, for the talented manager working in the appropriate culture. Treating employees as valuable assets is a good way to begin. Managers must demonstrate to staff that they are viewed as thinking individuals, i.e., those who deserve to be respected and to be challenged. This is a strategy which should pay solid dividends. Involving workers in decision making, while helping provide them with the capacity to improve other key skills such as building interpersonal relationships and setting goals, is a very tangible means of establishing an improved working climate, one that is most conducive to improved productivity.

Moving an organization away from entitlement toward quality can prove to be a very perilous journey. Bardwick advocates turning up the pressure in order to effect a transitional mind set among staff from entitlement to fear. In other words, she believes that organizations have to get the attention of employees before their appreciation for quality can be heightened. This is most assuredly a strategic enterprise, one that must be defined as the pervasive culture of the organization. Senior leadership will certainly need to be tough-minded. Maintaining a balance between rust-out and burn-out has always been a key to sustaining performance. Our current times are so beset by instability that care may be exerted in confronting complacency while not creating a state of total paralysis.

Bardwick recommends increasing anxiety levels via the following vehicles: requiring risk taking, establishing a climate based on the peer pressure of working teams, creating competition, assuring a meritocracy.

An organization must create the opportunity for individuals to excel before they can contemplate improving their productivity. If the organization assumes that people want to work and to be successful, then a culture can be developed whereby people define their success by earning more difficult and diverse assignments. All organizations, even those in the public domain, must learn to earn their way through performance. This is becoming increasingly difficult in a an era in which such performance cannot be bought, either because monetary resources are not available or because the work rules do not permit merit pay.

Making people visible, especially through teaming, is a means of increasing accountability because functional collaboration and mutual responsibility are required simply to get through the day. It is interesting to observe that many organizations have worked for years to achieve such a condition as a means of keeping functional the states of conflict which quite naturally characterize a workplace.

Establishing a meritocracy means much more than simply paying people bonuses. Rewarding differentially is a means of providing those incentives which are a keystone to productivity. Keeping some pay at risk to keep people from becoming too comfortable is an enhanced model for rewarding differentially. Intrinsic motivators play an increasingly powerful role in such models. Empowering people, through their performance, to participate, influence, motivate, discipline, and even worry about the corporate state of health is a mechanism whereby instability can be used as a tool for increasing pressure to abandon entitlement and begin embracing an earning mentality.

The experience of Johnsonville Foods of Sheboygan, Wisconsin is an interesting case in point. Ralph Stayer (1990) is rapidly becoming a legend for his success in moving an organization from entitlement to earning. He himself had to learn to give up control before he could effectively manage the resistance that is inherent in reshaping the culture of a large organization.

This case has become a favorite teaching situation for me because it represents a comprehensive depiction of the process leaders must follow in establishing a focus for change, establishing a culture which makes quality the only product, mitigating the barriers inherent in an overhead mentality, and making employees accountable. Stayer's self-announced goal is to make his position obsolete. This is the only point of contention between us because I value his brand of leadership as essential to creating and maintaining a sense of vision. Ralph Stayer has demonstrated conclusively that he possesses the courage to admit that new directions are necessary, the vision to welcome change, and the enthusiasm to motivate.

Johnsonville Foods was earning a profit but the workforce depended on supervisory personnel to tell them what to do and how to do it. They had no motivation to accept responsibility for their errors and tended to dismiss mistakes as "accidents". Stayer recognized that he had to hold himself accountable for the lack of readiness in his corporation to embrace change. Even he was not sure in what direction the company should move, how then could the staff possess the vision necessary to meet the critical challenge of effecting change while remaining operational? Stayer determined that each staff member had to be trained to take risks, to be empowered to make decisions, and to be held accountable for their own work. He also observed that structuring the organization around a base of work teams would create a climate conducive to establishing accountability pressure and mentoring capacities. My favorite "Stayerism" is his courageous stand in mitigating the negative influences of middle management.

He realized that each layer of management created still another barrier to pierce in combating entitlement. Managers were transitioned into individuals who were paid more because they possessed a skill that the organization needed as a resource. Those who could offer little more than an authority model were invited to join a more traditionally structured organization. The corporate quality control model is now based on the philosophy that those who implement a decision and must live with its consequences are the best people to make it. Staff proved eager to embrace ownership for the quality of their product. Incentive pay was established and related to a profit pool. The vision, the empowerment, the potential rewards of success were all established in the minds of the work force by Stayer in order to facilitate the transition from a longevity based compensation system to one in which performance mattered most. Training became a key ingredient in the success of Johnsonville Foods. Process, system, and technological procedures are the major domains in which training takes place. Those who would lead others in this organization have to have something to impart to others. Just imagine the investment in communication skills necessary to convey such a program of change throughout an entire organization! Johnsonville Foods revitalized itself via a paradigm of change that was based on training as an implementation vehicle. Maintaining that sense of revitalization will require a continuing commitment to change.

A Better Way

One very practical means of using stress effectively to combat entitlement is to increase the accountability of each individual for their actions through the challenge of the evaluation process. People need to be held accountable for doing meaningful work and deserve to have their progress in performing their duties measured in objective terms with some motivational aspects attached. Today, the valence associated with such motivation may be as simple as a combination of being treated with respect, being challenged, and being invited to return to work for a subsequent day. Measuring the extent to which meaningful work is being accomplished is the function of performance appraisal. Those organizations which establish an appraisal process which is based on developmental considerations are well along to reaping the value of employee evaluation rather than being hindered by the vicissitudes normally found in this process.

Unfortunately, completing a performance appraisal is not a strong suit of most managers. Why? Both managers and employees fear the evolution. No one likes to be appraised by another, especially when such a process is based on a policy of assigned liability rather than mitigating weaknesses through strengths and considering problems to be challenges that an entire work unit must labor to overcome. Jobs should be based on some description of essential work to be performed. These "essential business elements" should be made known, without any margin of misunderstanding, to those who would hold the position. They should form the basis of both soliciting and filling the position. Incumbents in the organizations form the most credible capacity for identifying these essential elements and the successful candidate should, over time, be invited to contribute their perspective as to how the job should be modified to enable the investment of resources behind the position to be well spent. Despite the fact that complying with the little scenario described above is both a legal as well as programmatic consideration, many companies either are unwilling or unaware that this is the manner in which they should proceed. The growing number of discrimination suits, soon to be swelled by those filed under the Americans with Disabilities Act, attest to the hiring practices which result in adverse impact. An even more obscure notion is that the ability to make an organization progress is dependent on its ability to develop its staff and that an effective performance appraisal process is a primary vehicle is achieving such a capacity.

Some of the commonly held problems to be associated with performance appraisals are presented in table four.

Table Four:
Performance Appraisals: the Process and the Problems

- ✓ Me vs. Them Perspective
- ✓ Emotional Effect
- ✓ Sitting in Judgment
- ✓ The Complexity of the Process
- ✓ Lack of Preparation
- ✓ Delegating Blame
- ✓ Multiple Choreographic Techniques
- ✓ Sidestepping Confrontation
- ✓ Inadequate Communication Skills

My own beloved United States Navy is a prime offender in this vital human resources area. The vast majority of junior officer fitness reports list those being evaluated in the top five percent of their peers. Among mid-grade personnel the problem is even more ubiquitous with those officers being almost uniformly ranked in the top one-percent. We now depend on a type of underground in-house jargon-type listing of adjectives to discriminate among those top one-percenters who should be advanced and those top one-percenters who should not. This seems ludicrous in a time in which the welfare of the service as well as the security of the nation depend on finding, nurturing, and retaining only the finest young women and men. The enlisted evaluation model is just as archaic. Personnel are rated on numerous attributes that are as subjective in nature as most you will ever see, on a scale in which a 4.0 represents the highest ranking.

We have so many 4.0 sailors in active service that it has now become necessary to discriminate among them by ranking the best of the best on even more subjective criteria which they hopefully have discerned as being important through some process of osmosis. This is akin to an organization of nothing but outstanding executives who command even larger annual bonuses while the company slips badly. Something is out of whack here!

I believe that a personal example will serve to illustrate the impact of the common problems associated with performance appraisals much better than any item by item discussion. I once had an experience as an assistant department head in a large Naval Reserve Unit in which a sailor, who was a marginal performer at best, exploded when he discovered that the department head had assigned him a grade of 3.6 on only one item, with an overall ranking of 3.8. I learned of this incident when the sailor in question arrived at a holiday gathering threatening violence on the officer who had "ruined his career". Once the facts were known via an investigation, I found myself in the role of attempting to mitigate this event by attacking the process which led to the confrontation. I testified that the behaviors noted were unacceptable, but not necessarily entirely on the part of our unhappy sailor.

The sequence of events unfolded as follows. The appraisal was an annual event. No performance expectations beyond those expected via the single word criteria and past practice had been established for an individual sailor. The chain of command was not utilized. This was an important finding because it meant that those closest to the individual, those best able to offer both challenging goals and the guidance to achieve them, were not employed in this vital role. Thus the developmental aspects were completely lost. No progress estimates were developed over the course of the reporting period and no effort was expended to communicate what should be done and why those "somethings" were important. The evaluations were thereby reduced to estimates of who looked sharp, was reliable and timely in attendance, and possessed recruiting poster military bearing. Three criteria which should have been considered as basic requirements for retention in the organization were being employed to discriminate among top performers and these were communicated via expectation only.

To complicate matters, the department head was uncomfortable in dealing with the process. He tried to mitigate everything that was negative and left at least this one sailor without a clear notion of even why they were meeting. Is it any wonder that our marginal performer resented what "they" were doing to him. Imagine how lacking in credibility his superior must have seemed as he attempted to dance to several tunes simultaneously before jumping on some rational for the grades which seemed to work with a particular sailor. The department head was so intent on sidestepping confrontation that he delegated blame for whatever grades might ultimately be assigned up the chain of command so that when our sailor received his evaluation at the end of a drill weekend, as a fait accompli, it was the first time he saw his actual grades. And his officers were on their way to a holiday party!

The final straw for me was the fact that the comments which are supposed to explicate the rankings were in conflict with those rankings. A review of the man's record indicated that the comments had changed little over the past few years and constituted little more than generic "bullets" which are used as a type of Chinese menu to discriminate among personnel.

This scenario is being replayed every day in organizations of all type and most particularly, in my experience, in the public sector. Managers have not been trained how to conduct performance appraisals, they sincerely doubt that performance appraisal can serve any viable purpose, they are unable to communicate the intrinsic value of appraisals for both the individual and the company, and they are certainly unprepared to deal with the resistance to change or even confrontation situations which their actions engender. How many so-called "difficult geniuses" are forever lost to their organizations because their managers were unable to cope with their intellect or drive? How many performance appraisals were prostituted into being employed as a tool for removing an employee who might be seen as a threat to an insecure manager? How many organizations who purport to be striving for quality can afford such waste?

There seems to be little doubt that developing and maintaining human relationships is a key variable in developing the kind of leaders who are capable of reshaping organizations to be more productive. Becoming relationship oriented enables an individual to influence the behaviors of others. *These others can be counted on to fulfill the expectations of the leader only to the extent that they are aware of and willing to go along with these mutual expectations.* That sentence should say a lot to you, i.e., the concepts of: having a say in the quality of life at work, the ability to exercise creativity, the spark that is necessary to make decisions, and the freedom to hold accountability are reflected in those few words.

Leaders must be continually sensitive to the changing needs of their relational partners, i.e., those with whom they have built implicit contracts, in order that they may update the nature of their interpersonal relationships. For example, those in authority over others will hold legitimate power for a period of time but only for a fixed period of time. Consider the case of the professor who greets classes during the first week. Even the most perceptive and cynical of students may give a faculty member a week to prove just how boring they can be before giving up on the lectures. Legitimate power is a transitory state of influence because it fairly quickly tends to move into a real power scenario. For example, our college professor may decide to act in a coercive fashion and threaten the students into attending class or he may realize his limitations and work harder to demonstrate his expertise and therefore make the class more worthwhile. In the latter situation he would be demonstrating expert power.

This scenario plays itself out each day in the workplace. One of the most devastating and professionally dangerous situations for an employee is to be caught in the trap of working for someone who is weaker in talent and bent on exercising their authority to overcome this inferiority complex. In this context, conflicts are managed by the senior forcing their will on the junior and the power base continuously employed is that of coercion. The response mechanism of the employee is to block the attempt of the superior to frustrate or even destroy them. Hence, the same behaviors are mirrored back to the manager and the productivity of that work team drifts in the wake of this all encompassing game of organizational politics. Coercive power as a sole influence profile has no place in any organization. It violates the notion of situational leadership, it engenders a huge overhead base to supervise the downtrodden, and its motivational quotient is a perfect negative correlation. The pirate crew has yet to be put together that can get up for every passing ship and those who work in a world of coercive influence patterns will soon display numbness to the experience and concentrate their efforts on destroying the enemy or otherwise obtaining relief. Could Ralph Stayer have treated his people as galley slaves and achieved what he knew had to be accomplished?

Quite unlikely. Instead, he pursued the norm of reciprocity in his inter-personal relationships, building commitment to his vision while remaining flexible to the needs of individuals and the changing circumstances that accompanied the rebirth of his company. Stayer is a motivator, he recognizes the value of this primary purpose of communication. As Kreps (1990) writes, by reciprocally fulfilling one another's expectations, we develop and maintain interpersonal relationships and elicit interpersonal cooperation. Stayer made himself a valued resource to his employees, especially those who sought to prosper via his compensation model of paying for performance. His role as CEO may have been redefined but it was hardly diminished. Any individual who can build relationships via motivational strategies is worthy of trust and commitment. Such individuals enrich our lives and restore credibility to the fundamental relationship between management and labor. Thus are the foundations of improvement developed.

I once had the distinct pleasure to be associated with the organization of my dreams, one of the finest school districts I had ever known. What made this situation so enchanting was the staff. These were the kind of people to whom you would trust your family and without qualms. There was a certain confidence among them, whether teacher, custodian, or bus driver, they seemed to know the extent to which the community valued them. The superintendent expended every ounce of energy which he possessed in creating opportunities for the staff to excel. The administrative team was kept at minimal levels and then functioned primarily as resource providers. Every paradise seems to acquire a serpent and theirs came in the form of a new superintendent, a cognitively dissonant individual who combined a certain blend of arrogance and ignorance. On the surface he was everyone's friend but as events would show he was not above conspiring to discredit those whom he viewed as a threat. The real loss was something quite intangible, the spirit to excel. Layers of managers were followed by ever increasingly strict standards to insure standardization. Control mechanisms flourished and were designed to stifle initiative. Confrontation soon followed and soon even long term observers of the organization seemed to forget what had been. There is an old saying in the British Navy, something to the effect that there is no justice aboard ship unless it sails in the heart of its captain. I believe that these words were used to describe the dissatisfaction of the British Admiralty with respect to the fitness of William Bligh, in reviewing the events of the mutiny onboard H.M.S. Bounty. It is incredibly naive to think that any organization will survive, let alone prosper, without total quality leadership.

The sober 1990's will provide for a leavening of aspiration, a return to more achievable expectations, a sharper focus on reality. This will provide an unprecedented opportunity for building organizations by developing their people, for training to provide a learning psychology. Those who would seize the initiative must find ways to communicate their sense of vision, their aspirations for change, their willingness to embrace others as equal partners in a total commitment to quality.

4

PLANNING INTERVENTIONS

Beginnings

The road to quality is long and steep. It must begin with a few small steps at the lowest levels of the organization. A movement toward quality requires patience, and that is something that organizations in this country normally do not possess in abundance. U.S. firms, in comparison to their Japanese counterparts, seem to plan, for purposes of capital investment, in terms of ten minutes instead of ten years. The journey toward quality will involve a complete restructuring of the attitudes and possibly reporting relationships of the firm. Leadership must impart to the senior executives a sense of striving and a capacity to manage resistance effectively. Lake Superior Paper (Houston, 1989) is a case in point. This firm has been described as a petri dish for the employee participation movement, an organization that blurs the traditional distinction between workers and their bosses. Lake Superior is striving to find a balance between industrial egalitarianism and the pragmatic imperatives of demonstrating a profit by grouping employees into teams that are highly functional units. At Lake Superior, these teams can resemble highly autonomous governing bodies, invested with the power to hire, promote, and discipline their own, along with the responsibility to set plant-wide policies such as arranging shift schedules and job assignments. This novel approach to enhanced productivity began with training senior executives to let go of their authority base and begin to see themselves as resource providers.

Once awareness training among senior leadership is completed, then skills development may progress throughout the ranks of the supervisory personnel who will remain after the inevitable restructuring. The successful completion of this phase will result in a new spirit in the organization, a culture in which individuals are respected for what they can contribute and women and members of other protected groups are recognized for the talent and initiative they possess. Only then may the real work begin, the development of work teams, support establishments, incentive programs, and appraisal systems which will lead to an earning society.

How important is this? Winston Churchill (Gilbert, 1992), in one of the most forlorn periods of his political existence, 1917, took the most unpopular position of introducing legislation known as the Munitions of War Bill. Special wage awards would be paid to those who displayed the greatest skills. No worker would be penalized for belonging to a trade union or taking part in a strike. To those among his colleagues who decried the cost of such measures, Churchill replied that the government would not win the war without the support of the great masses of the country. Further, the war of production would be lost completely unless the masses gave their support "...with a loyal and spontaneous determination." Munitions plants which adopted his bonus schemes had the highest production in Britain.

Henry Mintzberg (1990) has examined the facts behind the folklore concerning managerial responsibilities. His research indicates that, for the most part, managers become conditioned by their own work habits and eventually tend to submit to the pressures of the job. They work at an unrelenting pace, their activities are characterized by brevity, variety, and discontinuity and they are strongly oriented to action. Mintzberg also found that most managers concentrate their time in performing a set number of regular duties, with a special focus on passing along information which they possess to selected employees for their subsequent use. Such a profile does not speak well for the type of patience and culture development that is necessary for an organization to begin the quest for increased productivity.

No organization can be well run if managers must spend a disproportionate amount of their time in dealing with disturbances, yet conflict management seems to be occupying more and more of the time available to key staff. Making decisions effectively is another important aspect of conflict management. Seniors have to be able to negotiate, i.e., determine the impact of their decisions on others, build a constituency among those able to exert influence in the organization, and insure that resources are not over-expended. How much greater return on the investment placed behind the senior leadership of an organization would accrue if issues such as those described above were able to be managed effectively at lower levels of the corporate structure. Indeed, those who practice total quality leadership have made sure that their staff has been trained to accomplish such tasks at the lowest possible levels, the arena in which quality must be ultimately defined and practiced.

If managers are to profit from the growth of an information based society, they must adopt their talents to the coordination of relationships that enhance the completion of work, much in the manner of a symphonic orchestra. Even routine duties which involve interpersonal roles, that is, those which involve little serious communication, are important to the smooth functioning of the organization and cannot be ignored. Mintzberg has identified this as an area in which managers must adopt a leadership role, especially in the area of assuming responsibility for the training and development of their own staff. Much of this training should now be directed toward skill enhancement. Cognitive learning is, and always will be, important, but such learning is routinely based in the formal education which most employees acquire prior to and during their employment experience. The ability to take risks, make decisions in areas of ambiguity, negotiate, reason, resolve conflicts, establish information networks and develop peer relationships, are the areas in which firms must make a significant commitment to train each and every individual which they employ. In addition, organizations must develop internal consulting capacities to help their quality initiatives succeed. Managers must be trained to build bridges to total involvement and to assess the readiness of a work force to promote a quality oriented program. Creating self-directed teams and building a customer focus are very contemporary challenges facing the corporate trainer.

Does such a training paradigm require special skills and attitudes among senior leadership? Yes! Do changes have to be effected in the way in which business is routinely conducted to allow such training to be effective? Yes !! Will resistance to such changes be significant? Yes !!! Is such training too expensive, considering this list of questions? NO!!!!

Dobyns (1990) pictures Dr. Deming as a capitalist revolutionary, one who preaches that big changes are necessary if we are to drive to quality and such changes are needed in a hurry. Deming believes that improving quality automatically improves productivity. The first of the "14 points", creating constancy of purpose, is where senior leaderships begin the quest for quality as they begin rebuilding their organizations along the lines described by this book. By adopting a total quality leadership approach they actually begin to save money. Consider the following: after many years of first ignoring and then rationalizing their difficulties, American auto makers have begun to realize that it is inherently cheaper to design quality in rather than inspect it in. That means that those who build the cars have to do so from a quality perspective and they must be trained to behave in that manner. Typically, about 25 percent of the resources of a production facility are expended for re-work and repair. Would you like to realize such savings? Well, read on....

David Kearns (1990) has studied the means by which leadership can be, translated into quality as CEO of the Xerox Corporation. When Xerox began producing and marketing a copier that had been designed by a Japanese affiliate, Fuji Xerox, they began to realize how far they had fallen behind some competitors. What really got their attention was the fact that the rejection rate for the parts produced by this affiliate proved to be only a fraction of the rate for American manufactured parts.

Xerox took some immediate steps in the right direction by identifying and benchmarking firms that had developed a Leadership-Through-Quality paradigm, including Fuji Xerox. They found that quality in manufacturing actually decreased cost and substantially because it eliminated inspections, rejects, and field service and protected sales against competitors. The Xerox quality goal had a simple yet ambitious objective, to develop manufacturing processes that emphasized preventing defects rather than screening them out through inspections.

The senior leadership of Xerox soon realized that the quality process would have to pervade every operation and further, that the key to achieving this goal was commitment on the part of every employee. The work force was transitioned from stand-alone, quality of work-life circles to work-family groups composed of working together in discrete manufacturing operations. Workers were trained in interpersonal skills, group dynamics and problem solving techniques. The burden of evaluating challenges such as working conditions and production problems and development recommendation was placed on the workers. Emphasis was placed on identifying quality short-falls, the problems that caused them and the solutions needed to correct them.

The results have been impressive, as measured by cost savings. Production-line defective parts have been reduced by more than 90 percent since 1982. Manufacturing costs have been reduced by 20 percent and they are still dropping and timelines for bringing new products to market have been reduced by as much as 60 percent. This model has been adopted as a long-term process because everyone involved at Xerox realizes that only such a deep commitment will enable Xerox to survive in the global market of today.

Harley-Davidson represents another success story of a firm in competition with the Japanese (Reid, 1989). In 1975, Harley was spending as much as $1,000.00 to repair new bikes to the level that dealers could sell them for approximately $4,000. New customers just simply weren't interested in tinkering with vehicles when they could buy a Japanese competitor at a similar price and acquire an almost defect free bike. Manufacturing was the problem and it was not until Harley benchmarked their competitors that they realized that the Japanese simply managed their people assets better. Before embarking on innovations such as just-in-time scheduling, Harley realized that employee attitudes had to be changed. A program of "new wisdom" was begun in which the staff were involved heavily in planning and working out details of problem solving on the production line. No changes were made until the people involved understood and accepted them, and this included every department from engineering to maintenance. Harley's next task was to train employees how to define and monitor the quality of their work. Managers had to be trained to become team leaders instead of just bosses and suppliers had to be convinced to adopt similar methods. Last year, Harley celebrated their 85th birthday and they expect to recognize many more profitable anniversaries!

GM represents the other end of the performance continuum (Taylor, 1992). Despite technological advances that border on brilliance and a knack for developing new products, the company is foundering. Before he himself was replaced recently, former CEO Robert Stempel could only offer massive cutbacks as a strategy to offset the negative slide. GM lags behind its major competitors in almost every measure of efficiency. For example, on one key productivity index, the number of person hours required to build a car, Ford is 40% more efficient than GM. The GM plant in Doraville, Ga., which now builds the Oldsmobile Cutlass Supreme requires twice as many workers to assemble a car as compared to the Ford Taurus plant in nearby Atlanta. In 1991 GM lost, on the average, $1500 on every one of the 3.5 million cars and trucks it made in North America.

The United Auto Workers maintains a take-no-prisoners attitude toward GM and union locals will strike over every attempt to change work rules to enhance efficiency. A stubborn and very entrenched middle management force only complicates the scenario at GM. It is important to all of us that GM succeed. It is the largest minority employer in the private sector and is the largest consumer of items such as steel, rubber, glass, plastic, and carpeting. GM has historically tried to solve its problems by throwing money at them, a solution that can no longer be afforded even if it had any merit. After spending $90 billion on new plants, equipment, and upgrades in the 1980's, GM is broke.

GM must reorganize to eliminate redundant operations and must destabilize the workforce even more. By that I mean that a spirit of accountability has to be installed and the famous "frozen middle" is the place to start. Fewer than 100 salaried workers out of over 100,000 have been dismissed for poor performance during the last few years and these are the folks who give the competition such a head start with their errors. GM must develop new attitudes among its employees. Each has to recognize the danger that the current predicament of GM places them in and everyone has to begin solving rather than creating problems. A reproachment with the UAW is an absolute necessity. The current contract provides for GM to pay as many as 80,000 workers as much as 85% of their salary during slow periods. If the company cannot communicate the seriousness of the crisis now faced by all to its union then GM is surely doomed. At Ford quality is job number one for the workforce. It is difficult to believe that GM workers cannot be trained to perform in a similar manner and speed GM's recovery.

Total Quality

How do we set designs for total quality and overcome problems when we seek compliance to a vision? How do we involve our employees and remain flexible to the demands of our environment? While a commitment to quality should not be considered a panacea, it does offer a strong potential for success. David Oliver (1993) has studied the manner in which organizations mature and believes that each develops a persona or personality, which involves commonly held beliefs, goals, attitudes, and hopefully, corporate heroes. Common attitudes with a focus on quality will bring a performance emphasis to an entity. Ongoing development is the critical factor in overcoming the ultimate deterence to growth, uncertainty.

In *Keeping Customers for Life* , Cannie (1991) offers the following as a "creed" for Total Quality:

- ☐ A PROBLEM EXISTS ONLY IF IT AFFECTS SERVICE.
- ☐ WORKING IN A GROUP USUALLY IMPROVES THE PROBLEM-SOLVING PROCESS BECAUSE TEAMS CAN CREATE SOLUTIONS FASTER THAN MOST INDIVIDUALS CAN WORKING ALONE.
- ☐ THE FIRST STEP IN PROBLEM SOLVING IS BECOMING AWARE OF THE PROBLEM. RECOGNIZING THE SITUATION

AS IT IS BEGINS THE MEANS TO A SOLUTION.

- ☐ PROBLEMS HAVE MANY CAUSES; SITUATIONS EXIST BECAUSE A NUMBER OF FORCES PUSH THEM THAT WAY. IDENTIFYING THE FORCES MAY GIVE YOU A DIRECTION FOR CHANGING THE SITUATION.

- ☐ EFFECTIVE DECISIONS DEPEND ON ACCURATE INFORMATION AND ON GENERATING NEW WAYS OF SOLVING PROBLEMS.

- ☐ EVERYONE IS CREATIVE. YOU NEED TO LEARN HOW TO TAP YOUR CREATIVE CENTER.

- ☐ TO BE MORE CREATIVE, YOU SIMPLY LOOK AT THE SAME THINGS AS EVERYONE ELSE AND THEN THINK SOMETHING DIFFERENT.

- ☐ PROBLEM SOLVERS ARE FREE TO CONTRIBUTE THEIR BEST EFFORTS, BREAK RULES, STOP BEING PRACTICAL, MAKE MISTAKES, LOOK INTO OUTSIDE AREAS, AND HAVE FUN-WITHOUT PENALTY.

- ☐ SOLVING A PROBLEM ISN'T WORTH MUCH UNLESS YOU CAN IMPLEMENT A SOLUTION THROUGH YOUR STAFF CAPACITY.

Notice the emphasis on service? How many skills, knowledge areas, or functional abilities can you identify from this list? How many of those which you have identified can you expect people to learn from a degree program or on the job? Sound like training may be useful here? Correct!

I often begin my TQL workshop by reviewing this creed and asking the participants to describe the quality assurance function in their organization, how it is staffed and what mission is has been assigned. The blank stares, even among senior executives, is almost frightening to observe!

How may we define quality? Is 99% world class quality? Most students would respond with a resounding "YES" if we were discussing success on an examination and the grade in question was a "99". However, quality has to be defined differently for an organization that wishes to remain competitive. Consider the examples presented in table five.

Table Five Examples of Quality at a 99% success rate.

A 99% MEANS:

- ✓ ABOUT 1.5 MISSPELLED WORDS PER PAGE IN A BOOK
- ✓ 20,000 LOST ARTICLES OF MAIL PER HOUR
- ✓ 5,000 INCORRECT SURGICAL OPERATIONS PER WEEK
- ✓ TWO SHORT OR LONG LANDINGS AT MOST MAJOR AIRPORTS PER DAY
- ✓ NO ELECTRICITY FOR ALMOST 7 HOURS EACH MONTH

Total Quality has to be something more, at least in hospitals that wish to treat me or airports that I might frequent.

Does your organization have a formal definition or set of expectations related to total quality management? If not, a point of departure for total quality may be defined as: a process to create a demand for re-examining creaky procedures, and, an investigation capacity to remediate trouble spots which have been identified.

The significant participation of employee teams is the key to the process. Total quality must be based on a "bottoms-up" approach that emphasizes patience and distrusts obvious answers. TQL is dependent on an employee based improvement capacity. TQM should be viewed as the minimum requirement for staying in the game!

The manager's responsibility is to create a workplace environment that empowers people. Senior executives have to be trained to study the competition. Managers must act as if they live to be told how their unit is performing. What is required is not a "blame-us" approach, but one that conveys an overriding interest in quality. It is necessary to avoid the "posse ploy", i.e., managers must avoid the trap of analyzing things to death. For example, if your organization performs as follows, it probably has already strangled itself into a state of impotence.

Consider the task force which studies the recommendations of the study group which reviewed the objectives of a task force which met with representatives of work teams who had been participants in a quality circle. The manager who wishes to practice total quality leadership will create process action teams to solve problems, enhance communication, maintain momentum , and forever keep moving the organization forward.

Consider Picogna's Precepts:

- TQM IS A SELF-ASSESSMENT PROCESS. LEARNING BY PARTICIPATION ALLOWS EMPLOYEES TO ASK QUESTIONS AND PERMITS THEM TO COMMENT ON HOW/WHY THINGS CAN BE CHANGED.

- THIS SELF-APPRAISAL METHODOLOGY REQUIRES A PROACTIVE APPROACH AND PUTS MANAGERS IN THE ROLE OF ASKING QUESTIONS ABOUT HOW SYSTEMS WORK INSTEAD OF MAKING DEMANDS ABOUT WHY THEY DON'T.

- WHO HOLDS THE EQUITY IN AN ORGANIZATION? THE EMPLOYEES!

- THE PROCESS CREATES AN AWARENESS AS WELL AS AN APPRECIATION OF THE MANY ROLES OF

THE ORGANIZATION. THE TRUE "WORKINGS" OF THE SYSTEM: HOW PEOPLE GET THINGS DONE BY INTERACTING WITH ONE ANOTHER.

In today's environment, if your organization does not espouse this philosophy you had better become an agent for meaningful change or begin planning for a new corporate affiliation. The folks at Johnsonville Foods developed the right approach and thrived. Their solution to the quality dilemma is presented in table six.

Table Six THE JOHNSONVILLE FOODS SOLUTION

✓ LINE WORKERS WERE MADE RESPONSIBLE FOR QUALITY CHECKS. They readily accepted the responsibility and contributed numerous suggestions regarding the process. Product rejects fell from 5% to less than 0.5%.

✓ CUSTOMER COMPLAINTS AND QUESTIONS WERE FORWARDED TO LINE WORKERS. The staff began to correct the problems that customers had raised.

✓ PROFIT SHARING WAS PUT IN PLACE. The staff began to collect data about labor costs, efficiency, and yield. They developed process action teams to strengthen the performance of marginal workers.

✓ ANNUAL ACROSS THE BOARD PAY INCREASES WERE ELIMINATED. Performance bonuses were paid when people assumed greater responsibility, such as trainers, or acquired new skills, such as budgeting.

✓ MANAGEMENT WAS ASSIGNED THE ROLE OF RESOURCE PERSONNEL. Those supervisors who had depended only on authority to fulfill their role were asked to move on.

✓ TEAMS WERE DEVELOPED. Decisions about performance standards, budgets, capital improvements, assignments, quality measures and operations were delegated with decision making moved down throughout the organization to whatever level could best accommodate the process.

The staff of Johnsonville Foods experienced both education and training, i.e., they were given the capacity to profit from an empowerment model and further, their capabilities in selected skill areas were enhanced. This represents a true total quality initiative because of the unique blend of values, goal setting, accountability, and training.

Planning for Total Quality

How do we get there? The road to quality is not an easy path, persistence, risk, delegating authority, building relationships, and sharing credit can be a difficult proposition to master. TQL is a process or a change in the way things are done, not a program. Here are some tips that relieve some of the tedium and shorten your journey.

Develop a clear consistent notion of goals. Staff should not have to ask the question, WHAT DO YOU EXPECT OF ME??? Federal Express (Cannie, 1991) offers a very simplistic yet highly effective response to this question by employing universal goals throughout the organization:

100 % CUSTOMER SATISFACTION AFTER THE SALE!

100 % CUSTOMER SATISFACTION AFTER EVERY INTERACTION!

100 % SERVICE PERFORMANCE ON EVERY PACKAGE HANDLED!

Motorola won the Malcolm Baldrige award by achieving a standard of quality that equaled 99.999989%. By way of comparison, consider the following illustration. THAT STANDARD OF QUALITY IS EQUAL TO LESS THAN 1.5 MISSPELLED WORDS IN AN ENTIRE LIBRARY OF BOOKS!!! THAT IS WHAT WINNING THE MALCOLM BALDRIGE AWARD IS ALL ABOUT!!!

Another challenging question that normally pops up from both management and staff who have embarked on a "quality quest" is, "HOW REALISTIC IS ALL OF THIS?" People want to do a good job and will if they know what is expected of them and if they are properly trained. The company has to set the stage by providing the following:

- ☐ CHARISMATIC LEADERSHIP: THE ABILITY TO SEE WHAT IS REALLY IMPORTANT EACH DAY ON THE JOB AND TRANSMIT A SENSE OF MISSION TO OTHERS. INSTILLING PRIDE AND SELF-RESPECT AMONG SUBORDINATES WILL MAKE IT EASIER FOR PEOPLE TO BECOME ENTHUSIASTIC ABOUT THEIR ASSIGNMENTS.

- ☐ INDIVIDUAL CONSIDERATION: MAINTAINING A DEVELOPMENTAL ORIENTATION TOWARD STAFF IS WHERE IT ALL BEGINS. SHOWING APPRECIATION AND CONSIDERATION, PAYING SPECIAL ATTENTION TO NEWCOMERS. THESE ARE THE ATTRIBUTES OF LEADERS.

- ☐ TAKE SOME RISKS: ENCOURAGE EMPLOYEES TO TAKE ACTION AND ASSUME RESPONSIBILITY. THAT IS WHAT BEING RESPONSIBLE AND ACCOUNTABLE MEANS.

- ☐ PAY FOR PERFORMANCE.

The last variable is one of the most difficult to achieve. Recall Bardwick's advice to destabilize the organization before attempting a transformation to an earning mentality. TQL is of particular value to organizations experiencing transitions and downsizing because it identifies areas that are the least productive and restores credibility, i.e., even disproportionate cuts seem fair after such a thorough self-analysis. When a work force senses a destabilized environment they begin searching for structure. Total quality is the best tonic for combating the entitlement mentality which may afflict a corporation.

An organization characterized by narrow-mindedness expects managers to organize resources, both human and nonhuman, to maximize effectiveness. This is essentially an engineering task when it implies that people are either redundant or are objects that are used up as is the case with transformation based raw material. Employees soon get the message that their primary task is to avoid being transitioned. They become afraid to take risks and concentrate their behavior on self-protection and self-promotion rather than cooperation. Fear takes over as a driving force because of the inability of staff to respond to the changes they are experiencing and their need to remain in control becomes exascerbated. This process should facilitate movement from pay based on longevity to pay for performance. What happens when the money runs out, is a question that most organizations will struggle with in the near future. It is an issue that can become very distracting to a veteran work force that may witness newcomers moving beyond them on the compensation scale or once steady pay increases disappearing. Many consultants working in the area of compensation systems will recommend that pay increases not be tied directly and automatically to the performance appraisal process. Telling someone that they are the greatest thing since sliced bread and then apologizing for cutting their pay due to poor productivity of the organization is a sure way to take a proven performer and turn them into someone who is surely along for the ride. Once the total quality initiative is installed, those who remain will begin to see not only the task but also the rewards ahead. As stated previously, these rewards may amount to little more than survival at first, but right now that may be enough. Using appraisals to qualify people to participate in a performance pool is one way of keeping folks in the game. Building an outstanding quality of life at work environment will serve as a substitute reward and also contribute to the climate that work teams must experience in order to flourish. I recently had some personal experiences in this area with friends who headed small law firms and insurance agencies.

The competition for survival against similar-sized to even mega-sized competitors has become extraordinarily severe. Only by carefully developing a strong sense of awareness among the staff as to the essential ingredients of the business can these firms hope to remain in business. These business essentials differ as each defines its niche but training the staff via both awareness and skill development programs is the key to success.

The Saturn automobile is built by a company which follows a unique set of rules. There are five values which Saturn employees are expected to embrace: a commitment to customer enthusiasm, a commitment to excel, teamwork, trust and mutual respect, and continuous improvement. Sound difficult? Well, maybe it did four years ago, but now we know that Saturn is a success, they sell more cars than they produce so there is always a demand for their product. Saturn and the United Auto Workers formed a partnership to compete with the imports. An often overlooked variable in the Saturn story is the manner in which sales consultants demonstrate their credibility on the sales floor. The challenge is to take the ideal of a better way to build relationships with prospective customers and make it a reality. Sound like quality?! You bet, and training was the vehicle to success. Saturn has its own training facility in Spring Hill, Tennessee where both manufacturing and sales personnel complete seminars and self-study modules in topics such as conflict management and creative thinking.

Quality must be mathematically measured, tracked all day,

every day, and compiled throughout the organization. Striving should represent a state of mind and a continuing commitment, not a "half-time" pep talk. Each member of your staff should be expected to develop a significant list of measures for their job which should represent excellence. These are the bases for the existence of their job and represent the essence of the business necessity which their positions fulfill, i.e., the variables by which staff are hired, promoted or fired. Settling for less than total quality is dangerous, how much can each individual shave off from 100%? In that set of circumstances, striving for quality when it is more chore than vision can actually result in a demotivating influence.

To achieve total quality every employee at every level must: define quality from the perspective of the client or customer; develop standards by which actual departures from quality can be defined and measured; and, continuously track performance. Consider the following as a "quality motto":

WHEN PEOPLE ARE PLACED FIRST, THEY WILL PROVIDE THE HIGHEST POSSIBLE PRODUCTIVITY AND PROFITS WILL FOLLOW!!

What are the things that normally get in the way? Table seven [on the next page] presents the most common barriers to achieving excellence.

TQM cannot be done yesterday, today or even tomorrow. It requires patience, staying aligned, focusing on goals, using staff as strategic assets, and assigning work teams meaningful roles. Train to gain and then train some more!

Table Seven Barriers to Excellence

- ☐ POLICIES THAT EXIST FOR THE CONVENIENCE OF THE ORGANIZATION.
- ☐ JOB SPECIALIZATION, KEEPING THINGS COMPARTMENTALIZED.
- ☐ LACK OF COORDINATION OF THE PROCESS, PEOPLE WORKING IN A NON-ALIGNED MANNER.
- ☐ DECISION MAKING POWER THAT IS REMOTE FROM THE CLIENT.
- ☐ PREOCCUPATION WITH COST CONTAINMENT.
- ☐ INDIFFERENT, POWERLESS EMPLOYEES.
- ☐ NOT ENOUGH CREATIVE PROBLEM SOLVING.
- ☐ FAILURE TO LISTEN TO CLIENTS.

The Structure of Training

Training has become the *sine quo non* for the Anderson Companies (Galagan, 1993). Arthur Anderson and Anderson Consulting annually invest some 5.5 percent of their revenues, over $300 million, in training their employees. According to Lawrence Weinbach, managing partner and chief executive, training makes the difference between simply hiring smart people and learning how to invest in their abilities. The goal of the training, which focuses on people in their early career, is to mold a strong technical background with the ability to establish connections throughout the Anderson family, thereby increasing the ability of the organizations to satisfy a client by a geometric factor.

When Winston Churchill assumed the position of Minister of Munitions during World War I, his first goal was to streamline an incredible bureaucracy (Gilbert, 1992). He replaced fifty semi-autonomous departments with an "ordnance council" of eleven members who were made accountable for certain economies of scale and efficiency designed to speed the procurement of vital war materials to the front lines.

Challenging performance objectives were established for his ministry and maintaining close liaison with those business persons and industrialists who provided the actual manufacturing capacity was central to his administration. Churchill did not replace staff, he trained them to communicate with each other, share his vision, and to adopt his audacious methods of placing objectives ahead of all other considerations. In addition, Churchill set an example by his own behavior and attitudes. Once, when staff were dwelling on why certain things could not possibly be done in the time available, Churchill dismissed their efforts by stating that they were wasting time discussing obstacles which were obvious instead of working on solutions.

My favorite of Sir Winston's quotations was directed to his senior staff: " Power is achieved by giving it away rather than struggling for more." Churchill knew that the enormity of his task required that every available asset be operating at peak efficiency not standing around idle while bureaucratic infighting took place. He trained his people in both procedural as well as cognitive skills.

This attitude is as important today as it was during the crisis of 1917. For example, anyone interested in developing effective teams must be concerned with skills development, at the very least, job skills for technical performance and interaction skills to enhance communication, manage conflict, value diversity. Interested in site-based shared decision making?

The following topics would be training musts before any such initiative could be attempted: facilitation and team skills, influence, managing resistance to change, communications, and systems thinking. Don't worry, parts II and III were written to show you how!

How long does quality take? Probably the rest of your life if you are interested in continued improvements in productivity and hence profitability. Such improvements happen a little here and a little there but they happen continuously if you change the way you think and behave, as a leader of others. To be a leader of total quality you must change your understanding of how people learn, what makes them change, and their need to take pride and joy in their work. Part II will help you define the necessary steps in this process.

PART II

TRAINING EXERCISES

5

THE INTERNAL CONSULTANT

Analyzing Your Role

You have just completed your MBA degree and landed your first significant job, as a trainer with the Acme Storm Door and Airline Company. The pay is fine, you have a decent office, and your colleagues seem friendly. There are even a number of "singles" that offer promise of an exciting social experience. There is just one problem, you really have little idea just what a trainer is supposed to do. The interview was focused on your background in human resources administration and your boss seems to believe that anyone with a background in personnel should be able to take care of the corporate training function.

Your assignment is quite typical for a small to mid-size company. You are alone in the role, the human resources staff provide you with a working space and not much else besides some legitimacy and people are already expecting you to be productive. Your second day on the job you receive the following memo, reproduced on the next page.

MEMO

From: I. M. Boss, President, ACME Associates

To: Suzie Q. Trainer, Management Development Specialist

Re: Initial Training Plan

For your first assignment, I would like you to prepare a synoptic briefing paper which would describe your conceptualization of a training program which will raise the comprehension skills of our production workers. The company will soon transition to highly automated equipment and I am most concerned that our rank and file are not prepared to assimilate the necessary training programs. The failure to address this problem effectively was a major factor in the demise of your predecessor. My expectation is that your briefing will define the purposes of the training along with the anticipated outcomes, stated as learning objectives. Please provide specific examples of these for my review and approval. You will identify for me, by function, those managers who can act as resources for your planning.

This can be a real toughie your first time out. All of a sudden you must begin to produce and you really have no one to discuss this challenge with. What is my role? How do I define what needs to be done? What sort of design would be best? Who knows what outcomes are important? How do I measure results? How do I achieve long-lasting results? How did I get myself into this? These are all typical questions which the novice trainer might face on beginning a new assignment. Even the seasoned professional cannot be all things to all situations. For example, some people have been trained to broker programs from a consultant base. Some have been prepared to serve as stand-up trainers. Some have dabbled with a little of both. The pitfalls are extraordinary and the stakes for you and the organization are quite high. This chapter will help you establish expectations for the position of trainer and discuss the skills necessary to do the job effectively. Capturing the pulse of an organization is a always a difficult proposition but a necessary first step. Good Luck!!!

The role of the training coordinator in any organization is quite complex. You must learn to define and redefine your key behavior norms and responsibilities in terms of outcomes which the organization will value, i.e., in terms of knowledge, skills, and abilities. Achieving change, as measured by knowledge, skills, and abilities, is really a strategic function, one which requires you to build rapport with those who set the course for the company as well as furnish the commitment to quality, and also, with those who define the work which gets done and again with those who do the work. As we have seen in previous chapters, many times the commitment to excellence stops with the paper pronouncements. It is up to you as a trainer to translate vision into reality, to operationalize the specific goals of development for the staff, to act as a buffer between the challenge of total quality and the reality of limited resources, poor attitudes, and numerous commitments. To succeed, you must become the consummate staff individual, a person perceived as highly credible with a wealth of talent, the ability to capture a significant resource base, and no agenda to fulfill. Sound difficult? You bet, but the role is critical and the job can be great fun as well as most satisfying and rewarding.

Those who would coordinate training can be prepared in any discipline so long as they possess the organizational ability to plan and develop interventions and the interpersonal relationship skills to convince people to buy into their initiatives. Trainers must be able to set objective, highly quantifiable, and focused objectives. They must learn how to build rapport with line managers, be proactive instead of reactive with senior executives, and have a strong sense of being evaluative, i.e., know how to measure the true worth of a program. This last skill may be hardest to acquire, not in the least sense because of the courage involved in reporting results and using them as building blocks for future programming. Even a non-significant result has value in terms of the lessons learned and the real payoffs when a skill is institutionalized, that is, reflected in someone's work, or a needed behavior change is seen. Moving to a learning society via a total commitment to quality requires learning a different way of doing things, primarily among those who may be least well equipped to make the necessary changes.

The trainer who functions as the internal corporate development consultant to the organization must know how to buy external resources. As a professional trainer, I currently market eighteen different seminar titles. Even with such an extensive repertoire of offerings, I would still encounter numerous areas in which I would require assistance in terms of program presentation. Assessing needs is always paramount toward getting started on the right path. It is even more vital when that path must be geared toward a training program which will be provided by an outsider. You, in company with the management team, must decide on the proper interventions and the anticipated outcomes before you start shopping for a vendor.

Let's say that your work with line managers has indicated that production workers have problems with basic literacy skills. From your contacts with the strategic planners, you have ascertained that the company will retool its line with the latest generation hi-tech gadgetry, a tactic which will exhaust the capital reserves of the corporation. Senior management is staking everything on this very tangible improvement initiative and are concerned about the readiness of the staff to profit from the change-over. You now become the key to this major corporate initiative. By providing an appropriate training experience, you can solve the CEO's concerns and probably be regarded as a hero. If you confine your search to a subject matter specialist, you should also begin investing some time updating your credentials, because you are headed for a failure. What you need is a trainer, someone with a sense of presence, who can hold the attention of the audience while delivering a message. A trainer will entertain, establish an environment conducive to learning, and have a message related to the concerns of the participants.

If to an outside source you must turn, then be prepared to use great care in selecting a consultant. Trainers invariably have specific capacities which they will attempt to customize to your needs, for a fee. You can develop lists of prospective candidates in many ways. Professional associations and journals are a rich source of information. Word-of-mouth among peers, sampling through attendance at conferences, and purchasing a computer-match search are all good places to begin building a cadre of candidates to complete your assignment.

Once you develop a listing, the next step is to review the wares of each trainer who seems to have something worthwhile to offer. Trainers will attempt to provide you with a program that is really an information package. You must ascertain the adequacy of these programs to your situation and then determine how far a program can be adapted before it exceeds the parameters within which the trainer is proficient. You should only speak of learning objectives in terms of knowledge, skills, and abilities and force your prospective consultants to respond in kind. That is the safest means by which you may ascertain whether there is a fit between what you think you need and what your consultant would like you to think you need.

Once you begin to become comfortable with the information package which your consultant is marketing, it is then time to size up the professional capacity of the consultant as trainer. Interview him or her to ascertain what recent and relevant experiences they may have had. Find out what kind of information they require to tailor their expertise to your needs.

In what format do they require such information, with what degree of specificity? Do they have experience in sensing needs? Will they assist you in this area? At what cost? By determining the goodness of fit between your needs and what the market place has to offer you may then choose, with some degree of confidence, the option of having the program offered as is or paying to customize the program to some extent, hopefully within the expertise level of the consultants. Acquiring references, scrutinizing material from previous workshops, and having your consultant audition are all wise precautions. Yes, have them audition!

Trainers should build programs around selected skill modules. That is both professionally sound and financially efficient. You structure learning objectives and their enabling learning activities around a particular skill that you which to impart. Once a trainer has developed a number of such skill modules, it becomes relatively easy for the trainer to mix and match these skill modules as building blocks to develop entire programs. You develop the list of skill proficiencies and have them demonstrate to you how they intend to teach them to the participants. As part of the interview, have your finalists teach a specific skill module. If they cannot make you feel involved in the experience and able to demonstrate some enhanced capacity, how would you expect them to be successful with less capable or even less interested audiences? How do they intend to involve their learners? What techniques for providing practice in the new skills areas and opportunities for applying the skills and knowledge will they present?

Evaluate your needs before you comparison shop. Be wary of subject matter specialists and their pre-packed programs. Solicit assistance from established resources.

Remember, if you cannot deliver the program yourself, you are only as good as the person you select as your surrogate. Choose wisely and prosper.

Building Commitment

Okay, so you have been given an assignment to prepare your first briefing for a training program that will enhance the comprehension skills of workers who will shortly be tasked with operating fairly sophisticated equipment. You are expected also to define the purposes of the training as stated learning objectives and identify those line managers who may act as resources for the training. Where to start? Well, the key to completing this particular assignment lies in the definition of the assignment, that is, those managers who can act as resources for the training. While you may have the skills necessary to conduct a needs assessment and a discrepancy evaluation, the folks who work the line, most particularly, those who are responsible for production, can serve you as either a tremendous resource or an insurmountable barrier.

Functioning primarily in a staff role, you will be seen as anything from a threat to a nuisance, depending on how well you conduct yourself and how much talent you display. Developing a sense of the pulse of an organization depends on how well you can sense the life cycle of each work family within that organization. Line managers must deal with issues, you might even help them realize this. Your first job is to be seen as a credible resource among those charged with the transformation process in your company, that is, those who make a buck for the stockholders. Building a constituency among line managers will enable you to define needs from a learning perspective, much as they would define the improvements which the managers feel are necessary to improve their capacity to be productive. You move from threat to asset as you become more useful. For example, the training professional acts as an internal consultant when he or she might recommend a mechanism whereby workers are built into the needs identification process. Organizing a quality circle might take time, but it can serve as a vehicle by which a portion of a work force may feel comfortable enough to contribute their expertise to the cause. The results just might help managers focus their resource base a bit more effectively. You will develop some respect and credibility and the data may prove extremely useful in developing a sense of the real issues confronting this particular work family. As you compile such data from unit to unit, you can begin to place a structure on the architecture of an assignment which originally may have been rather nebulous, i.e., enhance comprehension skills. Thus, developing a training plan may involve dealing with a lot of non-training issues just to build some respectability and to determine essential training needs.

If you want to sell something, have something of value for sale, that is, give them what they need, even if they are not able to define it for themselves. For example, suppose a corporation wants to increase productivity, a highly sort after goal these days. It is reasonable to assume that the key decision makers of this entity would expect their program development specialists to be able to recommend a course of action to achieve this goal. Having been trained in the area, having worked hard to identify the current capacity of the firm, as measured by skills, knowledge, and abilities, and having become well versed in the culture of the organization, you are aware that the current practice is to assign work in small job lots to individuals who are then monitored closely by a rather large staff of supervisory personnel. This has resulted in compartmentalized functions, fragmentation in task assignment, and assembly line sequencing of activities.

From your professional training you know that in order to build quality you must develop your people. From your process training you are aware that teamwork is a promising vehicle to employ in any quest for grater productivity because of the focus it places on people. Further, you are aware of the literature which suggests that investing in teamwork promotes productivity, enhances awareness of quality, reduces waste and improves job satisfaction. Now you make your pitch to your superiors! By recommending that they commit to a team approach, they can combine smaller tasks to form new and larger modules of work which can be assigned to groups of workers, with a resulting increase in responsibility and accountability because of the skill variety, simplified task identity, enhanced task significance, and autonomy that is an artifact of the team approach. You can point to the value of having employees sharing a core of functions, working with greater clarity, improved effectiveness, and efficiency. These are outcomes which may be qualified as to valued and quantified with respect to improving the bottom line. You might even be able to deliver such a program yourself. Hint: I would consider such an elementary initiative to be a must for anyone who wishes to be taken seriously as a trainer.

Well, you have been noticed. Resources have been provided to support your training initiative, and everyone concerned has been informed that the company will soon see a greater commitment to quality as a consequence of the program which you yourself will deliver. Everything should be rosy, right? Wrong! You have only completed step one.

Managing Resistance

Here are some tips for overcoming the resistance which you will surely encounter as you attempt to build and maintain a quality training program. Always discuss production enhancements in terms of knowledge, skills, and abilities. Do try to explicate improvement needs which may be articulated by line managers in terms of behavioral changes, technical skills improvements or other measurable changes. Do not confront these managers in a manner which they would believe is threatening, remember, impact not intent is crucial. Do review the production aspects of their cooperation but do so in a non-evaluative manner, let them identify issues as problems. Once you build a track record they will begin coming to you with an idea to flesh out. Help them, identify their strengths and then show them how to use those strengths to overcome areas which are determined, via scientific analysis, to require attention.

Consider the following. The Aviation Supply Office (ASO) of the United States Navy, which has earlier in this text been used as an example of a "how-to and can-do" organization, submitted an application for the 1993 Presidential Award for Quality. With a new administration trying to make its mark, no awards were given but the team that examined ASO both applauded the efforts of the organization to strive for quality and strongly encouraged the command to reapply for the 1994 award cycle. The data package that is audited as part of the competition includes significant submissions in the following areas: vision of quality, strategic planning, customer focus, quality assurance, measurement, leadership, staff development, and employee empowerment and teamwork. Now I would argue personally that the last three variables named are perhaps a bit redundant as stated separately but, more importantly, they constitute the vehicles by which the entire TQM mechanism is driven. The chief executive of the command must agree with me because he chose to communicate the results of the audit to his staff by encouraging them to reenter the competition by building on the strengths identified in order to strengthen the areas indicated as needing improvement. (Davidson, 1993). Further, the very fine training establishment of ASO was charged with articulating the needs identified into employee development programs which would complement the vision of the senior executives for continuous improvement.

This scenario is being played out every day in thousands of organizations. Opportunities are plentiful for those who have the vision to see them and the skill to profit by them. The key to your success as an internal management development consultant lies in your ability to pull this off.

A self-assured, articulate employee will demonstrate confidence in himself, have greater concern for productivity and quality, and be more initiating in support of his employer. That is, people have to become part of the problem solving capacity or they remain part of the problem. Continuous training mobilizes the experience and knowledge of the employee for constructive improvement. You have a role in creating this type of productive climate for your organization but you cannot fulfill this role until you have proven to your constituents that the training function is deserving of a commitment of resources.

To best meet resistance to your initiatives, try to define problems in terms of needs, not necessarily in terms of solutions, with each manager whom you encounter. You can learn a great deal from other people's needs at work and their viewpoints will be invaluable, they will provide essential data concerning proposed solutions which you their managers should develop in a participatory fashion. By this strategy, you will make each constituent part of the solution, you will have succeeded in making them buy into the process. By focusing on problem solving you will also encourage creative contribution, i.e., the participants will be forced to look beyond their normal range of duties and apply their organizational equity in a more comprehensive manner. When such a model is employed effectively, the participants will experience a feeling of mutual understanding and trust will be nurtured. Remember, don't feel compelled to defend your viewpoints, let them work through their own agenda with you helping to shape the discussion by providing feedback that demonstrates how training can and should be an asset to their performance.

The internal management development consultant must be a facilitator when it comes to encountering resistance. Your goal should not be to eliminate resistance because functional conflict is one of the creative components of moving an organization forward. People need to feel safe in discussing issues with you and you must develop that capacity by being verbally encouraging and demonstrating a willingness to hear people. Listen for facts and feelings carefully as the other person expresses them and then act on them, while reinforcing the idea that so long as disagreement remains functional it is truly helpful. You have a role as a process consultant throughout the program development process. In managing resistance effectively you may perform that role successfully by modeling the types of behaviors that maintain conflict in the comfort zone. No one likes being attacked, therefore be hard on the issues and soft on the people. Argue for a principle not a position and deal only with issues. Consider the following illustration.

Some years ago during the Carter Administration, the heads of State from Israel and Egypt were invited to Washington to discuss a potential accord for settling the dispute for the Sinai Peninsula, a particularly worthless area of the planet that had been the scene of significant blood shed between warring armies. After some days at Camp David, Maryland, Mr. Begin of Israel and Mr. Sadat reached such an accord, the Sinai was to be demilitarized. Now the popular joke at the time was that three days with Jimmie and Roslyn Carter would make anyone sign anything. In reality, this was a diplomatic triumph for the President because he was successful in having the parties deal only with issues, in this case military security. When it was shown how to achieve military security without placing armies in conflict in the Sinai, the worthless piece of sand lost its significance as a reason for nations to spend blood and treasure. When you help your constituents identify issues and when you shape that discussion in terms of dealing with the issues to enhance productivity, then you are arguing quality not upsetting the political equilibrium of the organization. You will progress much further when you employ a collaborative problem technique for conflict management instead of using a "forcing" technique, one in which you make decisions for people when expediency or your personal perspective are at risk. Likewise, the internal consultant should

...ence people by their expertise, which will lead to legitimacy. If you are perceived as a threat then your influence style will be seen as coercive in nature, and you will not be successful.

Building Credibility

The commitment to training makes the work force receptive to change and innovation rather than resistant to it. How do we build such commitment? You will begin building commitment among managers and their employees as you demonstrate the value of what you are proposing. Here then is the value of stating outcomes for training in terms that the production people can comprehend, knowledge, skills, and abilities which they believe are essential to the quest of enhanced productivity. Yes, you probably will have to help the managers define their needs in terms of knowledge, skills, and abilities, and yes, you probably will have to beg them for an opportunity to show that training can be a vehicle to improve the skill levels of the work force. You will maintain your alliances with these key individuals by demonstrating a return for the investment they make in you, that is, agreeing to release staff for one of your programs. Even if ordered to produce an audience for a seminar or training g program, managers who do not see the extrinsic value of the evolution may not cooperate fully. You might not see the very best candidates for the program. Those who do attend may be infected by a negativism or parochialism which is devastating to your efforts, or, you may be plagued by the in and out game. People being called out for "key" reasons too numerous to contemplate so that the interruptions outnumber the training periods.

You can mitigate these problems by making sense in your approach. Showing the key decision makers some potential return for their investment, in terms that you link with the "bottom line" will create an opportunity for you to demonstrate the effectiveness of your training initiatives. The first success will enable you to effectively contract for change and enhance your ability to exert influence in the organization. Anticipating changing needs, maintaining commitment, and showing long-term impact are the keys to maximizing results and that is the key to staying in the game.

Let's return to our example involving training work teams. Line managers must be able to visualize benefits before they will upset their routine, let alone a very comfortable organizational structure, and support the crackpot ideas of some new kid on the block. You will earn their respect by making them aware of what you know and do not know of their affairs, and further, by enlisting their able assistance in explicating your ideas. By this I mean getting the targets of your training to help you move from a conceptual basis to a training basis, a deliverable that meets the needs of your clients, not the comfort level for a program which you established for yourself. The supervisors of the trainees can also help you immeasurably by providing background information concerning the readiness of the trainees. The concerns, strengths, weaknesses, and capacities of the potential targets of the training will all have to be determined if you are to do a credible job and their supervisors can provide the necessary data, if they are convinced that all of this is worth their while and you can ask the right questions.

Consider the following cases. Japan's Bridgestone Corporation, a noted manufacturer of automobile tires, employs over 80,000 individuals worldwide. One of the enabling objectives for the corporation is to maintain a leadership niche in its industry by offering a cost-effective product which has a reputation for excellence, a common denominator in the global marketplace. Training is the primary resource by which Bridgestone achieves excellence via its employees. Workers, including line employees, receive training throughout their careers and their career paths are constructed to fit the strategic plans of the organization. Currently, over 90 percent of the staff receive some sort of continuous training via specifically developed programs. Workers are provided instruction from experts in specific subject areas, from mentors, and on a broader scale, from in-house instructors.

Sumitomo 3M is another organization which maintains a winning tradition by maintaining a high-profile focus on training throughout the company. The HRD group is charged with developing career paths and training programs which may span three decades of employment. During the first portion of a career cycle, the training program focuses on manufacturing and technical skills. From that comprehensive base, employees then embark on a program which provides them with training experiences which sometimes enrich their technical base, sometimes prepare them to cope with new technological development and challenges, and sometimes prepares them to assume managerial responsibilities.

Companies such as Bridgestone and Sumitomo 3M maintain their training base in lean times and even increase this investment as a way of holding a business niche or conquering new markets. They will not engage in such costly investments if the training capacity available does not present a credible means of achieving some desired ends.

As has been stated earlier, the training professional cannot even assume that those who pay the bills or those who supervise the people assets who are the targets of training are even capable of specifically identifying what the needed outcomes may be. The training professional can help, not just with a discrepancy analysis or needs identification, but by learning the business of the business they support and providing recommendations on how to improve the bottom line. This technique is know as making your case at the top" and the suggested action profile is presented in table eight.

Table 8
Impacting the Bottom Line

- RELATE YOUR ARGUMENTS TO PROFIT AND LOSS
- PRESENT YOUR CASE FROM THE CEO PERSPECTIVE
- DEMONSTRATE THE CONTRIBUTION OF YOUR IDEA TO IMPORTANT CORPORATE VALUES
- COLLECT SUPPORTING DATA FROM THE COMPETITION
- USE SPECIFIC EXAMPLES IN DESCRIBING THE PROBLEM AND THE SOLUTION
- NEVER BE DEFENSIVE
- DON'T BE AFRAID TO SAY WHAT YOU THINK
- MAINTAIN YOUR SENSE OF HUMOR

Taken collectively, these suggestions are designed to build your credibility. That is, by demonstrating your willingness to tackle tough challenges by increasing the corporate skills base and your capacity to translate complex issues into outcomes that show impact in areas which the corporate leadership can appreciate, you have earned your chance. And, this technique will work with line managers because they can not relate to an enhanced bottom line but they will also react very positively to any program which mitigates the obstacles they face in achieving that increased production.

Projecting an air of confidence will build an appreciation of your professionalism. Inventory your skills to make them productive both in terms of the processes relating to the job of being a professional trainer and as may be necessary to understand the business of your business. Learn to be a good listener and give and take feedback. Those who might initially distrust or ignore you cannot long overlook a potential asset to their becoming more productive.

Never forget two key principles of the internal consultant: one, the managers and production workers/service providers, etc., are your clients; and two, the more indispensable you become, the greater the rewards and resources which you can command.

6

PLANNING THE PROGRAM

Determining Training Needs

So where do we start? Why, at the beginning of course! We know how to manage the training and development function. We know how to effectively present ourselves as a resource to those in authority. Finally, we have discussed the principles of establishing credibility in the organization You can never fully master this concept until you actually work through the scenario.

Planning a program is a complex and situation specific activity. It is situation specific because no two programs for any two organizations should be replicated. Each must be determined to fit a certain context for a certain group of needs and people, those who are the targets of our efforts because it is they who represent the payoff. The HR department should at least be able to provide you with job analysis data. Simple position descriptions will not due, you must complete a detailed analysis and the only legitimate means by which you may accomplish this is to proceed from a listing of the essential aspects of work that the company needs to accomplish. That is, whether or not the company has conscientiously determined where it should be going, a job analysis would have determined the knowledge, skills, and abilities necessary to perform the essential work of the organization and the current capacity of the organization to fulfill this expectancy set. Your analysis of the various tasks currently being performed must examine the potential for doing something better. This is the means by which a results oriented training program may be planned. It has to be results oriented or you and the program will soon lose the support necessary to keep your little enterprise flourishing.

The senior establishment of an organization should have a burning desire to find out what works and what does not. Therefore, planning a program without an adequate needs base or a meaningful set of outcome expectations is a useless exercise, one that will only frustrate your audience and severely damage any future interest in your efforts. Ideally, each of your initiatives should be planned with a measurement component. Measuring results represents one of the hottest issues in an TQM or TQL endeavor and one of the most difficult to capture. Ideally, your programs will be planned to impact on the bottom line. Converting results to monetary benefits allows you to play a central role in any analysis of return on investment for specific operational divisions of the company. This is true whether your parent organization is a private sector manufacturing firm or a nonprofit service entity. The potential value of such an enterprise pertains equally to all areas of organizational behavior, including: skills training, employee orientation, supervisory training, and, management development. While we will discuss program assessment in a subsequent chapter, setting measurable, reliable performance standards is an essential piece of the beginning.

One effective means of accomplishing this is to call on the constituency that supported your training proposal in the first place, the line managers and front line supervisors with whom you have established some credibility. Once again these folks can prove to be a highly capable resource because the most fundamental manner to establish a set of outcome measures for any program development initiative is to conduct a discrepancy evaluation. Use your colleagues to help you establish a baseline of data, i.e., define the status duo in the exact terms in which your CEO would describe a certain scenario if he or she were endowed with the same experience set that you are compiling. For example, your company may be tracking the progress of competitors in establishing inroads in your specific business niche, say, the manufacture of circuit assemblies for automobile computers. The firm has determined that the product lines of the two rivals are similar in capacity and attractiveness to the consumer and that production costs should be equally similar.

However, your competition is reaching the point where they will severely threaten your market position by offering the product with a faster delivery time and lower cost. Since most of the key variables in building these components are known and would not permit your competitor to perform at this higher level of proficiency, the most obvious place to search is the quality with which each of the companies approach the manufacturing process itself. Your strategic planning group has in fact done this and has determined that your rivals have no need for rework because they build the thing the first time and every time. Your company has that very slogan as the total quality motto but it seems that your competitor has actually institutionalized the kind of climate that enables them to achieve that lofty ambition.

The potential loss of this business could really threaten the survival of your firm because many end users of sub-assemblies are now mirroring the Japanese model of establishing long term relationships with suppliers, a guarantee of business in return for an acceptable level of quality and service. Thus, a failure to overcome the competition could cost you a customer for ten years! The senior establishment sends forth the total quality assurance team and they discover shoddy work practices in several vital areas. It is determined that you will be sent into the breech to correct these deficiencies. Now is the time to cement that relationships with those who really face exposure, the line managers and front line supervisors who must make things right. They will help you identify standards that are realistic but which will meet the challenge of the present crisis. While the corporate elite must accept your proposal, the line managers will be instrumental in setting the direction in which to move. They will help you define where the situation rests and where it has to be. You have to determine the means of getting there and the means by which you will know if you have arrived there successfully. And, you had better be right.

Developing Priorities and Objectives

When you approach the money givers of the company with your proposal, they will expect a definitive analysis of the problem as your constituents see it, your interpretation of the status quo in terms of knowledge, skills, and abilities, and a clear picture of what they can expect when the intervention is completed. That is what training is, an intervention primarily used to correct some deficiency. A true training professional needs to develop the capacity to lead the organization, that is a far cry from simply being entertaining in the classroom. Your training programs must affect the quality level of the organization, i.e., the programs should be seen as "must do" interventions, activities which will accelerate the changes necessary to keep the firm moving forward. Trainers must help develop strategy, influence the cost of keeping personnel productive, and keep performance visible as the means by which work force production may be increased. What all of this means is that trainers must help the establishment keep its pulse of those issues which are the priority challenges that confront every organization on a routine basis.

Determining priorities should become a programmed function for the training staff, an integral part of the ongoing needs sensing that must be the first capacity which you build. Sensing needs is a situation specific activity. The data shells are fairly generic but the purposes to which the data are utilized are quite diverse. For example, someone may assess the competition and you will assess strategic management capacity. The top brass may determine a new direction for the company and you will assess the ability of the staff to move into that arena. Exactly what you collect and from whom will depend on the structure which supports the organization at any given time. However, the data providers will not change, those constituents remain fixed, at least by position or function.

The parameters for data collection will become fixed by the nature of the company which you serve, its chosen industry, and the resource base which it builds. The process by which you sense needs will also remain fixed in that it is a replicating function. Here are some hints to get you started. You should have a definite goal in mind each time that you tap your data sources. Another way of looking at this component is to predict that which you expect your needs assessment to uncover. Mitigating conditions which may skew the results, market trends, staff vacancies, leadership changes, etc. should be noted both for their incidence and potential impact. Keeping your data base current will enable you to chart trends as well as accomplishments. Since training should be viewed as a continuum, each component must be designed as complimentary of the whole. This should indicate to you that each training program should be part of a set, a design that is never ending because the growth of the corporation should not cease during its existence. Data concerning needs, data concerning accomplishments, and data concerning expectations will soon assume a life of their own. Such information is the basis by which companies create and document their history, market their successes and perhaps even compensate their employees. The HR department should compliment your efforts by charting the training accomplishments of each employee via a human resource information system.

Once you have a notion of the current organizational capacity as it comports with expected growth variables, it is time to set some expectations for the training program. For example, in the program module presented in Appendix B, Braughler, Kennedy and Kowalick include a synopsis of their program which indicates that their target company is one that has adopted a focus of maintaining a competitive edge by enhancing the caliber of customer service. That is a goal that has been established as a growth scenario for the corporation. The training professionals have adopted this goal and explicated it by establishing expectations for the training, that is, an organization that can establish a strong response mechanism to the needs, inquiries, and complaints of its customers will convince those customers to provide repeat business.

Researching the topic, reducing it to specific learning objectives and outcome measures is the next step. Here you are operationalizing the expectation set which you have established for the training. For most companies, learning simply means taking in information Real learning, however, is about enhancing capacity, being able to do something that was not possible prior to a specific intervention. An important by-product of learning is to create also a capacity for effective action. The better trained individuals are, the more likely they are to act independently. This becomes ever more crucial as we move toward Drucker's notion of an information based society (1992). Even organizations which might be considered "successful" via a variety of criteria are very traditional in that they operate as a resource-based entity. That is, they maintain rigid systems of command and control, concentrate on the magnitude of value addition which results from their transformation process, and use staff as "human resources". Companies that conquer the total quality puzzle also use resources but they create knowledge in the process. And in so doing they increase their capacity which is the real key to survival and growth. They are simply better equipped to compete.

Training is the vehicle to accomplish this learning and you are the key to delivering the goods.

Braughler, Kennedy and Kowalick make the transition between the ideal of increasing business by being responsive to the current client base by operationalizing the specific skill areas necessary for the work force to carry out this ideal. They have reduced their necessary outcomes to specific skills that can be the basis of a training initiative as well as the target of appraisal effort. Most importantly, there is a causal inference base between the strategic growth goals of the company and the skills selected to explicate the target area of improving work force performance in this vital area. The senior establishment of the organization can visualize the outcomes projected for this program. The line managers who must increase the repeat business base can appreciate the value of having employees whose skill base has been increased to include aspects which seem to have some positive impact. For example, at Cummins Engine Company an initiative was begun to improve work processes and reduce operating costs (Taylor & Ramsey, 1993). It was recognized that to achieve this goal, the employees were the key and the readiness of the work force to fulfill their role was in serious question. It was decided to teach employees to eliminate waste by promoting creativity and building a culture of continuous improvement. Training became the vehicle to achieve this higher standard of excellence.

A needs assessment was conducted and the result of the design process was a five day training program, which was established around the core concept of quality. To date, over 200 employees have been trained in the new cultural paradigm, accountability modeling has been successful and inventory reductions alone have amounted to a quarter of a million dollars! This is offered as an example of a true team approach in sensing needs, charting a course of action, and delivering something that makes sense to the doers, the staff, and line managers. The something that was offered was a tangible benefit if the training is concluded successfully. Cummins Engine taught new skills and thereby increased the capacity of the entire establishment.

In summary, these are the keys to sensing needs and determining priorities. Analyze the data to detect discrepancies at the strategic level. Translate information into goals to increase performance at the tactical level. Develop a feasible, especially cost effective, training solution to the problem, and sell the solution to the key decisions makers.

When you are asked to develop a program in response to a need for some technical skill, think of an intervention that will fill the immediate need while also contributing to an optimization of the learning process, i.e., teach people to work smarter. Every member of the staff should possess the capacity to see beyond their own assignments, possess an ability to conduct inquiry, and maintain a leadership potential. Monitor your information sources to track trends.

The Subject Matter and the Trainees

No trainer, however, well prepared professionally, can fulfill the role of being an expert in every field. Some try and fail miserably. Others realize that their parent organization, especially if they are not cognizant of how a training operation should operate, does have some expectation that they should serve as stand up presenters Therefore, researching subject matter requires a mix of skills. Knowing your own capacity, resisting the temptation to force solutions to problems into your perceived areas of competence, and matching the right topic, the "solution" to the data trends which you have identified. Remember, you are in the business of helping your firm thrive or at least survive. The finest design and the soundness of the instructional component will avail you of nothing unless the training is viable. Big training efforts cost big bucks and everything that you do will be scrutinized very closely. Therefore, it must be visibly sound, that is, have a demonstrable chance of impacting on some issue of importance to the organization. Looking beyond the instructional objectives and viewing things from a systems standpoint will help you develop tangible programs.

The old notion of building a taxonomy has value to this discussion. If you can visualize a set of outcomes, then you can plan milestones to achieve these outcomes. Such milestones would be trainable skills which would be cumulative both across the organization and longitudinally for individual staff. Attaining a specific skills plateau would certainly be a benchmark for staff, particularly if their compensation base would be increased as a consequence of such achievements. In addition, you would be able to show progress toward accomplishment of building the corporate learning environment each time you reported that a new bundle of knowledge or ability was available as a new strategic or operational asset.

Okay, I know what I wish to accomplish but how do I select targets for my training and how do I get them to participate? Tough questions but ones which are easy to answer if the corporate environment is truly oriented toward quality. For example, after more than eight years as CEO of GE, Jack Welch had the business portfolio package which he desired but not the staff capacity which he felt he needed. The GE middle management corps was being compared to GM's "frozen middle". The solution which evolved is know as the "GE Work-Out", a massive behavior alteration paradigm. Welch expects his people to be trained in building work climates that are more productive because the staff has increased its efficiency and quality. Those who participate in "Work-Out", as planners, trainers, leaders, or trainees, profit because of the presence of a definitive goal which has been established for their efforts as well as a strong commitment to providing resources to achieve certain definable training outcomes. Such a scenario greatly facilitates the actual mechanics of developing training programs. However, few organizations will offer you an environment which so rich in vision and resources.

For organizations that are not quite "there", some form of assessment will be necessary in order to determine the appropriate subject matter. Hopeful, such needs sensing is an ongoing component of the strategic planning process. If you are reduced to doing things for yourself, try to reach the greatest number of people in the shortest possible time. A questionnaire can be useful but only if you have already done the ground work discussed earlier and built a constituency out of the line managers. They will have to run interference for you and help convince the respondents that what you are offering is worthwhile. Your target audience should be comprised primarily of those who are in a position to help you translate the verbiage of corporate mission statements into topics that are directly related to vital knowledge, ability, and skill areas.

Once you have moved from goals such as "increase productivity by five percent" to enabling topics such as increase the "communication potential of line supervisors", you are ready to develop some greater finite sense of a potential training program or series of training initiatives to meet your objectives. I have enjoyed some success in making this transition by employing a small group as a sounding board to facilitate the kind of brain storming that must be accomplished in order to hit a home run with your program. These are the people who will pooh-pooh ideas which are too parochial or too far field, they are the catalysts who will spark your creative juices and prevent you from spinning your wheels on a pet idea which just does not present sufficient value to warrant any expenditure of resources.

For example, let us speculate that your company desires you to develop a training session which will orient selected staff to the parameters of the Americans With Disabilities Act. Through your interaction with those who hold equity in the firm, you are able to determine that a simple orientation will not help the organization meet the mandates of the act. Your data base, daily interactions with line managers and your research in the target program area have provided you with sufficient insight to ascertain that real learning must be accomplished, both of a behavioral as well as cognitive nature. People have to develop competence in certain aspects of effectively managing a human resource program that must be adaptive to the specific needs of individuals as well as they must acquire certain vital information concerning the legislation. As a further example, consider the program presented in appendix A, Professionalism for Legal Secretaries . In this seminar, the author, Susan Carrochi, has very carefully delineated the reason why the program is important to the daily functioning of this most numerous group of employees. Further, she has identified one topic that represents a skill, communication, and has explicated the rational for having identified this skill as being crucial. She is using a tangible skill, communication, as a tool to equip secretaries to more fully appreciate their role, how to cope with the unique aspects of their position, and gain greater insight into how a law firm is put together and why every person is an asset.

These are the kinds of considerations which will impact on your ability to deliver a specific training program which will meet identified needs. What about the trainees? Who should attend? Let's return to the "most for the dollar" notion. Your objective is to satisfy certain key needs within the organization in a highly cost effective manner. The number of people, the time they spend away from the job, and the need for substitutes, as well as the background costs of the training, materials, group leader, refreshments, etc., all contribute to the cost.

Since the size of the training group is related in a linear manner to the ultimate cost of the program, you must be cognizant of the composition of your group. There are no easy solutions to this dilemma. One model which I would consider to be highly positive is the train the trainer approach. In this scenario, individuals are carefully selected to be participants in a training program for a variety of reasons. First, they are deemed to be appropriate targets for the training, that is, they possess the capacity and the willingness to profit by the training. Secondly, they are situated in key positions in the organization and can thus use the knowledge, skills, and abilities which they will learn from the seminar to the best advantage of the organization. Finally, they are sufficiently influential within their work families to be able to effectively demonstrate the new skills or knowledge areas. Very often they are assigned the role of serving as a mentor for more junior employees. best of all, some firms actually compensate there people to a higher level because of the extra equity that they bring to the work place. They are the ones who can be depended on to transition training initiatives into action on the shop floor. They are "professional" trainees.

While this model may be considered extremely useful, it is also extremely rare. The actual participants are normally determined according to the following paradigm, which actually represents a bit of a dichotomy from the ideal. Initially, participants are selected because of the positions they hold, a decision that is often confused as having been made because positions are normally seen as being indices of power and influence or maybe capacity. From this group, a few will be unavailable and a few more will be late cancellations. This will seriously disturb the "mix" which our novice trainer had in mind when she caused certain individuals to be invited in the first place. This "mix" is a vital consideration and it should be based on the strategic considerations of the training: What long term improvements am I seeking? What changes do I wish to have institutionalized in the organization? Should I invite bosses and their staff members? How about the posturing which will result if the program involves middle managers and senior staff? How do I combat the group- think problem? Such considerations are real and cannot be satisfied via heuristic models, rules of thumb. There is a goodness of sit profile for both the number and type of participants and these will be introduced as each of the microlabs are discussed in Part Three.

This chapter has presented a template by which a program may be planned. The focus of your efforts must be closely linked to a central theme, causing some change to be effected. These changes must demonstrate value quite visibly, both to the future growth of the organization and the immediate needs of those who manage the transformation process. Such a holistic approach will facilitate the identification of the programs which should enable you to become a "commercial" enterprise for your firm and win you air time, both from those who pay the freight as well as from those who must attend the programs. I use "commercial" in the sense that being an in house training consultant requires you to be an effective marketing agent, in effect, you are trying to sell what you have to offer based on some notion of value. Once you have a notion of where you are going, the "big picture," you can identify the training pieces that get you there. This will enable you to begin considering the issue of feasibility, can what you need to achieve be addressed by a training program or even a sequence of programs? You determine this by examining the possibilities available to you for instructional design, the cost of the training, measuring the results and reporting the results.

You must learn to bring a notion of science as well as art to the concept of organization development. The science aspect is the technocracy of imparting knowledge, the art is the manner in which a knowledge transfer is accomplished. Both must be handled quite deftly for your commercial interests to prosper.

7

WRITING AND ASSESSING THE PROGRAM

Topics for Training

At first look it may appear that something is missing from the title of this chapter. What about the delivery of the program? That is what Part Three will detail for you and no, we are not putting the cart before the horse by exploring the training components of presenting programs via this sequence. There must be a strong and complementary relationship between how a program is written and how it is to be assessed. Contemporary training initiatives, especially as they are designed to support the improvement of productivity, must be assessed properly. By assessment I do not mean asking participants if they enjoyed the meal, the room, or the events of the day. I refer to a comprehensive attempt to determine whether or not the deserted organizational enhancements have been effected and the extent to which change has occurred. This is the process of institutionalization, the real payoff for any training initiative, and a process which begins with writing the program.

Writing the program requires care because you are constantly juggling two considerations, that which you need to accomplish, the outcomes, as well as the manner in which you will set the stage to maximize learning. I have never been satisfied with the approach of first developing, in isolation, an expectancy set of outcomes and then turning to the approach, the style of the program. While it is quite true that the outcomes, which represent the value of the program, the equity which the organization is attempting to build by funding your great adventure, are the primary concern, the essence of the training initiative will be determined by how well you establish an experience which is conducive to learning. Therefore, I believe in the following paradigm for writing the program.

First, in consequence of all that we have discussed thus far, reduce the expectancy set to measurable outcomes which are reasonable in light of the potential participants. The primary concern at work here is to maintain a careful match between the capacity of the participants and the scope of the material which you plan to present. It is assumed that you have already mastered the consideration of determining the readiness of the staff and selected those who can both profit by a training experience as well as contribute something on the other end. By this I mean selecting individuals who can influence others and thus geometrically increase the impact of training.

It is to the next level of being sensitive to selection and assessment concerns which are issue here. This involves selecting material and experiences which are appropriate to the population which you have identified at the first level. While you are still working from the corporate expectancy set, you will certainly face the challenge of having to be flexible here. Consider the following example. I am often requested to teach an "on-site" section of a MBA course. This is a scheduling alternative which enables an organization to offer a training program in-house and to base that learning experience on actual credit granting courses. Such scenarios are always more of a challenge than meeting a traditional class with the diversity inherent in having students who may have met a few prerequisites. Many firms will even devote a portion of the work day to the in-house course in order to stimulate interest. For example, a course may be established with a 4:40 PM start time which provides a somewhat truncated day for the participants while still permitting them to leave for home by 7:10 PM and still earn credits. The best experiences are those in which the classes are planned to complement the strategic corporate development plan.

Some years ago I had an extremely positive experience with the Jerrold Corporation. They had assembled an extremely talented cadre of staff members who were very articulate and knowledgeable, extremely motivated, and well educated. Some already possessed a graduate degree in some technical specialty such as electrical engineering. By the time that I taught the course, quite a bit of planning had taken place. The individuals had been selected, the course sequence had been determined, and everyone was aware of the potential payoffs. The class was entitled "Management and Organization Behavior", a course which is offered via many sections each semester. What made this special was the student profile data with which I was provided. The estimate of the capacity of the group enabled me to set a situation specific pace, select certain cases to spur discussion because they seemed to be very pertinent, and establish certain performance thresholds. I was able to customize this training experience and hopefully the client gleaned a proportionately greater return for the investment.

Conversely, I have also taught off-site classes in which the participants may have been very willing but their capacity was not strong. This also entailed a custom approach, different materials, different learning modules, perhaps a different pace. In any event, the learning outcomes were the same set of expectations whether this was a traditional class, a more capable class, or one which needed a boost to achieve. This is the essence of the skill of training. Being ready to move to different levels or different techniques to take groups to a specific goal. The stand-up presenters will often have to demonstrate such flexibility in mid-stream, that is, while actually teaching a lesson. We will more to say about that later.

Avoiding Wish Lists

The second consideration of my writing paradigm really represents a reality check. By this I mean, insuring that what is actually developed as an set of instructional objectives for any program are skills or behavioral modifications which are truly useful for the intended audience. It is difficult to develop a program that will change science, save the world, or teach law. That is for late night television hucksters on cable. You need to deliver something tangible, something that has demonstrable worth, something that will renew the participants.

Consider the microlab presented as Appendix F. In this program, Jennifer Johnson is working with the concept of employee assistance programs, certainly a topic which may be considered generic in terms of the potential population which could benefit from the training experience, but also one which is extremely broad in scope. However, Jennifer has correctly determined that this program will be most effective in mitigating the problem of troubled employees if it were designed to appeal to those who hold power within an organization, those who can well appreciate the costs associated with lost time and disgruntled employees. Therefore, her program was specifically written with supervisory personnel in mind and contained learning experiences dealing with the process of identifying troubled employees and remediating the situation. Ms. Johnson also presented a unique offering, the concept of a supervisor serving as an "enabler", one who should serve as an accountable resource to solve this major corporate concern. This was her signature solution to the dilemma of delivering a solution to a sever problem and making that solution something useful, cost efficient, and effective.

"Making Your Firm's EAP Work", is an example of a program that was conceived at the primary and secondary levels of writing concerns. It addressed the primary issue, troubled employees, and it was designed to be addressed to the most appropriate population that should attend as participants. She could have moved in many different directions in writing a program once her superiors identified the issue of troubled employees as their target. Our novice program development specialists will have to consider this secondary writing issue in a similar manner as they develop their training own programs.

The third consideration of my writing paradigm is to plan techniques which will complement the task of causing learning to occur. I once was retained as a consultant for a law firm which requested that I provide an evaluation of the speakers, format, logistic setup, etc. for a seminar which they were sponsoring. At the last minute someone in authority realized that they would shortly be expending a lot of money and staff resources, and exposing the capacity of the firm to public scrutiny, without having dealt with consideration number three. My task was damage control and rework. Well, the first iteration of the program, in my humble opinion, was an unqualified disaster. Over 600 attorneys were jammed into a large ballroom with insufficient space or ventilation and were seated simply on chairs with no place to write or examine materials. The handouts were exact reproductions of the pertinent statutes and the overheads were transparencies of actual size copies of the handouts which made them impossible to read. The first speaker stated that his purpose was to welcome everyone and told several bawdy stories about Elizabeth Taylor's most recent marriage, which seemed to have nothing at all to do with the program and introduced the next speaker. There were three "next" speakers and they all shared a common technique. They apologized in advance for their supposed shortcomings and read excerpts from the law and tried to provide interpretations. A Q/A session was provided after the last speaker and most of the questions were lost in the din of the room so that those who were still awake heard only the answers not the questions. There was not a single example, invitation to offer comment or bit of comic relief. I could have written my analysis after the first five minutes! I am sure that most of us have experienced such a program and were pleased when it concluded. No one in attendance learned anything that they could not have by studying the law. A sidewalk round robin discussion probably would have had more value and would have been much cheaper.

Notice that I castigated this program without out ever mentioning the content. The potential transmission of the content was ruined by the manner in which the program was designed. The fix was fairly involved. It required some planning regarding the expectations for the seminar. Was it to achieve a heightened awareness of new tax laws? Was it to train attorneys to deal effectively with these changes? Was is to review the experiences of the sponsoring firm as a marketing endeavor? Or, was it a combination of some or all of the preceding? Those who controlled the firm chose the last alternative and were really surprised at how much time they then had to devote to identifying the real issues which the firm wanted to communicate. Once that was accomplished we turned to the issues of technique and style.

There is a sense of style inherent in every program and the trainer who is writing the outline of a seminar has an opportunity to place his or her special signature on the proceedings. Throughout the microlabs, which are presented as the appendices, you will notice the shared characteristic of variety, illustrations, discussion activities, group work, guided imagery, and feedback opportunities. Most of these techniques are present in each of the seminars, yet they are not interchangeable blocks which are thrown together without a master plan. These are the tools by which you make participants take notice, reinforce a concept, or assess your programs. They are the solutions to the design challenge.

The Design Problem

Silberman (1990) offers an excellent discourse on designing a program to meet identified needs by consciously planning to keep the participants involved and profiting by the experience, hence the title, "Active Training". Keeping participants in the game so to speak is no easy task. A sense of timing, a notion of balance, a capacity for imagery are all important components of delivering a successful design. How about the issue of relevance? How do I vary my learning approaches? Can I count on any feedback from the participants? Who do I use their expertise? Do I dare let them move too far afield? How do I keeping reinforcing key concepts and disestablish vestigial ideas? How do I deal with the realities of the topic while staying on course? Let's see!

Back to our seminar on tax laws. This turned out to be something which was really important to the firm. They had something to offer, partners and associates who not only were specialists in this area but who also had tried some of the cases which occurred during the transition period between the superseded and new sets of IRS regulations, as well as several of the early defenses which were now being cited as precedents. This realization was most important for two reasons. It helped shape the audience who should be invited and it impact on the design issue. It turns out that the most appropriate participants were corporate attorneys of mid-range sized organizations, companies which were too small to maintain highly specialized legal staff but who routinely employed staff attorneys or who retained small generalist law firms. The actual purposes of the seminar then were established as follows: to provide an awareness of new IRS regulations which could impact on the manner in which companies conducted their routine activities, to expose legal professionals representing such companies to the new challenges inherent in the regulations which would mitigate a successful defense, and, to demonstrate the capacity of the host law firm, i.e., convince people to expend their billable hours with my client.

We had now moved from a generic topic that was commonly accepted as being relevant, tax law changes, to a specific set of goals for the program, and we had identified those who should attend, those who had the capacity to profit by the program and who also possessed the influence to use the knowledge which they would acquire. The trick now was to develop the road map which would enable us to fulfill the expectations for the program.

From Point A to Point B

Our next step should focus on the specific outcomes which we would see exhibited by our participants as they conclude the training experience, whether it be a one day workshop or a seminar series. I have found it to be useful, perhaps essential, to specify such outcomes in behavioral terms. Words such as define, list, pose, operate, appraise, evaluate convey the sense of action inherent in achieving behavioral changes. For our tax seminar this posed some interesting challenges. We were not going to test the participants knowledge of the tax laws with a paper and pencil test. For one thing, retained knowledge of the new statutes was not a desired outcome. From a style perspective, we were about to embark on a marketing venture. We needed to develop a sense of need and then show the participants how to meet that need. We needed to demonstrate the worth of the host firm to provide certain services of quality. While the ultimate assessment would be based on how many new clients the firm acquired, the value of the seminar would be judged on how well the participants realized the need to change the way they conducted business and the role my client could play in helping them make this adjustment. Silberman (1990) refers to the three key ingredients of any design effort as being composed of : a purpose, a method, and a format. The design challenge is to address each of these components successfully while achieving a blend or feel for each throughout the program. Dealing with these ingredients transformed the tax taw seminar from a disaster into a successful marketing tool.

These parameters were all part of the mix which resulted in a program that satisfied the style considerations of delivering what was basically a sales pitch. We now turned to the design building blocks, illustrations, discussion activities, group work, guided imagery, etc., and began developing our strategy. Programs should begin at the beginning. If this sounds like a riddle think of how many presentations which you may have attended which started with a speech, an apology, or some mundane housekeeping activity such as handing out materials or viewing the curriculum vitae of the group leader? These are not beginnings but distracters. For example, I never have anyone introduce me. The name and a short biographical blurb is contained in the program and they will probably learn more about me than they care to know as we progress through the day by following along with each of my stories. I begin with something appropriate to the occasion, an icebreaker, a challenge, a story they can relate to, the description of a common problem, to name a few. Consider the opener contained in Appendix D. In "Closing the Deal", John Matlaga, got everyone in the mood by a role play and then transitioned to personal experiences related to the topic. We are dealing with salespersons in this program. They did not come for a lecture but to learn a variety of techniques which will enable them to persuade prospects to sign on the dotted line.

Our lawyers in attendance do not need warm up exercises in order to get to know one another or to get going. Lawyers had better be articulate or else they should choose a new business line. Since I was the only non-attorney in attendance, I was probably the only live prospect present. We got our program started by telling a few stories of firms that faced new tax burdens because they either ignored or were late in changing their procedures for sheltering profits from taxes. Then the audience heard a few success stories and were told that the purpose of the program was to show them what to be concerned with, how to convince their clients to change their routine and, the great untold truth, how the host firm could satisfy their needs. And so it went. For each point that the experts thought was important, a technique was utilized to probe, question, reconcile, review, and develop. At the end of the six hours of training the participants demonstrated an awareness of the new challenges that faced them. They had participated in a number of exercises which built on their anticipated knowledge base to a higher level of skill. They showed enthusiasm and confidence. They even offered some existing ideas for new tangent business lines, lawyers just love to do that. The program was deemed a success. It was succinct, able to be communicated in only six hours, and was designed to give the audience something to take away, in this case a realization that there was a new alligator network out there to gobble them up and an introduction to the means of keeping the beasts at bay. By empowering the audience to become active participants, we made them part of the solutions, we tapped their equity, we provided them with an opportunity to think about what had occurred, and we reinforced their learning. All of this with less than great trainers. I never had the opportunity nor the time to properly train those who presented the seminar, although, after their initial failure, they were more than eager to accept my recommendations. Aside from the false start and the necessary patchwork and retrenchment, this is a great model to use as a guide. The participants and the presenters joined together in a transformation exercise. Each gave something of themselves to the program and each took away a great deal more than they brought with them. A successful program possesses the characteristic of synergy, the outcomes are multiplied geometrically. However, such synergy is impossible to achieve if you insist on lecturing to your group, if you bore them to tears with inane material, if you fail to develop a partnership with them.

Variety is the Spice of Life

In Appendix B, Braughler, Kennedy, and Kowalick, tell you who should attend and what they will teach you by the end of the third page of the microlab description. Their program requires five hours and thirty minutes to complete but they are so good in delivering the seminar that it feels more like a celebration rather than a chore. Their own talents in presentation aside, the program could not have made such a dramatic impact on me had it been based on a truncated design component configuration, one which was based primarily on lecture for example. Note the variety in the approach proposed by Braughler, Kennedy, and Kowalick. They avoid repetition, provide time estimates, and never overplay their hand by attempting too much or becoming overly complicated. Another significant feature of this program is the use of the resident knowledge of the participants. In section "C, Importance of Training Employees", the trainer makes active participants of the audience by structuring a discussion activity around only one parameter- the content, i.e., the most recent training experience each participant can recall. The results of this discussion activity then become the basis for a transition activity, evaluating training based on the real life experiences of the trainees. There is a reinforcement component also, the trainer reviews in detail training programs of firms that the participants have heard of such as the Disney Corporation, which have highly positive components. There is quality participation represented here and that is the key to success. I have even had people attend a program and admit that the participation activities made the day worth while even if the material was not quite what they understood from the brochure. Being interactive throughout is the *sine quo non* of success.

How do I plan such variety? Remember one of our golden rules, active means participatory but pre-plan your flexible approaches. Each technique has a part to play in our little drama, especially lecture. Many students of the training course sequence attempt to develop their first microlabs with the absence of lecture. They treat this very viable approach to communicating information as a communicable disease, something to avoid. Yet information processing, lecture, is the most used of all the purposes of communication. If we define communication as a transfer of information to insure understanding, then lecture, information giving, starts to play a very significant role. We clarify what is to be done by processing information via a control purpose. We respond to questions by providing information and we keep things moving by telling people what they need to know when they need to know it. I have built a career by telling stories, they punctuate my use of lecture by grabbing the audience's attention and the humor aids in their in recall of salient points. Story telling is a form of lecture. Consider the following example. One of the skills which professional stand-up trainers need to master is that of imagery, the ability to create clear mental pictures in an audience. It is difficult to capture the attention of an audience, it is darn difficult just to get a program opened. Stories can help but only if they are good, relevant, and easily understood. To test the receptiveness of my group when I discuss imagery I often use the following example. I was once assigned to an active duty period in San Diego, California, certainly a garden spot, one whose very mention should spark some interest in a listener. During my stay there was a mysterious car bomb explosion and every military installation went on alert. I found out about the alert while during my laundry in the officer's quarters. A chief petty officer was calling my name in the passage way and he was carrying a weapon and a notice which informed me that I was to serve as something called a "senior watch officer" that evening. At the time I was dressed only in a still wet bathing suit and was anxious to put away the .45 caliber pistol and bring along my laundry at the same time. The only place to stow the weapon was in the suit. I tried the front but then thought better of the idea since I was not sure that the safety would work and decided to place the weapon in the small of my back within the waistband of the swimsuit. That seemed to work although the cold metal against my skin was not at all a pleasant experience. As I struggled with my laundry and attempted to return to my room, the gun slipped within the suit. It just so happened that the Navy was sponsoring a recruiting trip for nurses and they were assigned to the same building as the officers of my unit. While I was holding the laundry with one hand and fishing in my suit for the gun with the other, three of the young ladies happened to enter the laundry space, took one look at me and went running back to their rooms. That story usually provokes laughter, not because I am standup comic, but because I have the ability to enable listeners to visualize a middle-aged man in a very embarrassing situation. Imagery is the essence of story telling and story telling can serve to introduce or soften a lecture period. Stories are usually easiest to work with when they are true life experiences and they can be a tremendous way to transition from one component of a program to another. More about this in the next section.

Becoming Creative

How about the situation where someone is designing a program and they do not possess a plethora of life experiences which they can reduce to stories for the purpose of communicating information or illustrating a point? Well, this is the most likely scenario which you will face. Remember, lecture is a legitimate technique for imparting knowledge which can become deadly if abused. One of the ways in which a presenter can soften the blow of the lecture format is to place the intended use of the technique in a proper perspective. For example, the lecture will be much better received and have a stronger positive impact if it is previewed. By this I mean, tell the audience in advance what is coming, what to look for, and why is will be of value. I have some particularly astute trainers complement this strategy by inviting participants to interrupt the lecture with descriptions of personal experiences which are related to the topic.

Working from a posted outline is another way of making a lecture more effective. This helps the audience to follow along and you are, in effect, segmenting the material which helps because people are consuming the data in smaller portions. Let's say there are five salient points which require a lecture technique in order to be explicated fully and you have timed the presentation for 50 minutes. It would be much more beneficial to break down the lecture into five, ten minute presentations using each break as an opportunity to summarize and elicit audience input. Also, you have effectively created a change of pace five times instead on once and that is easier on anyone's attention span.

Silberman (1990) offers another viable alternative to "straight" lecture, a technique entitled "guided note taking." In this situation, the lecturer stops at intervals and invites individuals to take notes because of the importance of that particular component of the material. This creates copious opportunities to be creative, perhaps asking the audience to offer examples or even compare relative experiences, each of which are widely believed to help cement learning.

Many very accomplished lecturers believe strongly in a question and answer opportunity as a summative experience in the lecture and as a readily available method to elicit responses, clarify points, and transition to a new topic. To be effective, you must truly spark interest. Some people make the mistake of asking content oriented questions and answering each themselves as a means of expediting a program. Other problems associated with a Q/A include not being patient enough to wait for a response or having the skill necessary to provide a bit more seed information to help explicated the discussion. The classic fault, which is really quite insulting to an audience, is to simply attempt to check understanding by asking, "Do you understand?" The audience would have to be at an extremely high comfort level to respond in the negative. We will examine the technique of questioning in the next section, but the designer of the program can help the presenter in the following manner. Plan your questions just the way you would design in a break, transition, or some alternative to the lecture. At the very least, identify the content areas to be questioned to reinforce the anticipated learning and leave the technique to the presenter.

Attractive Alternatives

Your review of the microlabs should have indicated that lecture is not a preferred technique, however necessary it may seem. There are a number of alternatives and most program design experts will test the applicability of these before resorting to the pure lecture, especially as that technique might be used very extensively.

A promising alternative to lecture is the case study, especially if they are written around real to life situations. You are communicating information, just as you would in a lecture, and you have the ability to set the stage by highlighting the pertinent parts of the exercise. The reinforcement opportunities are copious and under the control of the trainer, who would be expected to develop questions to provoke a discussion of the case study.

A case study may be used to introduce a topic or even an entire seminar. Some of my misadventures with rental care companies are used to introduce programs in quality service, for example. People can relate to such a misadventure, and I can pause for effect or reinforcement whenever the opportunity presents itself. A simple rendition of this personal experience, along with pertinent data, opportunities for comment and feedback, and the need to develop solutions, either individually or via group discussion permits me to exceed the impact of a lecture, by a significant margin, often at no appreciable loss of time. People have been invited to participate in the activity by the nature of the presentation of the case. The variety of the approach helps maintain attention levels and the group may actually be practicing some of the skills you wish to develop through the forced interactions with a group.

Another positive aspect of the case study is that is can be prepared and disseminated in advance of the group meeting for the formal training program. I often employ this technique to provide a bridge among training days in a lengthy seminar or series of programs. Of course, the material has to be interesting enough to cause people to work with outside of class. This is true of the entire workshop agenda so make it a point to only use cases which can be construed as having some demonstrable value to the participant. Disseminating case studies in advance, i.e., prior to the first meeting of the participants, is normally only a good idea when you are dealing with an in-house group and you can properly brief and introduce both the case and rationale for having provided it. For this reason, I seldom use this approach in such circumstances.

Case studies do have drawbacks. Even real to life situations must be presented in a manner which is both summative yet inclusive of key data. Fictional scenarios are even more challenging. The program designer must use care in developing material which meets the test of relevancy yet does not appear to be overly done, i.e., so far beyond the realm of real life as to be dismissed as insignificant.

Another key point for those who would be writers of case studies is that of discussion questions. These must be to the point, based on actual data present in the case, and most challenging, required the respondent to interpret information, maker assumptions, and draw conclusions. There are some outstanding examples of case studies described in the appendix material.

Odds and Ends

In addition to case studies, effective alternatives to a lecture format include: group activities, especially inquiry; guided teaching; discussion activities; and, role playing, games, and simulations which are all of a similar genre.

Group inquiry is often confused with discussion but the concepts are more complementary than inter-related. Arousing curiosity or interest through the diversion of questions is the essence of group inquiry. The program development specialist may design a group inquiry exercise by introducing a topic, posing problems or alternative solutions to a dilemma and then providing from the group to generate its own questions as a means of exploring the issue. The group work would be based on a discussion of each of the questions, prospective answers that would be generated and their appropriateness in furthering the discussion.

Guided teaching involves using questions to further the lesson or prompt individuals to expound on their thoughts, feelings, or personal experiences. I have found them following to be most useful. Record the inputs from the participants on some readily observable medium such as newsprint. Use everything which you receive, as you would with a brain storming activity. Never critique or censor an idea. Let the audience react to each point. Reinforce salient ideas. Try to avoid being reactive. Plan to return to these points as appropriate whenever the evolution of the seminar permits.

Discussions serve a variety of purposes, and, depending on the skill of the trainer, can serve as a very positive activity. People may get involved via a discussion format. They can provide you with input based on their own experiences and this can be a very strong motivational tool. The careful program designer will plan the use of discussion as a progressive threshold of difficulty. That it, move from the generic to the specific, from the simple to the complex by developing a discussion shell and planning intervention by the trainer. New material, corrective material, enhancement information and program transitions can be served well by such interventions. The trainer must use care in not dominating the discussion format, a fault found in your author on many occasions!

Consider the program design presented in the microlab contained in Appendix B. The specific area of interest here is part "B" of the program, "Empowering and Involving Employees." In this scenario, the discussion period is introduced by a lecture type of activity. After introducing and briefing the topic, the participants become involved through an exercise in which they are asked to visualize a workplace containing the positive aspects of empowerment just described. The exercise blossoms into a complete discussion as the participants work on the specific task of describing a transition from authoritarian to participatory management practices.

Role playing, games and simulations are among my favorite diversions from the dull or mundane. These are situation specific exercises in which the trainer attempts to have the participants get a feel for a topic by living, however temporarily, some aspect of that topic. I once gave a class an assignment, based on work groups, to develop a role play which would describe the worst aspects of the performance appraisal process. Two of my more inventive students came up with the following. The manager invites a very nervous employee into office and offers a chair while asking, "I assume you know why we are here today?". While the employee stammers out his response, "To discuss my performance appraisal", the manager asks him if he would like some coffee. While turning to pour pretend coffee from a pretend pot, the manager looks back over his shoulder and states, "I am really not satisfied with your work over the past year so I am going to fire your ass. Would you like cream and sugar!". Such a vivid role play can easily be used to provoke a discussion. The imagery is obvious and so should be the value of the technique.

My favorite usage of this type of alternative (the three techniques named are interchangeable for our purposes) is the ubiquitous survival exercise. This provide such rare opportunities for learning because of the variety of skills which they involve. I am sure that many readers have played the game where they are supposedly ship wrecked and have to rank order a number of "survival" items and then work in a group to develop a consensus which is then measured against "expert" opinion. Decision making, communication, influence, bargaining, and imagery are among the many skill or ability areas challenged by such a simulation. A central design rule to keep in mind is to carefully plan the anticipated outcomes for the use of such a technique before designing it. While these are really fun, in the hands of a seasoned trainer, if they are used for the sake of a "break" in routine , or they are used too frequently, they will actually have a negative impact and serve as a distracter. They have to complement the seminar material or people will spend the rest of the day asking to do another one, or anything else that is preferable to the material which you have designed. Plan the impact you wish to achieve and then design the program to achieve it.

Assessment

The assessment area is probably the most challenging for the program design specialist. The purest assessment would involve designing an instrument which met acceptable thresholds of validity and reliability and which could be administered in some fashion to the participants. Even a single measurement opportunity would not suffice since the real goal of any assessment should be considered to be multivariate in nature. By this I mean that assessment should be viewed not as a single event but a compilation of information which should be used to examine the utility of a given training opportunity, to determine the extent to which the knowledge, skills, or abilities which were intended to be communicated to the participants have been institutionalized, and finally, that the results of the training effort as a whole have furthered the strategic interests of the organization. This brief description of the function of assessment should be enough to indicate that the totality of the process is really the responsibility of the strategist rather than a trainer. The level of training and experience requirements require professional preparation in the area and quite beyond our discussion. Besides, evaluation of the extent really required to insure true impact rarely occurs anywhere in the world of the soft sciences, even the public schools.

If measurable knowledge gain is not a sinecure for assessment and if assessment is so necessary, how should we proceed? Here are some important considerations. If the program is well planned, that is, if it is designed to meet some strategic considerations, then your primary concern should be to determine the efficacy of the design. By this I mean, you should plan to collect data throughout the presentation. One of the major products of any of my consultancies is a summative report which is based on the actual seminar which I have conducted. During the course of the program, I take note of the capacity of the group to complete the exercises. I also observe such items as the flexibility demonstrated during the problem solving sessions, the willingness of the participants to engage in discussions, and the tone of their participation. By this I am referring to the climate which results in the program as a consequence of the various profiles or other data gathering opportunities which the participants experience. For example, one of my most requested programs is a seminar on conflict management. One of the very first exercises which we complete is designed to have the participants identify sources of frustration in the workplace. I take careful note not only of the items which I elicit but also the demeanor exhibited as a consequence of engaging in that activity. In my report to the client, I concentrate on an assessment of the group, not individuals, offering opinions and recommendations concerning each knowledge, skill, or ability area that the program was designed to satisfy. Such reports often become the basis by which further training is planned and longitudinal assessments are conducted. This same set of data findings also provide me with the capacity to evaluate the program and rework whatever may be necessary when a similar program is offered for a similar population.

The technocracy of the design should also be evaluated. Here is a list of questions which could form the basis of any evaluation protocol:

- Where the knowledge, skill, and ability areas addressed properly?

- Did the time sequencing work? Were seminar components completed as planned? Did the entire program finish at the time advertised?

- If participant inputs forced the abandonment of some pre-planned exercises, did the resulting configuration still cover each of the learning objectives?

- Was the program designed with an adequate pace? Did each of the components flow easily into the next with each serving in a complementary role to the whole?

- Were the transitions adequate? Did the program suffer breakdowns when the trainer attempted to move from section to section?

- Did the pre-planned opportunities for participants to "buy" into the program prove successful?

- Where the knowledge, skill, or ability areas covered by

the learning objectives appropriate to the capacity of the group?

- Did the materials work? (Hint: this is an area which is almost totally dependent on the responses of the participants.)

In a summative sense, assessment is based on the "goodness of fit" theory, you plan to do something then you measure how that something worked out. Since many of these indices are based on the ability and observations of the trainer, we shall return to this topic in Part Three as we learn how to deliver a program.

PART III

THE DELIVERY

Delivering the program is the essence of a training initiative, it is the ultimate expression of communicating an opportunity for skills transfer. Thus far we have sampled fairly detailed descriptions of how corporations have organized their assets to build accountability throughout their ranks in an effort to improve their productivity. We have also seen some examples of archaic strategies which do not work and seem almost guaranteed to invite destroy in the forthcoming cooperate wars. Part One also provided us with some insight as to the role that training might play in helping us achieve this state of heightened capacity. In Part Two we experienced a step by step guide as to the development of the actual instrument that would translate the grandiose ideals of the strategists into the reality of skills improvement needed in the workplace. That component is a quintessential aspect of any effort to improve productivity, the means by which the tremendous investment in human resources incurred by every organization pays off. The ability to take somewhat global goals and refine them into a process by which trucks are routed more effectively or typist learn word processing is a legitimate role for the program development specialist. It is a minimum skill set for anyone who would aspire to this role.

The third part of this book is dedicated to the delivery of the program. While presentation skills in a variety areas are not to be expected in order to serve as a program development specialist, they must be available to the organization via some mechanism, in-house staff or hired guns. The last component of this text is written directly for those who would establish the logistics for a program and carry it out. However, while the style of writing is personalized to those "who do", it is also intended for those who have the responsibility to see that what is done is carried out in a professional manner, that it, delivering knowledge skills and ability sets to those who do the work that makes the company productivity. Part three is written in the same narrative style used in earlier sections but it represents the actual template of the book, the means by which someone with a minimum of experience can carry out the increasing important function of providing training to increase quality.

8

OPENING THE PROGRAM

Where do we go from here?

In the beginning there were managers who where trained in highly operational matters. Planning, controlling, staffing and financing various aspects of the corporate enterprise which constituted their training base. These were the skills which were prized, the abilities which seemed guaranteed to keep organizations profitable. Now that we have experienced the reality of that promise, we have to adopt what I refer to as a," train for gain" approach to excellence. Training has to be employed as a hands-on, value driven initiative in the style of Peters and Waterman (1984). Of the eight basic principles which form the basis of their work, I believe that one exists as an over-all goal within the context of this book. That primary principle, as I normally refer to it, is to develop a capacity to foster a climate where dedication to some central value set of the organization is adopted as a the goal and productivity through people is adopted as an enabling objective. The latter is another of the basic principles advanced by Peters and Waterman. Our immediate objective, the delivery of quality training, is dependent on still another of the eight basic principles, having a bias for action. This notion is a must for those who are committed to program development because it is the key to the new skills which those who would lead others must possess. In effect, those of us who ply our trade as professional trainers are fortunate, we now have clients who are interested in having us deliver programs which are rich in potential even if they are difficult to document as being successful. However, the people placed in our charge to develop may not share our enthusiasm for the adventure on which they are to share with us. That is why we, are program presenters, must have a bias for action, a capacity to make operational, concepts which may seem ephemeral to the uninitiated.

Getting Started

We have now reached the part of our journey where the rubber meets the road. We have learned how to build a constituency, identify needs, plan an attack, and design the program. Now we must experience the final step, taking all of the inputs which have been gathered and refined and using them to accomplish something. Achieving a state of enhanced productivity requires patience, the courage to chart a new course or way of doing business internally, a significant commitment of resources, and serious attention to all three of the components presented in this book. Many companies theoretically stop at the end of part one. They hear about something good, perhaps in a competitor, and they may even make a serious attempt to benchmark some promising aspect of how another organization conducts some aspect of their business.

However, they fail to catch the spirit and grasp the opportunity. This is readily observable because of the nature of their effort and how quickly that effort is abandoned. Other companies stay with us through most of part two but often truncate their potential growth opportunities by failing to commit the resources necessary to translate goals and objectives into programs. Unfortunately, few organizations make the leap to work with the concept of total quality all the way through to the inception of demonstrable benefits, that is, to implement the results of actual training into the daily routine of the workplace. For those of you with the willingness to learn something new, with the patience to make a significant investment of yourself, and the courage to be seen as a proponent of allocating resources for which tangible benefits may not be readily observable, here we go!

Program Descriptions

The imagery created for a program offering will often determine its success. You create such imagery by writing an effective program description. This is your primary marketing tool. This discussion is presented here to satisfy the situation in which the program development specialist, the program designer, and the program presenter are not the same person. The description of the program which is distributed is related, in a causal sense, to the delivery of the program and thus it should be written by the training professional who will conduct the actual training session. Only this individual knows enough about that which actually is be presented to effectively convey an accurate portrayal of what to anticipate to potential participants.

In the "classic" seminar situation, the trainer actually knows little about the participants and the group themselves are participants in a "public " program, one which has been advertised as being available at a certain locale and time, for a specific fee. The availability of such programs is advertised primarily through the ubiquitous catalogues which seem to arrive with ever increasing frequency to all who have had the misfortune to have been identified as a marketing prospect for a mailing list. Organizations with substantive training operations often circulate their own in-house training catalogues.

These catalogues are an item which deserves some attention from us at this point. The program descriptions which seem to provoke the most interest generally contain a comprehensive outline which lists benefits of attendance by posing questions which are directed at a limited area of focus and which provide only a "tease" of a response, i.e. an unspecified solution which represents a high comfort state of being able to solve a problem by attending the program. The program descriptions should also present some sort of section which identifies who should attend. For example, I have developed an entire series of programs which are directed at support staff. In recent years, many organizations have begun to realize that there is a significant and often untapped source of equity present in each of the office veterans who have served as clerks or secretaries. These people have had an opportunity to demonstrate their capacity for learning, their initiative, and their loyalty. It makes sense to build an advancement ladder based on skills to enable an organization to tap this potential, especially when you consider the inherent benefits in that these potential candidates for additional levels of responsibility are readily available and usually cheaper to employ. My programs are designed to teach specific skills that these folks will need to meet a specific goal such as "serving as the executive behind the scenes". That phrase seems to be an eye-catcher for those who read my program description.

I present a synoptic description of what I mean by this phrase and describe the kind of person that I believe would profit by attending this program. In the case of the example, this is an individual with enough service to know how things work, the ability to articulate well with the internal or external customers of her or his work unit, and a desire for advancement. Such a tactic is not only an effective marketing tool, it serves as a means for insuring that the most appropriate audience will attend the program. Both internal and external trainers have to be mightily concerned with their reputation, their job is to satisfy the expectations of those who retain them by delivering a quality effort. We have already seen how important it is to design a program to fit the capacity of the audience, and in the public seminar situation, this is one way to enable those who shop for programs to make intelligent decisions about whether to attend. There is a causal relationship between how successful your program will be and how appropriate the audience is for the presentation. Even those who present programs to in-house clients may face a situation in which participants may come from a fairly generic population. Preparing a concise yet specific program description will help insure that the right people attend the most appropriate training evolution. Total Quality initiatives involve a great deal of training and you must learn to avoid disappointing people if you wish them to continue to participate.

And so, the first step in support of effective program delivery is to prepare a description of the activity which stimulates interest by allowing people to gain a sense of how the program will be structured, what 's in it for them, and whether or not they are appropriate attendees for the seminar.

Beginnings

Delivering a six hour seminar is a taxing experience, one which will require much stamina as well as skill. I try to teach my students who are learning the skills of program presentation to see themselves in the guise of both a Broadway producer and director. Why? Because a one-day training experience can be as complicated to deliver as one act Broadway play. In fact, given the kinds of skills one would like to see exhibited in a trainer, perhaps the analogy should be based on a one -act comedy. To set the stage appropriately, we must open in a manner that will capture the interest of our audience, tell them something about what they are about to experience, and convince them that we know what we are doing. Sound tough? Well, that is why a number of plays never reach Broadway or close down shortly after they do. Let's take a detailed look at the concept of opening the program. And please remember, you will profit most from the sections to follow if you attempt to use the material as criteria to be employed as benchmarks in your own situations, whether or not you are an actual trainer.

Perhaps I am of a simplistic nature, but I tend to view this critical operation as being based on only two considerations, how well do I, as the trainer, know the group, and, how well do the members of the group know each other. We will examine this issue in each of its possible permutations.

Much has been written about the techniques that should be used to begin a program. If you know little about your audience, the "public" seminar situation described above, you must plan your opening variety of perspectives. First, since you have only your program description to guide you, look again at the type of person which you have identified as having the best prospects of profiting from the program. remember, your goal here is to get the show on the road, emphasizing the involvement of the participants and demonstrating your own competence. That should translate into an opening experience in which you get them talking but not at a level that is so simplistic that they will begin wondering why they have invested a day away from the office in exchange for the opportunity to be bored by you. Peters and Waterman discuss the concept of "foot in the door" research, that is, incrementally conditioning individuals into greater commitment. The opening experience of the seminar should be viewed in a similar manner. This is not only the first, it is the best opportunity which you will have to convince people to buy into what you have to offer.

I can recall a really miserable experience in which I was all set to begin the first of six days of training for senior staff of a large organization. This was a major contract for me and also a huge commitment for the executive of this department because the program had been designed to present an indepth experience in some rather contemporary issues of leadership. The participants all had, at least to them, extraordinary busy schedules, and a few had already informed me that they would not be able to attend each day or all of every day. This should be read as a major danger signal by every budding trainer. I had worked closely with the executive who had booked the program and felt that I had a firm grasp of all major contingency issues facing the group.

These included: the average number of years of seniority for the group, their typical career progression pattern, the number and kinds of people that they supervised, and the kinds of mission statements which they had developed for their organization. As stated above, I also had the "inside" information, the insights of their supervisor, a person who seemed quite capable and committed to change. He had identified certain problems which existed within the organization. He was uncomfortable with the manner in which his key staff dealt with people and new operating procedures. Resistance to change was a problem, which is not unusual in a contemporary bureaucratic setting.

The biggest concern was the fact that the organization was being downsized, more and more of their operational funds were being transferred to "soft" sources which had to be won via competitive solicitations and the response of the supervisors had been business as usual. This is a fairly typical scenario for the public domain where incentive systems are not comparable to the private sector and where the training investment is not very contemporary, at least as we have been defining the quality through people approach of this book. That is why this leadership program had been designed for my client.

Frustrations

Part of any opening is the coffee and muffins get together. You should be on deck early enough to be satisfied with the logistics and have all your materials ready to go. The coffee hour requires you to be extremely upbeat, greeting people as they enter, making small talk about the coming day, and making every attempt to get people used to you. You should not be in this business if you cannot meet this challenge. You also should be using this time to get to know the people with whom you will spend the day, especially if your pre-program knowledge base is not as extensive as that which was described for the program in the example. My experience with the group in the example was fairly positive. They all seemed bright and at least half voluntarily acknowledged that they were looking forward to the program because they had had no training in this area and they knew that "times were getting tougher", i.e., they were being pressured to do more with less and in the public domain this means a severe reduction in staff assets.

In trying to get everyone comfortable with me I was trying to identify some condition or issue that would get their attention. I noticed that the almost everyone was wearing a portable cellular phone on their hip and many of these were already being initialized, a lot of calls were coming in. I wanted to make my way into their group and I knew I had to put an end to the potential source of interruptions so I made reference to the phones by announcing that everyone should check their guns and phones by the front door. This seemed to have the desired effect and provided me with an entry to begin discussing some more pertinent issues with selected individuals.

By this strategy I was attempting to use of the principle of "foot in the door". By beginning to pull more and more people into the spirit or style that would be used in the workshop

I was working the crowd so to speak, getting them ready to participate and perhaps getting them used to me. I was also finding out some tidbits of office politics, certain workplace likes and dislikes. There would be invaluable to me as I choose stories, cases or examples as we progressed through each learning objective for the program. The less you know about the group the harder it is to customize your material to their interests but the more important it becomes to use such a strategy successfully. I was also making mental notes of those who seemed open to what I was trying to accomplish. These were the people on whom I would call when I got into trouble in the program, and no program ever goes as well as you would like.

Well, I was all set. I had several "openers" ready because flexibility is a major condition as we will see throughout the remainder of this section. I was still considering two ways of getting started when the door burst open and the boss of my contact arrived and announced that he needed a few minutes to review some administrative matters with his "troops". Well a few minutes turned into forty-five and I was about to throw a fit. This was the only time in my career when I was tempted to bag a program, that is, either cancel or truncate this day and try again some other time. Not only was I losing valuable time, I was losing my audience. This person had handed out copies of the federal register and taking the group away from their almost idyllic off-site setting back into the typical problems which they faced everyday in the office. In addition, he was putting great pressure on them to leave the program, at least mentally, by imposing a few deadlines which they had not been aware of previously.

The almost final straw came when he started talking about audits which had found that individuals were using governmental office supplies for private use, pens and pencils! Is it any wonder that my client was concerned that his supervisors were not equipped to handle contemporary leadership challenges.

I had to find something to get the group back as we were now one hour and fifteen minutes past the start time and even I was almost asleep. Finally the big boss left without even acknowledging what they were there to accomplish and without even noticing me. I immediately said "Good Morning" over the din which is indicative of a group out of control and stated that as a Naval Reserve Officer I had access to government supplies also and wanted to confess to having a "federal" pen in my pocket, which I promptly produced. They started to laugh and I felt that I had them to the extent that I freely stated that we needed a break to re-focus ourselves on the coming events so we took ten minutes for a lavatory opportunity and then got started in earnest. It worked out well and as someone told me at the end of the day what happened at the very beginning was a terrific example of what they needed to overcome.

Being Flexible

Flexibility is a major key to success in the business of training. Having my material available will not enable anyone to actually conduct a program because the content needs to be communicated via a certain style and that had to be refined throughout the day as you learn more about your group. The outline, lists and descriptions of exercises, etc. really do not constitute content because a training program is really composed of the talent of the presenter, the climate for learning which is established, and the style in which the designed exercises are presented and received by the participants. Making up discussion groups, choosing examples to use, and deciding on the appropriateness of the stories you were planning to interject are all critical ingredients in looking good on your feet. Getting started with an opener that works is difficult because you may know something about the background of the group but you usually know very little about their attitudes or capacity. Having a number of routes to pursue and making quick decisions about choosing the best of the best is an art that requires some practice to master.

My workshop on conflict management can be used here to good advantage as an example. Conflict management may be viewed as a growth industry. There is and has been great interest in this topic, so much so that I have created several different workshop designs to meet certain contingencies. The public seminar group usually profits by an experience in which they explore sources and solutions of conflict and learn how to manage confrontation in a manner designed to avoid the dysfunctional aspects of the problem. I teach the traditional concepts of "fight, flee or flow" and try to build a repertoire of response patterns which participants learn to use after a successful "read" of a situation.

Groups with a much more similar makeup usually have specific agendas to deal with in the area of conflict management. Here the notion of group think usually is important, that is, teaching the evils of false consensus and the means to avoid it. These groups usually profit by exercises in which they learn how to build consensus easily, to honor the existence of contra ideas without actually agreeing with them. Negotiation skills are also usually a major ingredient of such a seminar. These two program outlines are fairly diverse. The commonalty of materials does result in some overlap and my repertoire of stories is always there waiting. Which do I use? How do I get started?

If I am working with a homogenous group, especially one with a pretty strong learning capacity, I tend to open their version of the conflict management seminar in a different way. Here I am trying to create images of individuals who use certain styles which either mitigate or exacerbate conflict. One of my favorite examples is a true story about a statistics professor which I had for two of the last courses in the doctoral sequence, an individually whose style of being cognitively dissonant was legendary among his students. His favorite saying was : "A graduate student is like an oyster, you have to irritate it to get a pearl". Well, we heard this in class after class along with disdain for our capacity to master the material and some of the most obnoxious references to which backgrounds that I have ever encountered. For example, when we were made to introduce ourselves the first night, a tactic which I never use in my programs by the way, I was asked to admit that my ethnic heritage some three generations back was of Italian descent. That comment was married to my residence location and I ended being greeted by the phrase, "Well you live in ______ with the rest of the Italians who cannot read or write." That was over twenty years ago and even in a age when people were more generous about granting some freedom to individuals who had legitimate or reward authority over them, I, like most of my classmates who received a similar greeting, was less than enthralled. As an opener, this story goes on for approximately ten minutes stopping to ask participants to react, a bit of analysis concerning the dynamics of each situation described, and finally a discussion as to the purposes and value of such behavior. I know that I have chosen wisely when they are not only responding but also relating what was said to their own situations at work.

With groups in a public seminar that I don't know very well, I try to begin by soliciting some ideas concerning things or situations that are sources of frustration in their daily lives and then refine the topic by turning to similar areas of frustration in the workplace. This seems to work well because I get them talking fairly easily because they are relating to things which they live with on a routine basis and thus know well. The transition to the workplace gets them thinking about the kinds of things which I am trying to change, often by creating a realization that they cannot ignore their own potential role in causing conflict to become dysfunctional in the workplace. The list of items which I elicit in both part of the opener serve as focal points and I can refer to them throughout the day as we deal with many of them by exploring possible solutions or alternative forms of behavior. Thus I am underway on a positive note because I have taken ten to fifteen minutes to introduce the topic, tell some stories about my own frustrations, and get them talking. They are automatically ready to get into the first exercise, which is usually a discussion piece.

Openers

Openers can help groups get acquainted while at the same time induce a spirit of cooperation and interdependence. This would be especially helpful in a scenario in which you were working with intact teams of individuals from the same organization which contain both supervisors and their respective staff. If I were presenting my conflict management seminar in such a situation I might use a technique known as "group captions". This involves establishing small groups and having them develop a caption for a picture and then guiding the subsequent discussing concerning the meaning of the caption. One of my favorites is a picture of a giant elephant getting ready to step on a mouse. In the ensuing discussion of the captions, I try to elicit some role reversal feelings concerning who perceives themselves as the mouse. Often it is the supervisors and the staff have an opportunity to learn some of the challenging circumstances which confront their bosses on a daily basis. This is a major ingredient in teaching the concept of subordinateship, one of the techniques necessary to mitigate dysfunctional conflict.

You can build group interdependence through such exercises in which people are asked to share their most embarrassing moment and the others are charged with attempting to mitigate the imagery that caused the embarrassment. This promotes confidence levels which are necessary to spark the key discussions which are to follow. Exercises involving pairs can also be very useful. I sometimes have individuals introduce themselves to a partner who then chooses which facts about the individual with the rest of the group. By using such an exercise you have immediately created a bond between paired members of the group. You have developed what are referred to as "dyads", a term which we shall find useful as we move into the body of the seminar.

For groups which know one another well, you can set up very simple reporting exercises in which the members are asked to share something new about themselves. Again, they are talking and becoming more comfortable and confident and co-workers are seeing them in a different light.

Openers can also fulfill the role of providing the trainer with an immediate assessment capacity concerning the knowledge, skill, or ability areas which the participants are bring into the program. Having members share expectations, relate pertinent professional training or experiences, asking them how they have handled a certain type of situation in the past, are all very quick, and relatively safe, means in a technical sense, of getting the program going. The trainer does have to be especially alert to provide structure to the information lists which are being compiled and prompting people to participate. You have to push but you cannot push too far. Everyone learns this by doing so just get out there and practice.

Your only real worry is not to loose sight of your goal which is to promote immediate involvement. I have a program on time management which I start very simply by asking how many of participants keep lists or even lists of lists. From there I begin listing those things that people tend to worry about and have a ready made and highly personalized data array from which to transition into a discussion of how to weigh the importance of things which we feel compelled to deal with.

The microlabs contained in the appendices provide us with numerous examples of effective openers. In reviewing this material you should also note the considerable diversity which is represented among these exemplary programs descriptions.

In appendix A, Carrochi, gets her group into the swing of things by employing a diverse approach, combining information sharing with tapping group equity. The Shakespearean quote is an interesting twist, it creates awareness of the problems associated with being a support staff person in a law firm, but with a humorous touch. Braughler, Kennedy and Kowalick use a role play to get started. This is basically a skit in which the participants see something they already know about, discourteous service. While the content is well know to anyone who has needed help in getting something services, it has value because it breaks the ice while simultaneously focusing everyone's attention on the topic for the day. Matlaga, who also designed a program on sales techniques, choose a role play for his opener exaggerated poor technique is featured. The audience is sure to participate heavily when questioned about the role play when the errors are so obvious. In addition, they are unlikely to forget the lessons learned from such an opening exercise. McKeon, with another program in the area of sales, seeks to capture the attention of her group by presenting statistics which illustrate the perception that customers have concerning retail enshrinements.

Robson, in her workshop on stress, begins her program by building a list of common stressors that people encounter in their daily lives. In addition to facilitating her opener, she will be able to refer to this last as the program moves into the learning activity phase. Johnson also begins by eliciting input from the audience and builds her illustration from information concerning "troubled" employees which the group provides. The responses may not be exactly what she is looking for but the exercise is certainly something that anybody who has worked can relate to.

In summary, the opener has to satisfy the need for structure or meaning among the participants and you have to seize this opportunity to gain control over the program. The participants will react much more successfully if you give them the opportunity to get involved early and often. In eliciting their ideas use care in avoiding value judgment but use praise extensively in acknowledging their contributions.

Variations

The above discussion concerning openers was directed toward groups that have been assessed as possessing a significant capacity, i.e., readiness, the ability and willingness to get involved. Very often the decision as to the readiness of the participants cannot be effected until the moment of truth, that is, what do you do after saying hello! Another very pertinent question involves considering the number of participants who may qualify as being "ready". How many are enough? This is a Sodom and Gomorra dilemma, " Will you save the city if I can find ten honest people?" I think that can pull it off with only three or four people who seem able and willingness to participate, particularly if the design of the program provides for an early exercise which will be based on material initiated by you and explicated by the audience.

Do I go for the substantive beginning and try to hit a home run or do I ask them to write their names on a sheet of paper along with a favorite color and then try to form groups just to have everyone introduce themselves and thus start talking, at least about something. I once attended a conference of training professionals, people who do this for a living, including some who are very good. The participants were artificially grouped by sessions, each approximately five minutes in length and containing four people. A question was posed to each group and each member was directed to offer a response, usually an opinion. Two individuals from each group were always directed to move to another group and become involved in responding to another question. After a while this exercise ended or rather kind of petered out and we were treated to a rather clever poem involving types of birds with pertinent references to some aspect of the training process.

In reflecting on this experience, I cannot for the life of me, fathom the purpose of the first piece, if not to stimulate doubts concerning the advisability of having invested in the fee for the workshop. The second piece, which was much shorter, seemed to have some tangible value in that there was something for all to share in, a reference to what we do which was clearly inspired. However, we were only listeners at this point not participators and we were told why, time required us to move on! We can easily evaluate the success of these two techniques but observing that in the first there was nothing of interest to talk about and in the second we were not able to talk.

Openers are most assuredly situation specific. However well planned, they will not impact successfully or even n the same manner on an entire group. However, it is usually advisable to attempt something worthwhile than to use what I refer to as throwaway, as was described above. People of the caliber of those in attendance in that workshop had a great deal to share and this equity was not tapped. They will have to pay me to attend in the future. We will return to the program for some more "how to's" in succeeding sections.

A caution is in order at this point. While my experience indicates that I should advice you to be somewhat bold in getting started, do not place yourself at the mercy of any one technique. Have some sort of "speaker" ready, i.e., a means of provoking discussion from a frame of reference with some commonalty among the participants. At the very least you should ask them why they signed up for the program or what their expectations are. A list of expectations can easily be captured on newsprint and used to explicate the major topics of the program. Opportunities for participation, praise, and reinforcement are all here and you find something of value to transition to the next exercise or you may even garner a unique thought or different perspective which you can build on to further the program. More on this later but remember, you must be prepared to occupy the entire day as well as be flexible enough to drop something you have planned in favor of some teachable moment which may arise. By the way, being bold means trying not to underestimate the group instead of attempting something theatrical. Silberman (1990) provides some interesting examples of very fundamental activities to get people talking, especially when you are working in a public seminar scenario and you have ascertained that readiness is low. *Again, the primary rule for openers is to not risk losing the group at the very beginning by attempting an approach which is elementary to their readiness.*

Openers get you going. They set the stage for what is to come, both from a content as well as climate perspective. With some planning they can be most helpful and a lot of fun.

9

THE MAIN EVENT

Presenting Information

Well, you have gotten started and should be asking, "Where do I go from here?". It is time to start the actual teaching process, and that means communicating information for understanding. This is where the design function really begins to come into play. As a trainer, you have the dual obligation to present key data while varying the pace, i.e., maintaining an interesting presentation via a multi-faceted approach. The design function is the place to deal with avoiding copious lecture and there is a real danger that you will lapse into lecture as your information dissemination tool if you sense that the participation is flagging or your exercises may not be achieving all that they were designed to accomplish.

If you have used a successful opener, your next thought should be some sort of transition into the major topic for the day. In my conflict management seminar I often use a set of visuals to provoke discussion. Company slogans, cartoons documenting boss — subordinate relationships, and even short role play videos usually are good ideas to ease people into topical discussions. Programs have to be planned and then carried out in incremental stages, each building on the previous plateau which has been achieved. Thus, we find the opener fulfilling the role of creating opportunities for participation, the trainer building a sense of tempo and style for the program through their early interactions with the group, and the first transition getting the people into learning.

For example, one of my favorite cartoons shows a young supervisor being given an order from his boss in the first frame and the second frame shows him trying to delegate the assignment to his staff. The rest of the panels of the piece illustrate how people will tend to ignore individuals who have failed to build strong interpersonal relationships in the workplace. Invariably this experience will provoke comments from the group about personal experiences which they have encountered. Within such comments, lies a real opportunity for the trainer for herein are keystones on which to build your discussions. If someone is responding to a scenario by describing a real-life experience, you would be extremely foolish to overlook the opportunity not to further your lesson by using the key points of the response. Remember our golden rule of flexibility—take what they give you and use it because group members view the use of their material as positive reinforcement, and this acts as a stimulus to elicit even greater levels of participation. In my time management workshop, I use a transition from my opener concerning the making of lists which is based on some stories about the kinds of things people tend to dwell on which really should not capture their attention for a variety of reasons. The item may be beyond their control or some concern with a rather low probability of complicating their lives. I then use a tell and list exercise in which the participants provide input which I translate into the kinds of examples that illustrate the major points I am trying to make. The newsprint list which I develop from this exercise then serves as a further transition to the next major topic which is planning.

Another technique which has found favor among professional trainers is the short story. I recommend that you have plenty of personal experiences to use as the bases of your stories because reliving personal experiences seems to capture the attention and imagination of the group. Also, you will appear relaxed when you are conducting this type of exercise because you know the topic so well. Using the short story technique is fairly easy. Conceptually, you give data, structure the participation, and collect data. The first step, giving data is the easiest component of the three. The story will either have been pre-planned in the design stage or will have been prompted by the occurrence of a teachable moment, something offered by the crowd which causes you to redirect your plans. In either case, the story will represent something you are comfortable with. This is a confidence builder both for you as well as the audience. You can be at ease without referring to any notes and this may be a great chance to leave the front of the room and mingle with the crowd. Try to keep the story brief as well as focused on no more than one major concept and stress, especially by voice inflection, those aspects of the story which you wish to bring to the fullest attention of the audience.

The second step involves enabling the audience to participate. A sense of timing is a great asset here. In posing the scenario, raise an issue which invites commentary. In describing a problem as a part of the story, pause and ask the audience what they think happened next or how they would have reacted. Be supportive, energetic, and quick to channel a comment in the direction you want to go. Do not invite long harangues or even short speeches here. Keep them in the game by the manner in which you structure the exercise but not to the point where significant departures from the primary theme may occur.

In step three you are collect data which normally involves responses to questions. I try to employ questions which provide me with some feedback as well as those which may provoke more thought. We shall discuss questioning in detail later on but for now consider the following. Content type questions force the audience to reflect back on the story which hopefully was illustrative of a major issue for the seminar. They enhance listening by making the participants active, i.e., they have a role to play which is dependent on gathering information and assimilating it. Content related questions also provide with a multivariate assessment opportunity. From the quality and range of answers you can determine how well people are listening, how well you are communicating, and how well they are learning. Use care in making a mental note of how many people volunteer a response as well as the accuracy of the response. If you are not communicating effectively you probably will have fairly few volunteers. If the material is too difficult or has been presented in too complex a manner, you probably will not receive many quality answers. Combine types of content questions, i.e., ask the group a question which will force them to think about the material. You can accomplish this very easily by asking them to predict the consequences of a certain course of action or asking for recommendations for how they would have acted in place of some character in the story. Use care to structure this evolution by helping the respondents use important content in their discussion.

In addition to content area questions, the open-ended questions have real value in taking the workshop to the next activity or phase. One of the ways in which I try to accomplish this is through the use of small groups who are charged with either finishing or rewriting the end of my story. I set some conditions which force them to reconsider the material in a slightly different light and then ask them to go to work. I use group critique here, in that the relevance or value of each story's ending is reviewed and discussed by the entire group.

Each time an exercise is designed, a reinforcement or summary activity should be planned. The short story presentation obviously contains numerous reinforcement opportunities, however, I use care in summarizing what has transpired in each section prior to moving onto the next. As the program proceeds you should find it easier to have the participants do the summation for you. One of the stories which I use in the time management program revolves around my personal schedule. During the regular academic year I routinely work five days, four nights and more than half of each weekend. I work with the participants to explain why this is necessary, how it happens, and how I manage to deal with the situation. I invite them to place themselves in these circumstances and reflect on how they would react. I also ask them to discuss things like the impact on me or my family. This type of exercise again permits the participants to get involved but I have now introduced a higher level of involvement because of the interpretation of data necessary to respond to the scenario. This is stage setting for the more involved exercises to come. In addition, I have taught the concept of weighing activities in order to manage time more effectively and have introduced the concept of scheduling.

Do not forget reinforcement. Please consider the following. Before I move to a discussion of planning in time management, I take a few moments to review the good ideas which have been presented by the participants to date. We revisit their material on the keeping of lists, some of the concerns they have reported in terms of things which complicate their lives, and some of the solutions they have proposed in finishing my stories. I take pains to compliment them on the level of participation, attribute good ideas to their author. My role is quite active. I must refer to my mental notes for this component which I developed as part of the design work and I am forced to make a judgment about how well the group mastered this plateau and whether they are ready to move on.

Since programs have to be designed around an incremental progression, it is essential that you ascertain whether or not a key concept has been mastered before you move on. It is rare in any seminar that I will always be able to move immediately into the next phase each time I complete a component. Each group progresses at a pace which is defined on a given day. In addition, the material which is being presented in a major part of my life work and I may have overestimated how quickly certain concepts can be mastered simply because I know them so well. Again, flexibility is the key. It is far better to attempt to teach one or two concepts well and perhaps abandon several more which have been planned, than it is to follow the schedule for the sake of covering material. In the time management program by this stage, the participants have to understand the importance of making value judgments concerning the relative importance of the routine occurrences in their lives before they can attempt to plan effectively the means to mitigate these complications.

Before I transition to the next level of complexity in the program, I have to ascertain whether or not some other exercise is needed in order to cement the concepts which form the basis of the next component. It is vital to the success of the program that you design your activities to complement each other. Using a base line set of knowledge, skills, and abilities to progress to another level is not crucial to the learning process, but is crucial to the involvement process. the participants will begin tom sense how well they are mastering what is happening. Their sense of accomplishment will keep them involved, create a sense of confidence for the challenges which they are yet to encounter, and, in general create a more appropriate leaning climate. It is important that you monitor the learning climate. it may be possible to reach further into your bag of tricks and use a technique which involves more advanced learning concepts. Remember our discussion of the bus driver-do not let the schedule or your pre-planned activities rob you of the opportunity to embellish your program and thus serve your clients better.

If the audience is becoming more confident you will start to feel better about your self and this in turn will be quite demonstrable to the group. There is a certain bonding between you and your audience which has to take place in order for a program to be truly successful. By this time of the seminar you should be well on your way to creating the leave of acceptance and mutual trust which I have tried to explain here.

Transitions

This is both an important as well as interesting concept. Transitions have to be considered in the design phase, they are that important. They provide a smoothing between exercises, an excellent means of ensuring continuity and fulfill a dual role of reinforcement as well as an introduction to the next task. Transitions should be viewed as a value adding or transformation activity. In order to be successful they must contribute to the learning experience by bridging the gap between program components. Jokes are not transitions any more than coffee breaks are. In fact, while breaks are a necessary ingredient of any program planning process, they are serious digressions which require an even stronger transition experience to overcome.

In the version of the conflict management workshop which I use for groups with a fairly high capacity and which are of an in-house composition, the program is very challenging in a number of areas. There are a number of learning objectives. The skill outcome expectancy set is severe to the extent that participants are expected to actually be able to demonstrate certain conflict management techniques. The pace for such a program is inherently fast, which means that the group is taken through a series of exercises which provoke interpretative thinking without a great deal of time being available for each learning component. Such a schedule is a purposive design feature because talented people both need and deserve to be challenged. However, they should not be challenged to the extent that the program becomes sloppy and disjointed as you move from section to section. The key to effectively maintaining a fast moving pace is the use of successful transitions.

Silberman (1990) suggests that transitions must appear to be seamless and flowing, easily connecting what you have covered and what you will be covering next. He recommends doing an agenda check to indicate how far the program has progressed and what is scheduled for the next evolution. While this may appear to be a digression it actually can be quite useful because it provides an opportunity to remind the audience how everything is supposed to tie together. Using a new visual aid to begin a new component is also recommended by Silberman. This technique normally signals that something new is now beginning.

The microlabs offer some interesting transition activity examples. Carrochi, in appendix A moves from a discussion of coping with attorneys to a major learning activity on taking and understanding directions, by using a transition exercise based on listening skills. In appendix F, Johnson has designed her program with the role of the supervisor being paramount in dealing with troubled employees. She introduces the concept of supervisor accountability for this issue by using a discussion technique which is designed to elicit input from the participants concerning the impact on performance when troubled employees are ignored. Holt, in appendix G, needs to communicate the advantages and disadvantages of owning a franchise as a knowledge outcome of his seminar. He transitions into this learning activity by having the audience review a case study of McDonald's, Inc. Yesko, in appendix H, wants his audience to realize the importance of document design and quality in improving the quality of publications. He uses several communication exercises to transition into major learning activities in this area. Lieb, in her seminar on "humor", offers a hypothesis based on her principle that more positive, "fun", work situations, lead to more productivity and fewer performance and attendance problems. She introduces this concept via a transition exercise which is based on employee reaction to criticism.

In my program on conflict management I often move into

the main body of learning experiences with a transition exercise that is designed to build on the opening exercise by using a transition which forces the group to focus on work place centered frustrations and get them involved in managerial level concerns about the consequences of dysfunctional conflict. After years of research in this area, I have a tremendous reservoir of data that has been collected on conflict aspects such as work place sources of frustration. From this sampling of information, I have created an exercise that is built on four dimensions. In the first, the participants are asked to respond to a questionnaire which provides fifteen sources of frustration in the workplace, along with prompts inviting them to add their own. The group is provided with directions for completing this questionnaire along with information concerning the source of the categories, that is, that the items listed were gleaned from hundreds of respondents who preceded them in this type of workshop. They are directed to identify the three sources of frustration which impact on them at work in the most significant manner.

The second dimension of the exercise is a group activity in which we drive to a consensus among the small groups as to the three most important sources of frustration which lead to conflict in the work place. Here we are learning the technique of consensus building which should also be viewed as a skill which has worth to the ensuing aspects of the workshop as well as to the participants who will be able to apply what they are learning in their own work situation. The results of the deliberations from each group are then compiled and discussed by the entire population. This yields a list of workplace frustrations which will be referred to later in the day as "their inputs" as they are used for reference purposes.

The third dimension replicates the first except that we turn now to solutions or reactions that individuals normally turn to or have in dealing with frustrations. Building a consensus in small groups here normally results in a series of interesting debates as the range of personal choice reactions to frustration is almost as large of the size of the population in the program. In some cases I am able to introduce the building relationship profiles among the variables of frustration reaction, personality type, and rank within the organization or status.

In the fourth dimension of this exercise, we build a list of consensus solutions to work place frustrations with the added dimension of assessing the worth of each solution in mitigating dysfunctional conflict. This completes the transition activity. I have now employed at least three different types of learning experiences in taking a novice group to the level of recognizing the danger of permitting natural work place competitiveness to be exacerbated to the level of serious conflict and have exposed them to the inadequacies of their own natural response mechanisms.

A note to the trainer. Thus far I have introduced conflict as an artifact of having naturally aggressive individuals at work who are competitive and vying for limited resources. I have done this by the use of short stories that describe work place conflict and the consequences or outcomes of the same. I have also used self-immersion techniques which personalize the concepts within the reference framework of each participant and challenge them to critique their own heuristic base of reactions to conflict. Never have I laboriously taken time to define functional and dysfunctional conflict, yet by this portion of the program they know where we are heading and where we have been with a great deal more certainty than if they had been lectured to and required to memorize selected data on their own as we progressed through the program.

Break and lunch times offer some interesting possibilities for the trainer. Please use care in not breaking in the middle of an exercise for refreshments or lunch. That is a design issue per se, but since you never truly know in what direction you will be moving, you must use care to reach the climax of any activity before creating such a gross interruption. I always welcome the group back from a break. This is a forced transition activity and you should take advantage of this chance to review what has been accomplished, in tangible terms and then move on. Forcing them to do some actual work is a good transition technique after a break. Before lunch I preview what we shall be doing in the afternoon. After lunch I review again what has been accomplished and compliment them for what they have demonstrated.

Once again, after lunch, I usually plan something which will get them personally involved. This is a quick way to regain their attention and have them focus on the material.

Learning Activities

In communication theory, a speech is developed around certain theoretical concepts of which one of a crucial nature is known as the "peroration." Succinctly stated , the peroration represents a key concept which the speaker wishes the audience to retain, it is the primary learning objective which the listener should retain or take away from the program. A successful training program has to be built around a series of perorations or major concepts that the participant is expected to "take away" from the program. The consequences of the peroration concept in a training program are perhaps more critical than those of a simple speech and not just because there are many more of them. In training for gain, the type of program development experiences to which this book is dedicated, participants are expected to "take away" knowledge skills or abilities which they will be able to demonstrate or replicate in the work place. These skills should have been identified as being critical to the advancement of the organization so the stakes are very high and the trainer is the person who had the accountable position in making all of this happen.

These "happenings" occur through the teaching of objective and tangible skills, things which are transferable to individuals. These are the heavy duty training experiences in which pertinent skills are built, especially through practice which replicates the learner's work environment.

The essence of the conflict management seminar, which has been used extensively herein as an illustrative example, is built around a number of comprehensive learning experiences. People who are responsible for increasing productivity through the maintenance of a healthy work environment need to be familiar with a model for diagnosing and dealing effectively with conflict situations. I could just introduce such a model and have them write down certain things and even comment on them but then I would be guilty of teaching the audience to do as I say not as I do. To cement the skills which I want them to learn, I must make them experience them along with all of the nuances my years of training have made known to me.

Before I move to any discussion of a model, I try to make them experience just what real conflict is and how challenging it can be. One of the techniques which I use for this is a small group exercise which is based on a relatively short case. The scenario involves a true to life incident involving the somewhat notorious college basketball coach, Bobby Knight and an incident in which he allegedly was involved in a shoving incident with a player from another team. The script contains all kinds of sidebar descriptions of areas of confrontation, name calling, and threats of legal action, just the stuff to make headlines and make league commissioners wince. Our discussion of this piece is focused on a number of criteria or decision points. First, I establish a template to determine whether conflict exists and whether or not the situation(s) is/are of a nature which can be ignored or of such severity as to warrant some intervention by a higher authority.

Once we determine that there is a problem and that it ought to be dealt with, the game begins to turn really interesting. At this point I introduce a series of questions which are really proposed solutions to the case. It soon becomes obvious to the group that they cannot begin to assess the relative worth of the "solutions" until they determine just what they are attempting to solve. This leads to a mini-lesson on determining the real nature and cause of the conflict. The teaching is based on a case which they are cognizant of and just happens to correspond to the first step in the conflict diagnosis model.

At this point I introduce an exercise which is based on the earlier inputs of the participants. This "recycling" of their own ideas offers many benefits. It represents a change of pace, it provides a sense of pride concerning the worth of their participation because it is being employed as an integral part of the program, and it offers still another heavy involvement opportunity for the group as I work to reinforce these key concepts. The exercise is aimed at reviewing their responses concerning the manner by which individuals usually react to confrontation. I return to their earlier inputs and reuse them with a focus on the case and structure a discussion which is geared to reaching a three category classification of responses which I entitle, "fight, flee or flow".

We then apply these generic terms to the case and I provide data concerning the utility of the categories in judging which of the proposed solutions which they have been examining fulfill our primary objective, offering some permanency in mitigating the conflict. Armed with these data and having worked with the case on a personal basis, the group members are prepared to assess the relative worth of each of the proposed solutions to the case. Their responses no longer constitute mere guesses. After a period of discussion, they are prepared to state whether or not a certain alternative will work and offer a rationale to support their contention. If this exercise is successful then the participants will have learned a fairly simple category system for classifying means of dealing with conflict, a template which they can use to facilitate the development of their own response network to conflict management. This is an example of a "peroration", something which they can take away from the program and begin using immediately as they return to the workplace.

The next learning objective in this seminar involves mastering the use of a variety of conflict management techniques. I am interested in having the members develop this capacity because this objective is a stepping stone to a larger issue, one that is a primary performance expectation of the seminar. That issue involves being able to recognize a situation which has the potential to become dysfunctional and choosing a particular strategy which offers the greatest potential to mitigate such dysfunctionality. This is an outcome which could be approached directly, especially via a lecture approach but that would violate one of the technical considerations for this program, to develop numerous templates which the participants might employ in their own work situations. What I am saying is I could use a number of approaches to present the terminal material which I feel is necessary for them to master. But in order to optimize their learning, I need to create an environment in which they can actually experience what I am talking about through self- immersion. To do that I have to break up the program into teaching segments that are consumable, i.e., pieces of a puzzle which people can understand, readily practice, and then employ. The programs with the most effective designs always build a foundation at one plateau as a prelude to exploring the next.

The transition exercise which I use for the extent example is referred to as a focus case. Simply stated, it is a comparison of two individuals in a similar managerial scenario who use quite opposite responses to certain stimuli, the behavior of others who are composed of peers, seniors, and subordinates. We read and discuss the short stories and the commentary usually provides a pretty fair critique of the response which seems to be questionable. The group is normally very confident about this exercise because they have used everything that I worked with. At this point, I begin referring to selected parts of the short story text which contain descriptions of situation specific circumstances for each party. I ask questions which force the participants to begin considering whether or not the listed circumstances might have influenced the kinds of responses which they had just been critiquing. Murmurs turn into commentary and finally some agreement. the group is once again unsure of themselves because a nuance has been introduced, a variable which has complicated their quick responses to the challenges which I have been posing because they require some new data to cope with the uncertainty. This is another example of why a seminar needs to be put together in the manner in which I have described. The participants complete one component only to discover that they need to begin working again to conquer another. The experiences which I give them at this particular juncture are designed to create the impression that those responsible for others must respond to each person in their charge in a manner which may be dictated by circumstances and the context in which two people find themselves interacting. I almost want the group to experience the realization that mitigating conflict is not only situation specific to individuals but also with regard to the rank of the individual.

If it sounds as if we are pretty far removed from that terminal objective which I described above, you are reading the situation accurately. I have at least two levels of learning objectives and three to five exercises to go. I start with a program component that requires a good forty to fifty minutes, one of the longest exercises, time wise, which I employ. The first piece is built around a questionnaire. The participants are asked to describe how they react to a series of preprogrammed situations involving potential conflict by keeping a certain individual in mind as they address each item. When they complete the questionnaire, they are given a scoring sheet which categorizes their responses into one of the five types of conflict management techniques which we have been studying throughout the day. Each individual then builds a profile of his or her response patterns and we have a discussion concerning the results.

Each of the participants now has prima facie evidence concerning their own response patterns to certain influence situations and conflict occurrences. They have experienced some hesitancy in choosing a conflict management technique and each time that happened they realized that it was the nature of the relationship between themselves and the person they were mindful of that had resulted in the complication. They had experienced, in a very personal sense, the kinds of mitigating circumstances which I had introduced as part of the case transition piece. They were equipped with a heightened awareness of the complexities involved with managing conflict successfully, and, more importantly, they were ready to move on to another plateau, another learning experience. And so it goes, each piece building on the other with the transitions tying together all of the segments.

The appendices offer us a number of examples of sound practice in teaching major learning objectives. As you review the material, keep in mind some of the following salient points about learning activities and note how effectively they are used in the examples. Learning is facilitated greatly by a sequencing approach, i.e., building on previous principles maintaining a good mix of material, and some stage setting. The microlabs chosen as demonstration designs for this book were chosen, in part, for the highly effective manner in which the teaching of challenging topics was organized.

In appendix B, Braughler, Kennedy, and Kowalick are trying to convince people that empowerment is a managerial tool which should lead to more capable and accountable employees. They provide some information which includes a definition of "empowerment", which they explicate by discussing the paradox of empowerment and its virtues. They get the audience "ready" to learn that participatory management is the key to success by having the group visualize how an organization would look if quality, productivity, and creativity were its primary characteristics. They set the stage for learning by introducing the topic and then backing into the learning by establishing an awareness and then reinforcing the notion. The sequence of activities, how they are blended, and the means by which they serve as a foundation for introducing the topic of training, is very sound, as a training methodology.

Jennifer Johnson, in appendix F is dealing with employee assistance programs. Her orientation and awareness information is handled well but is clearly subsidiary to her major deliverable, the role of the supervisor and the knowledge, skills and abilities needed by that person to assume an accountable role for mitigating the impact of troubled employees. This is a heavily charged program with several major deliverables in terms of skill enhancement. People do not leave this program simply having heard a sob story, they know what to do about the problem because of the variety, complexity and sequence of learning activities which they have experienced. Note the comprehensive nature of her exhibits, the utility of form #5 for example, a performance appraisal for a fictitious employee, which forms the basis of the subsequent referral interview.

Notice the blend of science and art. The science aspect of the training model is seen in the manner in which the exercise is structured, i.e., people cannot deny that poor performance cannot be ignored. The art of training is seen in the advice to the seminar leader to have each person in the audience document the performance behaviors listed. This also provides a rich source of feedback data which the trainer can incorporate into the evaluation report developed for the client.

The exercise dealing with barriers to referrals has been designed in a highly personal manner. The participants have been asked to respond to a film which depicts the need for action, i.e., making decisions. Barrier noted that the performance of the supervisor shown in the film are not just noted, they are assigned to people via a process of being listed and attached to the foreheads of group members via post-it notes. people become immersed in their learning in this manner. Their attention is captured, they are on display, they must perform.

The material is presented in a hands-on format and contains just enough structure to insure that it can be managed appropriately, without smothering any potential for good ideas flowing from the audience. A supervisor in attendance in this program would be hard pressed for raising a credible argument as to why they should not assume responsibility for maintaining effective EAP's.

Summary

This chapter has explored the means by which you deliver what you promised, the advertised performance outcomes. If you wish people to be able to demonstrate a skill, possess new knowledge, or increase their ability levels, you must program their learning experiences to help facilitate their understanding. You must give them the opportunity to practice. I have many students lose control of a program and rush to cover outstanding material by resorting to straight lecture and telling people that they ought to practice something on their own. Bull curses as my son was permitted to say in his preteen year!. It is your responsibility to create the opportunity for the participants to expand their behavior portfolio to include the new skills which are the topics of your program.

If this seems to be an imposing task, it is. However, there are some fairly simple means of acquiring the proficiency needed to design high impact learning activities. I maintain a data base which is composed of codes which refer to learning modules. Each of these modules has been categorized by a functional area, for example, communication, conflict management, leadership and supervision, etc. The sum total represents the architecture by which I construct program designs which are within my area of competence. When I conduct a search of the data base and derive a list of learning modules, I then have the references to complete design documents which resemble the microlabs contained in the appendices. These are the templates to which I add my individual touches such as stories, commentary, etc.…things I need to deliver the program, while at the same time, meeting the peculiar needs of the client.

When someone requests a program, I take the client through the steps described earlier in this text. Ultimately, the negotiations end up with a list of functional areas, the concepts and performance outcomes which the client is interested in purchasing as behavior modification experiences for their constituents. This kind of data base is a must for everyone who wishes to succeed as a program development specialist. The data base need not be automated, mine certainly was not for many years, and if you are a novice you must start at the beginning. This is the research type of activities which we have already discussed. You need to have expertise in translation client expectations into learning modules. You do this by your training, your experience, or by purchasing the service via a consultant. You do this by planning and designing your first program, that is the start of your data base, and each subsequent initiative simply adds more key information to your records.

Remember, no one working in this capacity as an in-house program development specialist can be expected to have sufficient expertise to develop or even present programs in a wide range of topic areas. However, if you have learned your lessons well in working through this book, you have the keys to developing and maintaining the kind of information system which will lead to success.

One final thought before we press on, when you book a

program from an outside consultant, make sure that you retain the rights to the product which is purchased, whether it be materials, objectives, or even an overall design. People often confuse copyrights and royalties. Someone may have a copyright on their material but you can establish a capacity for extended use when you purchase the service.

10

PRESENTATION SKILLS

Establishing a Bias for Action

Performing as a stand up presenter is the essence of the art of program development. The science aspect of your skills base will be reflected in everything that transpires right up to and through the big day, i.e., the manner in which everything is brought together. But, standing on your feet and delivering something of quality is an art, one which requires some skill and a great deal of practice. I am quite weary of those who write that a trainer is there to instruct not to entertain. Without a personal touch, without building strong interpersonal relationships with the participants, you are better off sending everyone a commercial video and a pre-packaged assessment questionnaire. You are not expected to be an entertainer, you are expected to use the positive aspects of entertaining to create an effective learning environment, one that facilitates achievement.

If you are saying, "I understand and agree with everything that you are saying but I have stage fright. Maybe I should stick with program design?", you are probably in very good company. Remember, we said that the skills required to plan and conduct a successful seminar combined a knowledge of the science of program development as well as some training in the art of program presentation.

Presentation means communicating, the transfer of information for understanding. People accomplish this by encoding a message, selecting some mode of transmitting the message, insuring that effective listening is taking place and ascertaining that an understanding occurred. The last step of the process is the most overlooked and represents the area of feedback. One of the best means to provide for receiver understanding, the encoding phase, is to focus on your goals for the seminar. Asking yourself, "What do I need these people to do?" will help. If you are unsure of where the program is heading, of what you want to say and how you wish to say it, then the audience will begin thinking of better things to do.

There is a golden rule in communication theory which is often violated by novice program presenters. It reads as follows; *overcoming barriers to effective communication involves both what is said and how it is said.* You must concentrate on the impact of what you are communicating on the audience, not the intent of what you would like to do. To fulfill this mission requires some skills in overcoming the nature barriers to effective communication.

The biggest barrier to effective communication is the sender himself or herself. Feelings of power as the key figure in the training program will quickly be communicated as a negative to the audience. Your job is to form a bond with the audience as a colleague not to try and maintain some sort of status role over the audience. Values which you communicate which may be differentiated from those of even a single member of the audience establish emotional walls between them and you and therefore between them and effective learning.

I recommend concentrating on the purposes of communication and the program format as a means of avoiding making yourself into a barrier to effective communication. The commonly applied purposes to communication are the emotive, to ease tension; motivation, which is necessary to secure commitment; control, used to clarify what is to be done; and informational, that is providing data which will spark effective decision making.

The key here is variety. Unless your audience is highly atypical they will be used to communication patterns which are highly control and informational in nature. The use of motivational or emotive attempts at communication cannot help but build a stronger set of interpersonal relationships with the participants in the program. Emotive behaviors are fairly easy to apply, they are the positive strokes of communication. Being seen as genuine, specific and precise, being timely in giving feedback, and most importantly, being honest. Acting without pretense is the most recommended manner of being seen as honest, that is, being credible. A lot of survey research on leadership traits which employees most prize in the supervisors is that of credibility, being seen as honest. Following the suggestions contained above will help you in this most important of areas. If you are not naturally given to displaying or projecting the so-called "positive strokes", you may find it easier to simply avoid negative strokes. These include: being indifferent, being plastic, that is, conveying insincerity, being hostile, read this one as arrogant also, and most of all, being a qualifier, using negative remarks to follow positive communications.

The art of motivation is the essence of leadership and also a major purpose of communication, or one that should be a major purpose of communication. Therefore, it seems safe to assume that you will never reach your full potential as a leader unless you master the art of communicating in a motivational manner. Diversity of approach is one means of accomplishing this. In appendix "B", Braughler, Kennedy, and Kowalick have developed a program outline which offers a rich variety of learning techniques. They begin using a dramatization, and illustrations, discussions, guided imagery, and group activities are all found in abundance. Similar diversity is found in each of the other microlabs. Thus, motivation can be built into the design of the program.

Communicating Effectively

The greatest source of motivation for a program is you, the trainer. You must view the program as a huge challenge, one that will require you to be constantly on call. The smile of the entertainer, the enthusiasm of the cheerleader must be present in your makeup. You may not come to such an approach naturally, your personality may be more control than freedom oriented, but you must deliver on the appointed day. I view each class that I teach as both a technical as well as artistic challenge. I would no more offer the students over two hours of straight lecture than I would stand on my head. It is my responsibility to plan opportunities for input, the variety that reinforces learning by increasing attention, and to lead the performance. A seminar to me is equal to one-half of a Broadway play in terms of the planning which must take place. In reviewing my road map for the program, I prepare a cadre of anecdotes, stories and examples and polish everything until I am satisfied that it will work. Then I put on my game face and concentrate on the climate which I am establishing.

A major control factor in such climate setting is the kind of communication patterns which I exhibit. By making people comfortable, I am able to ease tension. By indicating the worth of the material to be covered, I am securing commitment to see the events of the day through to a successful conclusion. Most of all I try never to dampen whatever enthusiasm I am able to build by ignoring the impact of my contacts with the audience. That is why movement about the group using a nice easy style is critical not only to display proper communication patterns but also to maintain a data source to evaluate how well the program is progressing.

I accomplish this by following these recommendations. I realize that the words I choose to communicate may not mean the same things to me that they do to other people. I always concern myself with the appropriateness of my message for the intended audience. I assess readability levels, the amount of challenge involved in my exercises and always try to be conversational and work directly with individual members of the group, even when I am lecturing. By this I mean, to plan to make direct contact with everyone, on a rotating but equivalent basis.

I am always cognizant of whether or not I am being understood. I consciously avoid the use of slang words or euphemisms in my speech. Jargon is another no-no, it tends to discriminate against anyone who is not privy to the short hand language which I am attempting to employ. I am cognizant of the fact that how I say something may be just as important as what I say.

This point leads us to a discussion of non-verbal behaviors. I believe that nothing is more important than establishing rapport with a group than the impact of your non-verbal behavior. How I dress, stand, conduct myself, the sincerity of my smile are all parts of this agenda. As a novice, you will have to rehearse your gestures, movements, even the manner in which you portray a response to ideas which may not be something you value or agree with. Your non-verbal behavior probably will impact on the audience far more than your spoken words. If the portrayal is negative or even hostile or if your non-verbal behaviors do not support your spoken words, then your presentation will be in trouble because your motivational impact will approach zero or perhaps even a negative index. Be cognizant of your stance and gestures especially. If you appear stand-offish or maintain a posture with hands continually folded across your chest, you are sending negative signals. With respect to gestures, I have noted two types of problems in preparing prospective trainers. They either pre-plan their program to be conscious of using gestures and wind up waving both arms frantically or they cling desperately to a podium, from which locale they rarely depart. I recommend using only occasional gestures, and then only for emphasis and you cannot emphasize everything. Effective non-verbal communication depends on the totality of cues concept. You do not want to be distracting, i.e., the totality of cues which you present must be consistent. Attempt to compensate for your own biases and prejudices and always be cognizant of the context of a situation.

Motivated trainees want to learn. You can help them achieve that state by using positive reinforcement, establishing positive expectations not dire threats of doom which will accrue to those who do not complete the program successfully. Above all, be interesting.

Practice will make perfect only if the practice is correct. Try to plan your opportunities to be emotive and always use a motivational perspective. We have discussed means of using lectures effectively an alternative to this technique. As you review the microlabs, you will see a great deal of diversity, but each represents some attempt to transmit information for understanding. The best design, the best script will amount to naught if the trainer cannot stand up and be entertaining and be understood.

Another communication consideration is that of promoting effective listening. While the receivers bear some burden here to participate actively, the quality of the message and control barriers to effective communication are the sole corner of the trainer. Allow the audience some spare time to summarize what you have been saying. Suspend judgments while receiving inputs in order to maintain the vitality of the audience participation and also to maintain your credibility. Limit your own talking and encourage others to do the same. Here are some additional keys to promoting effective listening: find areas of interest for the audience, marry effective delivery skills to your worthy content, listen for ideas which you may use to further the lesson. Resist distractions and be mindful not to create many yourself. and facilitate conversation not argumentation.

A skill area in which you will have to become proficient is the art of questioning. Asking the right questions in the proper manner, can dramatically increase the impact of your training. Questions can be incredible power tools for the trainer. A question is the most effective way to get people talking and to derive an answer to an area which you wish to interrogate, especially from the perspective of assessing mastery of a concept. We have seen how the use of diverse questioning techniques is an important consideration in the design of your workshops. You can improve your questioning proficiency simply by asking questions which invite people to think, to use higher order skills, and to interact with you, rather than the succinct and highly focused directive which invites only a one-word response, if you are fortunate to have the group on the exact same wave length as yourself. Open-ended questions are the best way to get participants to open up to your initiatives, divulge hidden resistance and provide base line data on which you may build your lesson. A goal of every program presenter should be to identify questions which lead to response which further the lesson.

Don't be abstract, use specificity to structure the area of interest, just don't be too confining. The concept of vocalics can also be helpful. Vocalics refers to the meanings which are carried by your voice. Varying the pitch of your voice as well as the rate of speech will help create a sense of emphasis, this will improve active listening, add a touch of emphasis and invite your audience to join with you. You therefore turn an opportunity to ask a single focus question into a discussion opportunity in which ideas flow and the seminar can actually progress with even greater participation.

Effective Feedback

Effective communication also depends on the perspective which you maintain toward the program and its participants. Maintaining perspective requires an understanding of the motives and goals of the receivers. This means insuring that you have a firm idea of the background, experience, and talent level of the members of the audience. Also, their attitudes and values will provide you with important cues in establishing the context for the program

Trainers must use feedback constantly if they are going to have the inputs needed to adjust the program along the way. To do this successfully you must understand the feedback, accept it, and act on the data which you should be receiving. You can help increase the flow of information by the use of your own feedback mechanisms for critique or praise.

Here are some rules to follow in providing constructive criticism. The critique should be specific, i.e., the individual should not be criticized only the issue. This will help you focus on what ideas may be too far field or deleterious to the program. Be descriptive not evaluative or judgmental, be emphatic but also equalizing. That is, do not communicate a feeling of superiority over the person receiving feedback. Qualify feedback which represents criticism, do not adopt a know it all attitude. One way of doing this is to be free in your use of praise.

In our achievement oriented society, failure is upsetting. That is a primary reason why you should not judge the person only their ideas. Find something praise worthy, if only the effort put forth, in as many input areas as you can. Tend not to be blasé about success, try to take note of every opportunity in which a success has been achieved. Praise for only legitimate reasons and in a timely manner. Explicate your praise, that is, make sure that the entire group is aware of something which has worked well and explain the value of the contribution or finding. This is an excellent opportunity to reinforce the worth of a learning objective to the real work situations of the participants and to invite feedback which may provide additional bases to further the lesson.

If you are inviting feedback, you are also inviting challenges, especially in the question and answer components of any program. There is a fine line between permitting people to respond and monopolizing the agenda or attacking you or another member. Here are the keys to addressing challenges. Listen to every person without interrupting. Answer only those questions which you understand, and most importantly, answer only questions not objections. Refer to any visual aids which will help you to respond, especially if they represent inputs from the audience. Maintain your credibility, don't be defensive. Look your challenger directly in the eye, and remain calm always remaining aware of the positive aspects of your presentation and opposition. Never allow any individual to monopolize the QAS.

Establishing a Road Map

The easiest way to plan an effective presentation is to develop a road map. This strategy represents the use of guidelines for adapting a presentation to a specific audience and program. The three main stages of a presentation are the introduction, body, and conclusion. I am not referring here to the entire program but for each point or learning objective which you wish to make. The introduction is the means by which you establish interest, rapport and indicate the major points which you are going to pursue at any given point. You establish interest by creating a need in the audience to participate in or learn about what comes next. Therefore, a preview of that which is to follow is very important. Rapport is dependent primarily on you, your persona, although it can as effectively be developed by eye contact, enthusiasm, or animation. Finally, let people know exactly what is coming. state your thesis In order not to be distracting, this statement should be short , clear, and focused much more narrowly than anything which you covered in the opener.

The body of any presentation is where you will find the substance. You build this substance by elaborating on three or four main ideas related to the primary topic which you introduced through your thesis. Fewer than three or four main ideas probably disqualifies the item as a major topic. If you try to tie together many more than three or four, you probably are being too complex for the audience, at least with the presentation of this primary topic. The most common form of organization of such material is known as problem solution or need fulfillment formats.

- First, demonstrate that a problem exists or at least that something is worthy of the attention of the audience.

- Secondly, examine the cause of the problem or the circumstances which contribute to the importance of the issue.

- Third, propose a solution to the problem or show how to employ your item of value, especially with respect to a back in the real world setting.

Finally, just as you would bring a program to a close, so to must you conclude the presentation of a primary topic. This involves summarizing the major points and delivering a peroration, or that which you wish the audience to take away. The peroration is the behavioral change, knowledge, skill or ability area which has been derived as a consequence of your reviewing the presentation of the primary topic. Perorations are cumulative during the day and their sum total represent the performance outcomes for the seminar.

Once the design of the program is complete, you can plan the construction of your presentation, topic by topic by topic. I recommend that you prepare this in outline form because this will spark spontaneity. Reading from a prepared script is guaranteed to put people to sleep. It makes you appear stiff not sufficiently knowledgeable concerning the topic and prohibits you from exercising freedom of movement. You must train yourself to work extemporaneously, that is, delivering a quality presentation because you are the presentation. Your notes consist only of casual reminder to jog your memory as you become burdened with managing the program and the mass of data which will become available as feedback. Develop the outline and then mark it up. Even experienced trainers write reminders to themselves to look up, smile, and make eye contact.

Here are some pointers to help you prepare superior contact. *Make sure that your intended meaning is expressed with clarity and precision.* If you fail in this area, you may know what you intend to communicate but no one else will. What exactly is the purpose of presenting this material? What action do you wish the audience to take as a consequence of listening to this information? Such questions must be addressed before you write your presentation piece. Use vivid language, speak in an active rather than passive voice.

Courtesy is the next variable to be considered. This refers to putting yourself in the listeners shoes and preparing material which they can comprehend without struggling. You have already been trained in ascertaining the capacity of the audience. Now adapt to their mood, react to their needs, communicate at their level.

Conciseness refers to the communication barrier of redundancy. While it is necessary to continuously reinforce important learning concepts in a program, especially if they are cumulative, developed in preparation for the next topic, you do not wish to accomplish this reinforcement by redundancy. I am referring to the tendency of repeating the same points over and over again. Introduce the material, build awareness through an involvement exercise such as a discussion group, and then use some sort of learning exercise to reinforce the key ideas.

Confidence is a matter of style. Plan to be assertive but not overbearing. You accomplish this by using emphatic rather than abstract language. Write your presentation outline to include references to using clear statements of purpose throughout.

Correctness should be a given. Proper syntax, speech patterns, format etc. This is the reminder to avoid jargon and some of the other language barriers which were discussed above.

Establish a comfort level with yourself in terms of stance, movement about the room, the pace of the presentation, and the volume of your voice. Use care to create a feeling of intimacy, a collegial approach to training which is based, to a great extent, on maintaining eye contact with every member of the group, the primary bonding weapon in your arsenal. Use your road map to identify the points to be emphasized with voice inflection, and try to recall any annoying body movements, phrases, or verbal "tics", such as "You know?!", which should have been practiced out during rehearsals. You want the group to see you as someone who challenges them, who makes strange material seem relevant to their needs, who mediates differences and pulls together many potentially diverse opinions.

Present the material in a conversational tone. When people ask me for advice in developing a job application letter or preparing for an interview, I tell them to be conversational and then explain that this means addressing a person as if they were an acquaintance with whom you were speaking in your living room on a familiar topic. The key here is to develop clear, specific images for your audience.

Additional Considerations

As a trainer, you will be called on to handle equipment and even props from time to time. Our discussion on logistics will cover this area but I do wish to concentrate for a bit on the issue of training with videos. This has become a popular venue for training. Some very large and highly effective training houses now publish catalogues which contain nothing but videos, either for self-development or for use by group leaders. I am not a big fan of videos under either circumstance. The very essence of program development is a highly personalized approach to each individual placed in your charge. You may learn aerobics via videos but I will wager that the experience in a gym with a real life instructor is more challenging and satisfying.

Even in the hands of an experienced trainer, a video will detract from the program format, unless you have built your agenda of learning activities on electronic media, and that is not really training. Videos can play a part in training if they are handled smartly and for limited purposes. For example, video presentations can be highly effective counterparts to role plays. I have used the technique myself to display characters interacting in various scenarios and had the audience pursue a series of exercises which focused what they saw in terms of what I wanted them to learn.

A case in point is the movie, *Twelve O'clock High*. This has been a favorite of individuals teaching supervision and leadership for some time. The technique is really too time consuming for me to use in a single-day presentation, but fits in well during an extended program. In this particular exercise, the characters portrayed by Gary Merrill and Gregory Peck are extremely interesting, especially as they react in changing ways to a similar set of stimuli. The exercise is very beneficial to the teaching of situational leadership, wherein you wish the participants to experience the necessity of building a repertoire of different response behaviors. Despite the value I am attaching to the video, I use it only in small pieces and to complement the involvement exercises. the video is never an end in itself!

Humor

There is nothing sadder than to observe a program leader actually dying on stage by attempting to use jokes to get a program underway or to establish some sort of learning environment. I have never seen this strategy work effectively. Stand up comedy is a skill reserved for only a few of us mere mortals. If you are any good at it you really should be in Hollywood and not wasting your time pursuing a real job. Even when a joke may work, it usually does not fit the program and I have already provided a lesson in this by the discussion in an earlier chapter of the program I was once retained to evaluate. There is no substitute for projecting warmth, humility and collegiality and humor can play a very important role in this.

A very positive aspect of humor is to set a tone for the program, a contribution to the learning climate. You want to project the idea that this group, of which you are a member, has come together to experience something spiffy. I always refer to group members as colleagues when speaking about them or their contributions.

It is vital to create an atmosphere in which you are viewed as a resource, the "learning" leader. Humor can help you accomplish that by showing your humanity, your foibles, and your equality within the group. All of us have experienced humorous incidents in our lives in which we ourselves were the object or the cause of something funny. On the day this section was written, I had attended a reception at a beach house and was wearing heavy sunglasses while following someone through a screen door which I believed was opened. Well, the person who preceded me through that portal must have been real quick or I must have been distracted because with all of the glare, I walked right through that screen door. The rest of the day, I capitalized on this notoriety by placing my hand out in front of me each time I entered or exited, as I gingerly felt for the presence of a screen

Humor must never be used when it is targeted at someone in the group. Remember, impact not intent matters! A joke at the expense of someone has the same result as criticism which is highly personal in nature. That is one reason why I provided all of the do's and don'ts of communication patterns earlier in this chapter. A single slip can not only be devastating to an individual member of the group, it can really upset the dynamic of trust which you are attempting to build with the entire group, probably irreversibly.

Humor is a typically American characteristic. We tend to make jokes when we are happy, when we are frightened, but usually, as a rule of thumb, when it fits. Don't force humor, it will seem artificial. When it occurs as a consequence of a mild digression or as part of the telling of a story, it can be very useful. Humor is highly personalized. In reviewing appendix I, you will notice that Lieb writes of the value of humor in relieving tension , improving concentration, and counteracting boredom, just the prescription for keeping people moving along with you in a training program.

This program description should also tell you something else, that humor is a most situation specific phenomena. This is true both for the circumstances in which humor can be employed effectively, you can artificially schedule a humorous interlude, and, the manner in which people employ humor. Lieb's program description is unlike any of the other microlabs presented, for this reason. It is difficult to be very prescriptive with this topic but it is so important that it was included even though the program was described in much more truncated length and breadth than the other examples contained in the appendix.

As an example of using humor as a teaching technique, please consider the following. One of the problems associated with using humor in the workplace is the tendency for its use to go unchecked, i.e., for individuals to become too familiar through the use of humor, which then may be considered antisocial behavior. To illustrate this point I tell my Las Vegas story.

In the mid 1970's, I had occasion to receive speaking assignments at conventions which were being held in Las Vegas in successive years. The atmosphere was always charged with excitement but I found the gambling did not capture my interest. Not so the group I was with, which included my wife. Each night after dinner everyone would make their way to the lowest cost dice, blackjack, or roulette tables.

After numerous evenings of petting the MGM lion, sitting in lounge shows and hoping to see somebody famous, I decided to try my luck at craps. The game did not seem complicated and after a while I was wagering five dollars a roll! Eventually I accumulated some chips, struck up a conversation with a cocktail waitress who was bringing me champagne and in general quite forgetting all the reasons I had developed for not gambling. Soon after, my wife arrived and in a manner that only wives can display asked me in succession, why was I gambling against myself, who was the woman I was speaking to, and hadn't I had too much too drink. She also picked up all my chips explaining that anyone could come buy and take them.

At that point a security guard approached her, grabbed the arm whose hand held most of my chips and said, "Madam, please do not disturb the patrons". My spouse asked to be released and stated that she was my wife. Things looked tense and I thought to mitigate any hard feelings by injecting some humor. My comment was something to the effect that I had never before laid eyes on her.

Well, things went downhill pretty quickly after that and I had a very difficult time convincing the security guard that she was my wife, all of which only exacerbated the growing tension between us. Even spending all my winnings on presents and flowers did nothing to soften the blow. I had gone too far in her opinion. Is it any wonder that I have never gambled again?

I know that this story had the desired effect of teaching that concept. People pay attention because they are entertained and they remember. I know that because some years after, I had used the story in a class, a student from that group met my wife and told her how much he had enjoyed my story about her exploits in Las Vegas. And I was out buying presents again!

The ability to poke fun at one's self makes us appear very human. It is good advice for a manager also, as we have seen. People who can be self-deprecating, to tell a story at their own expense are using a priceless resource as they attempt to get others comfortable with them or their work.

In summary, preparing and delivering a successful seminar depends on the group dynamics which you are able to establish. That in turn is dependent on the environment for learning which you establish. Which, in turn is a direct consequence, a linear or causal result, of the skill which you display in presenting the program.

The success of your presentation can be measured by the performance of the group in meeting outcome expectations. That represents group effectiveness, which may be defined as the sum of the individual efforts of each participant, magnified by the impact of positive group dynamics, and lessened by any process loss, which is usually caused by poor communication or loss of control over the group.

You are the key. I have never seen a program of the importance and complexity as the type which we have been discussing run effectively via a video leader. I also sincerely doubt that this is a field in which robots may be expected to replace the human factor.

11

GETTING AROUND THE LOGISTICS

Preparing to Get Ready

We will now take a break from our discussions concerning the learning activities associated with program development to review the behind the scenes activities which are as crucial to success as any learning objective. Most people who are novices in the program development business make a vow to sweat the details in preparing for their first program and then end up kicking themselves when they end up forgetting a few vital considerations. This chapter will help you prepare a checklist of things to worry about, within the proper context of the training professional.

You are really already aware of the first consideration within the world of seminar logistics, the program description. Potential participants within your firm should receive a prospectus for the program well in advance of the magic date. I have enjoyed the most success by developing quarterly plans for clients. Major strategic goals for the organization and production objectives of the various operational departments are a necessary ingredient for successful program planning and thus need to be known in advance in any event. Major corporate happenings such as conferences, stock holder meetings, etc., are also known in advance and can usually be avoided when you promulgate the quarterly plan. Quarterly really means semi-annually in terms of lead time and schedule availability. The Temple University Office of Extension Services does an excellent job in sensing needs, projecting prospective interest and in publishing a document in time for the information to be useful to those who manage training in their client organizations. Their publications are normally seasonal in nature and are superseded when necessary by updates. This seasonal approach corresponds to the quarterly schedule for program description publication.

How long a time frame you will have to employ really depends on your specific organization, most particularly, its capacity to redefine needs and change the context within which the organization operates. The type of logistic preparation and time frame also depends on the spirit in which training will be offered. I have developed program designs as much as six months in advance, worked with key executives to plan programs for months before the actual seminar, and planned, designed, and delivered a program in less than a week.

For example, I have witnessed many commands within the Department of Defense in which a plan must be developed on an annual basis, is required well in advance of the start of the programming period, and is immediately filed away. Fortunately, this is changing because of a new commitment to achieving excellence through people improvement. Now commands are expected to take the initiative to audit the quality and actual completion of the training. Even if the planning document may be obsolete when a specific training period occurs, careful, committed people take the trouble to keep the training useful by maintaining their flexibility and they annotate their records so that progress may be effectively monitored. They also do not tolerate avoidance of training by sub-echelon entities who attempt to beg off from even required programming by stating that they are too busy to train.

The organizational development specialist has a role to play in creating this commitment to excellence and one of the program logistic requirements is a key variable in the process. I am referring to something which we have already studied, building strong relationships with the line managers who have to release people to attend your programs and who, in general, constitute your ultimate base of support. Well in advance of the program the supervisors need an indoctrination as to how the program will work, i.e., what are the performance outcomes that are expected, who the program is intended for, etc. It is also a good idea to be shrewd enough to remind these managers that everything which you have described via this extended outline of the program was developed in response to their recommendations! I always make sure that people in this category have an opportunity to review and have input into items such as objectives, the kinds of training activities being planned, and especially any suggestions for institutionalizing the material within the work place.

It is extremely foolish to ignore this feedback opportunity. You risk missing key nuances about the prospective participants that may be critical in the program design phase. In addition you risk alienating your primary constituents by wasting an opportunity to cement your relationship development and another chance for them to buy into the process. The effort which you expend on a supervisory indoctrination will also prove extremely useful to you the day you actually train. The more the supervisors know about the program, the better prepared they will be to "sell" the program, based on the value of the concepts which you will be teaching as they may improve productivity back on the job.

Keeping contact with the supervisors is also important if you wish to really formalize the relationship between your training and their productivity by developing a performance contract. These can be very simply written and really constitute a promise or two to monitor certain conditions in the work place which the participants in your seminar will be expected to encounter on their return from your program. The observation scheme is based on noting items such as more appropriate influence techniques, more effective communication, or enhanced commitment to excellence, by collecting data in observable areas which correspond to the learning activities covered by the training program.

For example, as part of the evaluation phase of the conflict management seminar, I normally ask participants to provide me with a listing of work related behaviors which they can predict ought to be handled differently as a consequence of the training which they just completed. The supervisors have been well briefed on the components of the program and the participants, supervisors, and I often plan some performance improvements to be expected via attendance at the program. We brain-storm a listing which becomes an observation instrument back in the world. Ancillary data such as problems encountered with the implementation of the learning activities and the appropriateness of the skill, knowledge and ability areas identified for the training are data which can help you assess whether what you have trained people in is being used as intended, to benefit even if modified locally, ignored, or seen as an additional obstacle to the daily routine of work.

Care must be taken to avoid this technique in organizations which have a high degree of tension or mistrust. Such a data collection activity which has been described here can only be used effectively when an organization has moved from an entitlement mentality to a learning and earning psychology. The data collected from the implementation of these performance contracts is normally used only as an indicator as to the utility of the training, not the worth of the employee. In any event, they are an important logistic consideration because of the planning and negotiations which must precede and follow the actual training experience.

Getting Ready

Once the date for the program has been established and the participants have been selected, you ought to consider sending them a special invitation. I have used a short written communiqué introducing myself and the program, with special emphasis on the fact that the program has been especially designed just for them. I also take pains to identify the benefits which I believe will accrue to them as a consequence of participating. I try to be confident about my expectations for the day, provide a short overview of my relevant expertise, and let them know that I am acquainted with the work they do. I also try and reassure them that I know they will perform well during the seminar and that I am personally looking forward to working with them. If I am confident of the capacity of the group and if the ability range of the group is fairly homogeneous , I will invite feedback concerning the agenda. Some trainers advise never to do this and there is danger in having people state expectations and then be dissatisfied when those expectations are not fulfilled.

The value of this invitation lies in enabling the trainer to discover any resistance which has previously gone unnoticed and to glean further insight into the backgrounds and personalities of the group which I shall be faced with in the not too distant future. That is why I do not use this feedback alternative if the group is a mystery to me or their ability range is too great. Since I will probably be unable to correspond with the invitees again, I take pains to structure and delimit their response potential. By that I mean I invite feedback concerning the learning outcomes only and then only within the context of soliciting information concerning the prospective use of the learning outcomes in their routine work environment. Responses elicited in this manner can be most helpful in further customizing the program. While this is another means of serving the client to the best of your ability, it is a strategy that is best left to the experienced trainer.

Another evolution in getting ready, and one which cannot be ignored, is the preparation of materials. I greatly favor having a manual with the planned exercises, group discussions, and questionnaires already in place. The participants are used to seeing a pre-planned agenda and I try to satisfy this expectation by including a copy of the skills array which I intend to cover. Because I place a great deal of emphasis on keeping the pace, i.e., moving the program along by concentrating on learning experiences, time is a premium ingredient of my presentations and I only grudgingly waste any of that which is available on non-instructional activities. Therefore, I depend on the program description and the opener to orient the audience to the seminar and do not spend time reviewing an agenda.

The instructional materials package should also include documentation of key learning elements, the kinds of things that people have to be cognizant of in order to have profited by the seminar. If you are presenting a leadership influence model, it should be included in the materials package so that the participants have a future reference base. While I never teach directly from such exhibits, I want them there for the gratification and betterment of my audiences. Every trainer establishes a highly personal style of program development and my signature has evolved into a sharp focus on personal improvement for each participant. Therefore, the materials package which I assemble for each program has been designed to establish baseline data for each member of the group. When they leave the seminar, they not only take the knowledge they have acquired, they also have a series of profiles which document their position relative to certain challenges which they encountered and recommendations for alternative behaviors.

Everything that I use is of my own construction and has been created via the wonderful world of contemporary personal computers and their equally magnificent software packages. This permits me to present a client with a camera ready copy master that has been customized to their needs, looks fresh, and has a high consistency and homogeneity factor. I cannot conceive of a situation where a professional trainer would present a cut and paste appearing document to a client. I use a loose leaf-letter sized page format, it presents a smart appearance and permits the participants to remove the numbered pages for reference while completing a subsequent exercise. Many clients insist that their corporate logo be imprinted on the cover of the binder. I encourage this. The cost is minimal and it presents a caring image to the participant, especially if their name is also imprinted. Only that which is needed for participation, reference, or reinforcement is contained in my material packages.

The selection of the content for this vital instructional tool was determined during the design phase. The logistics aspect is to get what you need ready for publication.. Plan to use enough material to occupy the entire time frame for the program. I have never observed any program in which no participation occurs, and I have seen plenty of lousy efforts. However, being logistically literate means planning for any eventuality and this includes perhaps talking for six hours without much support from the audience. If you are ready to carry the entire program, each participatory experience will be a bonus.

If you are going to need materials which are not your own or commercially available, you must secure permission before using any copyrighted document. This can be a time consuming and also very frustrating process. I advise trying to avoid depending on this materials source if possible. One further tip. If I am convinced of the reliability of the client organization, I provide them with a camera ready copy. It is usually cheaper for them to use an in-house copying capacity and I do not have to lug around three dozen binders with up to one hundred pages in them. If I have any questions as to whether my material will arrive, any question at all, then I lug them myself.

A good logistician never panics in the face of a crisis and being a professional trainer will place you in the position of having to overcome any number of crises. Make sure to preview the finished product of your material. I always schedule an opportunity to review a copy of the materials set which has been prepared for the participants. This provides a good opportunity to check whether or not everything looks good and has been duplicated properly.

However, no safeguards offer complete insurance against disaster. Try this experience out and see what happens to your blood-pressure. I once was scheduled to present two entirely different workshops on successive days to different populations in the same organization. I had previewed the completion of the duplicated set and had carefully earmarked each box of materials for delivery to the appointed place and at the right time. I had worked for these folks before and had a great deal of confidence in their support establishment. The first program was scheduled for a Sunday and here the story takes a turn for the worse. The materials had been delivered but they were for the second day of training and there was nobody available on a Sunday to correct the problem. I opened the box swallowed hard, and spent a few moments thinking of my options. I decided to tell the group what had happened right after the opener which is when I usually say hello and handle logistical matters including handing out the packages. My quick review of the package indicated only five pages of exercises which would be of even the remotest use to me. I then decided to change plans and conduct the program "dry", without any materials set, to progress as if nothing had gone awry. This was my only experience with such an initiative but it worked out so well that I now use it as a teaching technique.

Since I had developed the program, researched the capacity of the participants, and written all of the exercises, I had an intimate knowledge of where I wanted to go. As it turned out, the only thing which I was lacking were the printed sheets which displayed models and data collection items such as questionnaire. The stories which I had planned to use worked equally well without the materials set and the inputs from the participants went a long way to helping me to keep the program as rich as possible. I included the key printed sheets with the follow-up material which I forwarded to each participant for the longitudinal analysis.

While I would not want to do this on a routine basis, the experience demonstrated to me that if you do your research, if you know your material, if you have polished your presentation plan, then you are ready to go. You are the key, the materials set greatly facilitates your work, compliments the work of the participants, and increases the reinforcement potential of your efforts. However, in my absence, the materials set could not have carried that program. I have proved this to my students any number of times. I disconnect bulbs from overhead projectors before their presentations. Also, VCR's strangely remain silent, handouts disappear and still they go on and perform quite well, if they have done their homework.

Choosing the Location

Where you train is almost as important as how you train. The rule of thumb is to get the participants away from their regular place of work, especially away from the routine interruptions which can ruin any sense of continuity which you are working so hard to establish. My experiences with the furniture company which was discussed in the first part of the book are a case in point. The facilities were the worst that I have ever encountered. I was so concerned for the participants that i called in a few chats and convinced a nearby organizations which I serve as a client to agree to donate suitable spaces for free, as a sort of good neighbor policy. The CEO of the furniture company would not agree, he did not want people to be removed from the workplace in case he wanted them and he felt free to interrupt early and often. Of course, I subsequently found that there was never any interest in staff improvement only in creating a facade for the bankers.

In house groups should be steered to a suitable off-site location. The investment of assets in this type of program are enormous and if you are trying to create an image of concern for staff improvement, booking a professionally oriented training space will pay dividends which far exceed the cost. The external environment will contribute to the kind of atmosphere that is conducive to learning. people will be free to focus on the material being presented, not on "crisis" phone calls or even rather routine matters that can become exaggerated in importance if you are proximate to them with time to dwell on them.

External sites also serve to even things out. By this I mean, each person enters a new location without any baggage. Even the most frustrated worker can experience a fresh start away from the office. Coffee and snacks at the breaks, a nice lunch in the same general area will greatly contribute to a relaxed posture, a high comfort state, and a realization that the organization is serious in its attempts to improve productivity through a training initiative.

There is one exception to the goal of getting people into a new climate to enhance the impact of the training program. That is the situation in which the company maintains a suitable training suite which can be complemented by the normal amenities which accompany a training experience of the type which we have been discussing. I am not speaking of the large, impersonal, formal room where everyone receives their orientation workshop. This type of situation is too familiar, too close to the normal work routine. What will work is the special room, perhaps the area in which senior staff meetings are held or where the board meetings are convened. Such a setting is usually comfortable enough and equipped well enough to work quite nicely.

If you are planning for a "public" seminar, the choice of location becomes dependent on many factors. Proximity of public transportation, availability of parking, perceptions of the accessibility and safety of the neighborhood, and travel time are all variables which must be considered. Part of the motivation of attending a workshop is the day away from the office syndrome and you have to make sure that you use that motivational tool effectively by establishing a central location with a significant attractiveness quotient, someplace people would like to visit, a locale which confers some feeling of status, after all we want people who attend our program to feel special.

Temple University has solved this challenge very effectively. The upper floors of one of the center city Philadelphia campus buildings has been completely renovated to serve as a conference center. There are different sized rooms with all of the necessary accouterments. Food service is available, the atmosphere is positive, and access from all parts of the city and suburbs is quite easy and economical. In addition, using one of the campus buildings helps keep the cost low.

Very often a client will opt for a total immersion program in which training is provided off-site and for a number of days. This adds the additional consideration of sleeping quarters, communication capacity, and relaxation facilities. Even the no liquor rule is often modified. Wine with dinner, even with a speaker, is acceptable. The "happy hour" can still be dangerous if you have planned a serious evening. That evening or extra session is nothing to ignore. In the situation where people are traveling a good distance and are checking in the night before a program, a dinner, accompanied by an introduction, followed by a work session, can greatly increase the impact of the program. Two days and two evenings can save a day for the office, although the design will have to accommodate the special nature of such a structure, which means longer hours for the participants. More group work and more self-paced exercises are fairly simple solutions to the problem. Keeping the pace moving while keeping the program interesting are keys. I often start this type of design with the goal of establishing smaller increments in the learning process through the first day or until the participants determine that they can handle the burden. This is the one situation in which I try to use an occasional video, a technique which we shall discuss later in this chapter.

The overnight training experience does pose some unique problems but with some extra care, the results will again prove worthy of the investment. The higher degree of intensity, the more comprehensive situation specific problem solving activities, and the "extra assignment" potential are key ingredients in escalating the impact of this design. Giving people something to think about as they interact with colleagues is an excellent way to increase your effectiveness. Even multi-day programs that are not sleep overs can provide a scaled down version of this higher intensity model simply because you keep people in the game for a number of consecutive training experiences and you have the extra benefit of being able to assign homework.

Sizing Up the Room

There are as many recommendations for room configuration as there are books which have been written about the subject. Actually, I believe that the room set up is a matter of personal preference for the trainer. The primary considerations are as follows. The size of the group is a primary reference point. For the type of program which we have been discussing, in which the goal is to achieve actual transfer of demonstrable skills, the group size should not exceed thirty participants. Larger groups are actually easier to accommodate in a room because you are then limited in the type of activities. If you are preparing for a sizable group in which they will be lectured to or exposed to examples via video or overhead projector, you simply need comfortable seating. You really ought to provide for padded seats arranged in rows with not too many assigned to a given space. The people from the host facility will usually set up the chairs right next to one another. That is easiest to deal with and requires very little effort on the part of staff. take some time before you begin a program in such circumstances and remove a chair or two from each row. The participants will really appreciate the extra room and every source of distraction which you remove will pay dividends with respect to learning impact.

The limit of the group size is a direct consequence of what you are trying to do. I have never seen an effective situation in which an overhead projector was being used in which more than sixty people could effectively see the material. All transparencies have to be prepared with large size type but there are technical limits with respect to how large the print can be, how large the screen can be, and really how much material you can communicate. An overhead is really only useful in outline form and the participants will still need a materials set to follow along with. Nothing is more uncomfortable than the situation in which you are sitting in a crowded row with no place for your materials other than your lap, listening to somebody droning on, referring to a projection on a screen in which the type is not readable.

Presentations which are dependent on video projection involve their own particular problems. The size of the screen, the clarity of the audio, and the quality of the video itself are all variables which are difficult to control. Just the number of monitors and playback units necessary to convey information to even a moderately sized crowd involve considerable expense. This is the kind of equipment which is normally rented. That means something extra to check on before the presentation and if your dog and pony show is quite complex, you may even need operators. As we saw in chapter ten, the impact may simply not be worth the expense or the trouble. Don't forget, any kind of visual presentation can be as much distracter as it is an aid. One of the easiest ways to lose the crowd is to call time out while you fumble with a major distraction such as a broken projector or monitor. For those of you who are slide projector advocates, your time seems to have passed. Having slides made, using them effectively, and keeping audience interest long enough to justify the technique is extremely difficult. I have seen slides used to support learning activities and for openers which are based on getting acquainted exercises but for little more that is productive. Again, you risk losing control of the audience. Just think, no matter how hard you work or how good you are, if you open the program with a video or a slide tape presentation and never return to such media, the audience is bound to be disappointed.

For even larger groups, select some college lecture hall or even an auditorium. You will accomplish little more than talk to people but that will be okay for a short period of time, maybe as a general orientation or program opener before the audience moves to a the actual training situation in a series of break out rooms. Such facilities routinely come equipped with everything which you may need with respect to media.

For the programs which are the essence of this book, true learning experiences which place a premium on practicum work, we should be shopping for a comfortable training room which will easily sit twenty or thirty people. I look for something which will allow for some break out space, say for up to six groups and room for refreshments. If possible, I never schedule a program in a facility which has to be reworked for lunch or in which the lunch will be served in the other half of the room. The potential for wasting time or distraction is simply too great to risk. I do like the refreshments to be local. This saves time and keeps the group together and provides several more opportunities for you to mingle in an informal manner.

Don't overlook your role with respect to lunch. If lunch is the responsibility of each participant, be ready with a preprinted list of nearby restaurants, including type of food served, price ranges and directions. If they are going out, you can look forward to 75 to 90 minutes for lunch, depending on the distance of the places which you recommend and the crowds. The starting time for lunch has to be somewhat flexible because you do want to effect closure of whatever learning activity you are working with.

If you are fortunate enough to be involved in circumstances which will permit lunch to be served on site, you have the advantage of saving time, keeping the group together which will increase their camaraderie, and you have an extended opportunity to interact with the participants. Please plan to have lunch with the group. If you appear to have important things to do during lunch, you can expect the group to do the same, perhaps even during the rest of the day. Get involved with the menu. Keep things light, no cream sauces, cocktails, or other consummables which will increase the sleep quotient in the afternoon.

Establishing the Ambiance

The room set up is also an important factor to be considered. Your goal should be to establish a certain intimacy between you and the group and among the group members. I like tables which seat up to six members. With a nice comfortable chair that swivels, people can simultaneously interact with me and their group and they have little difficulty listening to whole group discussions or case reports from other tables. The round design of the tables and the distance which is required between them satisfy the break out requirement, and I spend a great deal of time working in groups.

Tables also facilitate movement by the trainer among the tables. During a group exercise, it is vital that you move about interacting with the members. People may need clarification concerning the directions, you may need to step in and settle a debate or gently nudge a group back onto task. This kind of contact is a superb teaching opportunity. I use what I call sub-stories, examples which may explicate what I see happening as I move among the groups. These necessarily have to be extemporaneous and they should be of such importance as to warrant sharing them with the entire group. I have found that contact which is of a supportive nature with small groups seems to facilitate their progress, however, my experience with addressing the entire group during an exercise has not been as successful. This seems to serve only as a distraction and worse yet, an invitation for everybody to get into the act.

If I can not have tables, I go for a "U" shaped table set up and pray that I will be able to move them into a break out situation. You have to watch out for the table cloths. They sometimes are fastened in such a manner as to preclude moving individual tables around. Obviously, you will need more time and more room if you have to move tables. This has some impact on the design. If you are locked into a "U" shape or rows or some other configuration which will necessitate movement, plan your learning experiences accordingly.

Don't force the group to keep moving from small to large group settings. Group kinds of activities together so far as the learning sequence will permit and use the breaks as periods of movement whenever possible. A "U" shape enables people to keep close to you as well as each other. In chapter ten, we learned the importance of moving into the group, particularly when you are lecturing. The same effect can be established, although at a lesser degree, with rows of tables. If forced into this configuration, I stagger the setting to improve sight lines and facilitate my movement. Remember, you have to be among the troops to support and guide them and to collect the kind the kind of visual records which will contribute to you assessment activities.

My equipment needs are normally meager in nature. I like to use newsprint easels to record and save participant inputs.

I like to scatter these liberally around the room because each of the groups will have need of them as the day progress. I also usually book an overhead projector but my use of this device is becoming rare. When I do use the projector, I normally put up a transparency of something they are working on as a reference or background data source. If I feel the need or sense the opportunity I may reach into my bag of tricks and put up a cartoon or some other aid. These are items I would not ordinarily include in the materials package. Hint: if you are a heavy projector user, I recommend having copies of the transparency or slide for the group. You should also have an extra bulb handy in case the darn thing burns out.

If possible, try to book one of those erasable marker boards which also copy whatever is on the writing surface. These are very handy in making copies of lists for distribution around the room. Make sure that you do not use permanent markers on these display boards. I have been fortunate to get away with this twice. Either they were very pleased with the programs or haven't figured out who the culprit was!

On a few occasion I have used computer labs as a learning aid. The technical capacity of such devices is enormous as are the planning considerations. they can be powerful competitors to you and you are the key to what learning takes place. If you find their use to be appropriate, group the learning experiences involving the machines together and segment their use into a particular period of the day, before lunch at the afternoon break, etc.

Polishing the Presentation

Well, we have decided on a program description, date, location our equipment needs, room set up, even lunch, can anything be left? There sure is, and that is something I call polishing. This is an actual dry run of the program in which you try, and I mean only try, to time exercises and brain storm possible problems and questions or concerns which may be raised by the audience. In the next chapter we shall discuss closers and the dry run can help prevent running out of material an hour before the scheduled finish or face the end of the day when everyone is running for a train and still have several exercises to run. By polishing the presentation, I also mean practicing the use of a story to judge its impact. We all have favorite experiences which we would like to include in the program. *The rule of thumb concerning use is quite simple, if it does not add anything of value, drop the idea.*

Anticipating problems is really a design function but the dry run can help prove the efficacy of your design. Obviously, solving a problem at the practice stage is the way to go. I find that the designs usually hold up but the dry runs help me anticipate participant needs with respect to additional directions which they may require or areas in which digression is possible. In considering what may happen I try to act like Tevia in *Fiddler on the Roof*, always considering what may happen "on the other hand".

After all of these years I can usually time an exercise right out of the gate but I still check my work. This involves actually completing a questionnaire or case problem, weighting the results to account for familiarity, motivation, and knowing the answers. I never use third parties, mentors or friends because since I teach "training the trainer" workshops, I need to know how to instruct them in self-polishing activities, since most trainers will not have access to a pilot audience. This mostly involves being careful and introspective. this is not the kind of thing that you run to a line manger with and ask their help in assisting your preparation.

When people describe their logistics arrangements to me and ask if I think they are satisfactory, I tell them to run the program and see if they can complete the day without missing a beat because of a glitch in the logistics. Develop a checklist, review it for accuracy and then do two things, implement your list and pray that things work out. Your only real worry is to deliver a "seamless" program, one which supports the learning process not the technocracy of learning.

12

ENDINGS AND SUMMARIES

Closing Up Smartly

In chapter ten we learned how to develop a road map for our program. Even if you are on time, you may find it difficult to bring the program to a close. The seminar, and your reputation, will nose dive if you leave the audience hanging without closure or worse yet, simply fade out. Getting started in an effective manner is tough, presenting worthwhile learning activities is challenging, delivering a quality presentation will test your skill, but the closing is what they will remember.

Throughout the course of this book we have discussed the topic of program development from a theoretical rationale which can be summarized by the following: give the participants an opportunity to practice what you are trying to train them in. As you progress through the day, each exercise should build on the preceding, each new experience should be more challenging, forcing the participants to use higher level skills such as interpolation. You have been taught to encourage participants to express themselves and take risks. Each learning activity should include a feedback opportunity and a reinforcement sequence. That is how you build a foundation and move to the succeeding components

In microlab "F", the program on EAP's, Johnson uses a group discussion as a closure. her design emphasis is to reinforce the performance expectations discussed in the program by having the participants relate the material to their own work situations. Holt (appendix G) ends his program by providing a checklist of questions which are based on principal characters from an exercise that the group has been working with. This technique enables the participants to assess their own potential to become involved with franchising as they complete the final activity of the program. Lib uses a notion of fitting humor within the culture of the organization as the concluding activity of her program. Such a strategy is best implemented by employing a technique of introspective discussion in which the participants must come to an agreement about the "goodness of fit" of employing humor within the work place. Braughler, Kennedy, and Kowalick wrap up their extravaganza by having each participant review the key points of the seminar, developing a sort of checklist along the way, and using these data to assess the quality of service which is being provided by their organization.

After spending a day stressing group processes and sharing an unprecedented level of enthusiasm and energy, it simply would be a disservice to all concerned to end a program in a manner that is disjointed or divorced from all of the previous activities The closing should be viewed as a muti-faceted activity, a series of evolutions which are designed to facilitate recall of key ideas from the program and reconsideration of the routine work process or even the work environment which the participants are about to return to.

Here are three suggestions which I have found to be quite helpful in planning a sequence of closing activities. This material refers to the end of a program, not necessarily to the end of a day, which should be treated as was discussed in chapter eleven, primarily as a slight digression or pause in a program, similar to the manner in which you would introduce or attempt to recover from a lunch break.

The key consideration in any closing is to give the participants one last chance to reinforce their learning by tying everything together. If possible try to develop a cumulative as well as summative exercise. By this I mean, not just a finale that provides some review but a penultimate experience which ties things together by stretching the group even more, an exercise which hits on as many of the key concepts as possible. For example, if I am teaching a workshop on leadership and supervision, usually a one-day model, I will have necessarily covered influence and decision making strategies. If my group processes have been working well, some competition has developed which we would have recognized and used to further the training experience, perhaps by using the healthy competition which has developed in a sequence on the problems associated with the "group think" syndrome. A nice way to give them one more opportunity to experience that which I have been discussing would be one of the many survival exercises which are available in such abundant quantities. A component such as this will enable everyone to see, in a quantitative sense, the quality of their decision making and the magnitude of their influence capacity.

A second consideration is to compliment the climax exercise with an opportunity to prefocus their attention on the work situation that is awaiting them. In addition to serving the need for a transition back to the real world, this provides another valuable feedback experience to the trainer, i.e., how well people can make reference to improving their work situations by applying what they have learned during their time with you. In order to prevent this last learning experience from turning into a new source of problems which cannot be dealt with effectively in the time remaining, I recommend structuring the exercise by using very definitive operational parameters.

Once again, you want to create a synergistic effect by tapping the equity that is available throughout the entire group. The vehicle which I employ to accomplish this is a type of quality circle, in which I raise issues from the knowledge base that I have acquired from the participants themselves, about their work situations. The audience should know quite enough about the dynamics of groups to handle this, after all you have been sponsoring group work all day.

Basically, the result I am looking for is to have someone describe a situation as it is now at work and explain how they will seek to improve that situation from what they have learned. The trainer must be at her/his best to sail safely through these uncharted waters. Be especially careful not to force "pat" answers, things which you want to hear or which would fit nicely with the climax of the program. Encourage people to list obstacles which still remain in the way of their progressing according to the objectives which you have set for the program. This will provide you with an opportunity to explicate the program material, i.e., to stretch their conceptual understanding of everything that has happened. You may also reap the ancillary benefits of having some fresh or follow up topics suggested which you may put to good use either with this client or in the future.

The third suggestion is something you have been expecting since you started reading this section. Review the day! By this I mean tell the people what they have learned and how it may be put to use. You and they have come a long way together and you have created a product, the sum of all that has transpired. They will remember the commentary, the stories and perhaps even the jokes. Your comments here are a last opportunity to put the learning into perspective, to build a bridge from seminar to reality.

Your final sentiments should express appreciation for their courtesy and cooperation and to offer encouragement to them to continue that which they have started, a program of self-improvement. This encouragement should be complimentary, that is, try to phrase this not in the manner of a pep-talk, but in a way that quietly establishes the notion that they are capable people who have now significantly increased their capacity. If the "quality circle" closing has worked well, refer back to some of the examples which you have gleaned from that exercise.

Assessing the Day

We have already discussed the means by which the worth of the program will really be measured, the longitudinal implications. If there is an opportunity to conduct follow up activities, remind the participants that this will be happening. You should accomplish this in a formal setting, that is, let the people know that you will now be discussing what comes next. I always close the program to the extent that I express my final sentiment before moving on to assessment. I provide a description of what, if anything will follow. If nothing purposive was able to be planned for implementation, I spend some time reviewing the strategies which I have provided during the course of the program, as self-monitored feedback opportunities.

With that completed, I turn to the evaluation of the just ended course of events. the forms which you see in common use can be both boring to the respondent as well as deadly to their remembrances of the seminar. I try to tailor any questionnaire to the circumstances of the specific seminar, the topic, participants, length, significance, etc. of the workshop. I try to combine different types of feedback opportunities. Writing a paragraph or two on the impact and implications of the program usually is a good way to open this assessment activity. It gets people into the exercise and you may elicit data from their perspective. Short answer questions normally follow, i.e., suggestions for improvement, changes in technique, different definitions of the program, i.e., the type of learning activities chosen to teach the material. Also, this is a good place to ascertain what was most or least helpful and the reasons why or suggestions for improvement. The third section of my questionnaire is usually a forced choice inventory which elicits information from the participant about operational items relating to the technocracy of the workshop. I collect data on the pace, the language, the understandability and the readability of the material, and the utility of any visual aids used. I also request data concerning the quality, as measured by usefulness, of each of the learning modules which we have studied together. This is a major deliverable for the evaluation report on the program which gets communicated back to the client and also serves to assist me in reviewing the adequacy of the category system which supports my data base of skill areas and learning techniques.

I believe that confidentiality is a must when dealing with participant responses which are designed to evaluate you and your program. That is one reason why I conclude that the instructional portion of the program before moving on to the assessment. I allow people to complete the questionnaire and leave on an individual basis, leaving the documents in an area that is removed from my position in the room. At the place where they drop off their questionnaires, they can pick up a program synopsis which I have prepared as a final deliverable. This is both a summary as well as a reinforcement document and also contains information on how to contact me in the event they have additional questions or concerns. This is a no obligation service which I began offering on the day of my first program. Yes, after all these programs, keeping up with this correspondence can be difficult at times, but I believe that the benefits far outweigh the work involved.

Summary

This book was written to accomplish three discrete yet complementary purposes, which are reflected by the content of the various sections. The first part was designed to provide the reader with contemporary examples and philosophical rationale for the current emphasis on quality. This was deemed important because while many view quality as a passing fad, indeed the concept has already been abandoned by numerous organizations, the conceptual basis of the trend should be regarded as the essence of improved effective organizational behavior. *Total quality leadership is a term which has survived for an eternity as far as management improvement theories are concerned, but in reality, it is something to which we have turned to in desperation in the past decade, perhaps as a final attempt to regain our lost productivity.*

The notion of building a strong organization by increasing the capacity of the work force is certainly not new to behavioral scientists. Indeed, many universities have business school departments along with social science, political science and education departments all quarreling over why their discipline should be considered pre-eminent in the field. Remarkably, all of these areas of study have something to offer to the research base which supports our continuing efforts to survive in an age of diminished resources. The reason for that is all of these areas involve people, those wonderful assets who turn up each day and who, for the most part, would much prefer to be productive and active in an environment where growth not dismemberment is the watch word. Part One of the book presented real to life examples of outstanding attempts by organizations to increase their capacity to be productive by strengthening whatever cadre of employees they deemed to be necessary. We also have reviewed some not so celebrated examples of organizational behavior and designs which I have encountered in companies who have yet to see a relationship between long-term growth and a significant long-term investment in employees. Where organizations treat people as being redundant, management is usually short-sighted, and these are the entities whose survival is in serious jeopardy. I certainly would not buy any of their stock.

Quality means people because it can be achieved only

through people. If you cannot buy into that relationship then you should at least attend my workshop on the subject before attempting to leap onto the bandwagon of the next mega-concept. You probably will not embrace the next buzz word for long either until you gain both patience and insight. I sincerely believe that the current "craze" or emphasis on quality may not be a last chance but a golden opportunity to advance both because the term has captured the attention of resource providers and because behavioral scientists are prepared to address the implementation issues, it is what we do. This is why the second part of the book was designed with an emphasis on training. If you are interested in advancing and you believe that your people are the greatest untapped resource which you have, then it is only natural to strengthen that resource via a focused and yet relatively inexpensive manner.

Part Two presented a comprehensive discussion of the relationship between training and quality. Program development may be seen as a comprehensive effort to insure survival and training is the tool or vehicle by which this development takes place. Training is only the embodiment of a long and challenging effort to improvement in which the entire organization must play a role. Those who circulate training brochures and pamphlets without a strong rationale for some demonstrable gain for the organization may actually be causing more harm than good. Part Two presented the means by which constituencies are built, participants are selected and programs are developed. It represents the means to an end, translating goals into specific learning activities which will support the acquisition of knowledge, skills and abilities which are necessary for growth.

Part Three is yet another different yet related component of the quality puzzle. It is in this section that we learned the material necessary to complete the translation of good ideas and the best intentions into reality. As was stated earlier, training is a thirty billion dollar annual enterprise in the United States. Each organization conducts its fair share of training so it may as well appear on the credit side of the ledger, as a resource well spent. The physical act of training requires a special person, someone who can display enthusiasm and warmth to strangers, one whose competence and confidence is readily observable. Part III demonstrated how to operationalize your program development activity and make training a reality.

The "leadership", in Total Quality Leadership: A Training Approach, refers not to individuals, but to organizations, those entities who correctly define their priority as staff development, then train effectively to achieve it.

Final Thoughts

I have spent a year of my life working on this book and here at the close of this effort, I realize that the writing was more celebration than labor. I have always sincerely enjoyed that portion of my life which has been devoted to program development. I have been employed to administer program development funds supporting entire R & D networks, worked on the design of individualized programs and trained, trained, trained, trained. While I have enjoyed every aspect of this work, it is the joy of experiencing all three components which has been the real thrill. That is why I always recommend that even those who have no intention of becoming a trainer need to know all the information they can acquire about the process because no training program can ever achieve success without the seminar leader. If you are not going to be a trainer at least you should know what to look for in one.

The person who greets the equity at the beginning of a program has to be someone who truly enjoys working with people. The trainers are the talent, the persons who make things happen. The art and science of program development must be a total capacity resident in the individual who will facilitate the transfer of learning to others. Being on display, working on the edge of the unknown, can be an extremely exhilarating experience. You work intensely all day and then cannot believe that the program is over. All the months of building relationships, the weeks of preparing designs and materials, have all coalesced into a blur of activity. You accept the plaudits, perhaps even the applause, and then it is over until the next time. What have you accomplished? Well, you have had a chance to be an entertainer, a group leader, problem solver, and maybe even a cheer leader. But most of all you have participated in a contemporary drama that appears to offer the greatest potential for regaining our lost initiative.

This book was written in a narrative style. It was not designed to preach, to compartmentalize your thinking by proscribing every aspect of the training process, but to expand your horizons. Pages could have been taken to present checklists but that would not have represented learning. All the information which you need to do a credible job is contained herein. Read and synthesize the model, pick out the best for you and discard the rest, at least until you encounter some of the situations which I have related. That choice was purposive in order to offer the best alternative of presenting both the successes and failures which make this business so challenging and to personalize that experience set for those who come next.

To all of you who someday will plan strategy, design a program and greet a class, I envy you those experiences to come.

About the Author

Joseph Picogna has served as a management consultant since 1976. He first started teaching at Temple University in 1970 and currently concentrates in the area of human resource administration. Dr. Picogna has taught classes at the M.B.A. level in effective organization communication, negotiations, labor relations, program development, organizational design, staffing, and macroquality design.

He currently offers eighteen seminar topics which are designed to increase the productivity of organizations by strengthening the capacity of the people they employ. His client base numbers over 60 organizations in the public domain and private sector for whom he presents workshops and conducts organizational audits.

Appendices

The "Microlabs"

A

PROFESSIONALISM FOR LEGAL SECRETARIES

By: Susan M. Carrochi

About the Program

The legal secretary faces many challenges in a typical day. Knowledge of the basic tools of the secretarial profession is not enough to ensure success in the law firm environment. Legal secretaries must interact with lawyers and paralegals from inside and outside their firm; clients; firm administrative personnel and court personnel. He or she must be able to take and give clear directions to accomplish a task; cope with changing priorities and deadlines; have knowledge of court and agency filing requirements and at all time maintain composure. A legal secretary can and should be an important player in the legal team providing service to the client. This workshop is designed to address the non-quantifiable but important skills a legal secretary must posses to be a successful member of the legal team.

One of the most important skills a legal secretary can possess is the ability to communicate effectively with all of the people he or she comes into contact with. This workshop teaches communication skills directed to a law firm environment.

Benefits of Attending

Participating in the workshop will give the attendee a new way to view the role of the legal secretary; develop new skills for approaching and fulfilling that role; provide methods for understanding and coping with attorneys' needs and developing relationships with attorneys, other secretaries, support personnel and administration. Participants will learn how the roles of all individuals in the firm fit together and into the goals of the firm for providing legal services.

TIME	TITLE	METHOD	FORM
	A. Openers		
20	The Law Firm Environment	Illustration & Discussion	
10	Who is in Group & Why?	Discussion	
	B. The Legal Secretary's Role - Overview		
20	Assessing Your Role	Guided Imagery	Organization Charts
20	Refining Your Role	Group Activity	Organization Charts
20	Identifying Stress and Conflict	Illustration & Discussion	Flip Chart 1
10	Break		
	C. Communication Skills		
10	Understanding Lawyers	Illustration	Handout 1
20	Barriers to Communication	Discussion	Flip Chart 1 and 1A
20	Non-Verbal Skills	Illustration & Exercise	Flip Chart 2 Non-Verbal Exercise
20	Listening Skills	Exercise	Flip Chart 3 Listening Test
20	Verbal Skills	Discussion	

TIME	TITLE	METHOD	FORM
	1 hour Lunch		
	D. Skill Development		
15	Taking/Understanding Direction	Exercise	Listening Exercise
20	Giving Direction	Group Activity	Drawing
20	Communicating with Clients		
	Customer Service		
	Orientation	Illustration	Flip Chart 4
	Telephone Contact	Guided Imagery	
	Telephone Courtesy		
	Personal Contact	Illustration	
10	Maintaining Confidences	Discussion	
15	Stress and Conflict Techniques	Group Activity	Flip Chart 5
10	Team Concepts	Discussion	Flip Chart 6
30	Contributing to the Team	Role Play	
	E. Wrap Up		
15	Achieving a Professional Demeanor	Discussion	

Program Directions

A. Openers

1. Law Firm Environment (Illustration and Discussion)

a) Start with the Shakespeare quote - The first thing we do is kill all the lawyers - relate experience with being frustrated by confusing message sent by lawyer but we can't kill them all - no jobs left for us. Have group relate similar incidents - list on flip chart.

b) Describe typical law firm set-up.

Lawyers - Partners/Associates - Distinction

Associates enlist paralegals to help sort documents, research, review testimony or agreement. Lawyers and paralegals enlist secretary to help organize file, get documents prepared/filed, mailed

Others - Messengers - copy - hand deliveries

Administration - billing/accounting; personnel

Solicit input from group re: assignments/duties - list on flip chart

c) Introduce self and give background - law firm experience.

2.

a) Have participants introduce themselves and reasons for attending - list on flip chart.

b) Discuss the reasons for attending and how program will relate.

B. Overview of Legal Secretary Role

1. Assessing Your Role (Guided Imagery)

Give each participant two sheets of paper - on one have a typical organizational chart layout (dotted lines, reporting assignments). Have them fill in the typical layout with how they think their office is set up and where they fit in. Tell them they can make changes if they feel it is different.

On second sheet have them list all persons within the firm who have expectations of them, what they are, and where that person fits in the organization.

Solicit examples of organization charts and put on flip chart - discuss why they put various people in places.

Expectations. Have participants give examples from their lists of the people who have expectations and what they are. List on flip chart for use in application section.

2. Refining Your Role (Group Activity)

Refer back to organization charts. Break into groups (3-4) and have them prepare, on blank paper, an organization chart for a hypothetical firm.

Have groups present reasons why they put the various types of employees in various slots. List reasons on flip chart for use in stress section.

3. Communications (Illustration)

Solicit participants' definitions of communication. Supplement with examples from flip chart of types - explain sending/receiving.

4. Types of Stress/Conflicts (Illustration/Discussion)

Have participants relate typical stress and/or conflict situations in their daily work. Some typical responses may be - conflict between two attorney's rush projects; being blamed for missing part of a file.

Refer to organization chart and communication flip chart and discuss how they may relate.

C. Communication Skills

1. Understanding Lawyers (Illustration)

Have hand out with legal terminology. Solicit input from participants on lawyer's use of the terms and what they mean.

2. Barriers to Communication (Discussion)

a) Discuss typical barriers to effective communications. Refer to flip chart from communication definitions.

b) Have participants discuss barriers they have experienced and ways they could be avoided.

3. Non-Verbal Communications (Illustration/Exercise)

a) Discuss the fact that the spoken message conveys less than 35% of the total communication between two people.

b) Solicit types of non -verbal communication. Refer to prepared flip chart.

Appearance - manner of dress affects how people view you - first impression

Body Motion - non-verbal signals

Space - the closer you are, the more private or intimate the conversation is

Eye Contact

Voice - pitch/loud/speed/quality

Touch

c) Have participants pair up. Have each pair complete the non -verbal exercise.

4. Listening Skills (Exercise/Discussion)

a) Have participants take the Listening Evaluation Quiz.

b) Discuss results and importance of active listening - relate to taking directions.

c) Review active listening techniques (from prepared flip chart).

5. Verbal - Saying What You Mean (Discussion)

a) Solicit examples of phrases that if taken literally mean different things.

b) Review importance of being clear.

D. Skill Application

1. Taking and Understanding Direction (Exercise)

a) Give each participant the handout with boxes. Review the instructions and administer the exercise.

b) Review the results and discuss why they may have been misunderstood - would they have done better if they could ask questions?

c) Solicit input from participants of situations where they misunderstood - emphasize importance of clarification .

2. Give Direction (Group Activity)

a) Review importance of clear communications and relate their feelings with unclear directions from lawyers to how messengers and clerks also need clear instructions.

b) Ask for volunteer - volunteer will sit at front of room with back to group. Describe drawing and participants draw what is described - no questions.

Compare results.

c) Volunteer turns around and describes second picture - participants may ask questions.

Compare results.

3. Communicating with Clients

a) Relate to general customer service - ask participants to discuss examples of good service they have received; relate those to client. (Flip chart 4 - Customer Service)

b) Telephone contact - review basic telephone skills (Handout)

c) Personal Contact - review appearance, voice, introductions - social skills

4. Maintaining Confidences (Discussion)

Give examples of discussions taking place in public places that were overheard. Emphasize need for confidentiality of client information.

5. Stress Techniques (Group Activity)

a) Have participants break into groups of 3-4. Refer to flip chart made earlier and have groups discuss new ways to address the types of conflicts and stress identified. (10 minutes)

b) Have groups report on suggested new methods. Refer to communications skills and list on flip chart.

6. Team Concepts (Discussion)

a) Ask for input from participants on their experience in or on teams and what made them successful.

b) Review basics of effective teamwork and apply to law firm setting using flip chart 6.

7. Contributing to the Legal Services Team (Role Play)

Have participants get into groups of four and select roles - one each - lawyer, secretary, paralegal, messenger. (If a group has more than four, the additional person should be a lawyer). They are to work out the following scenario:

It is 9:00 a.m. A summary judgment motion must be filed by the end of the day. You have the first draft back. You still need to find and copy all of the exhibits, have the client review and approve it, get in final form with all copies, bound and filed in Federal Court by 5:00 p.m.

Allow 20-25 minutes for the role play. Have groups list skills they used in the role play.

E. Wrap Up

Achieving a Professional Demeanor (Discussion)

a) Review the results of the role play and have each group report on the skills they used.

b) Review the roles and charts made in the beginning of the seminar and see if their views have changed; will they use new techniques?

c) Distribute evaluation.

Attachments

Typical Law Firm Organization

Partners - are owners - may also be shareholders

- ☐ Make decisions on clients and types of law firm will practice;
- ☐ Make policy decisions on personnel; location; spending;
- ☐ Determine which associates will practice in which areas of law and new partners;

Associates - handle cases (litigation); prepare agreements;

do research; witnesses;

Paralegals - assist lawyers in discovery matters (document organization, depositions), preparation of documents and agreements; may do preliminary research; interview witnesses.

Messengers - file documents with courts/agencies and other lawyers; copy and collate documents.

Administration - handle business and personnel affairs of the firm - supplies; bills; payroll; insurance; office accommodations.

Organizational Chart

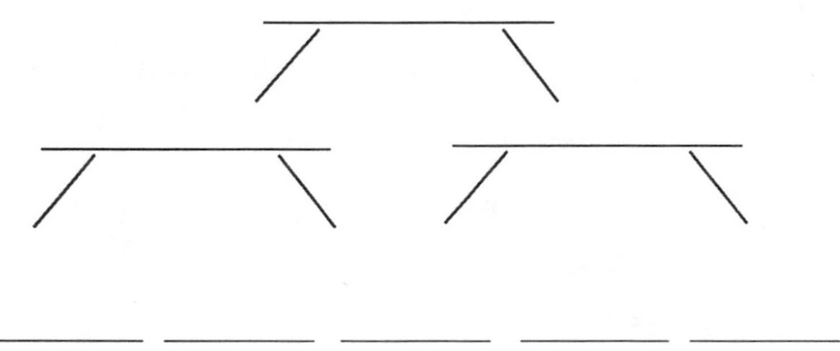

Flip chart 1 Communications

SENDER Message - Encode -Transmit	RECEIVER Receive - Decode - Understand

FEEDBACK

Message — What you want to communicate — Be CLEAR —Clarify your ideas first.

Encode — Putting the messageinto verbal or written words.

Transmit — Actual communication — should it be written or verbal?

Receiving — hearing or reading the message — Hearing needs to be effective.

Decoding — Translate message to thought — Find the meaning of the communication.

Understanding — The culmination of the process.

Feedback — closes the loop.

Flip Chart 1A — Barriers

SENDING

✓ Vague language
✓ Method — nonverbal clues
✓ Disorganized communication
✓ Overtones
✓ Actions must support your communications

RECEIVING

✓ Boredom
✓ Sender and receiver's position
✓ Time
✓ Interest in subject
✓ Perceptions

Handout 1 — Legal Termonology

Pleadings — Documents prepared in litigation

Discovery — Proces in litigation in which each side exchanges information relevant to the case.

Filing/File — Have certain pleadings entered into the court record.

Motion — a litigation document.

Party — One of the individuals/companies involved in the lawsuit.

Brief — A document that sets out the law supporting a party's position.

Caption — Part of the pleading that gives the names of the parties, the court, and the file number.

District Court — Generally refers to the Federal District Court.

Common Pleas — in Pennsylvania, the state court.

Deposition — A pre-trial procedure where a part or witness is examined under oath.

Docket (Dockets) — A summary sheet kept by the Clerk of the court listing all pleadings filed with the court.

Service — The physical delivery of documents in a lawsuit to the opposing party.

Subpoena — Court dicument directing a person to appear as a witness.

FLIP CHART 2 — NON-VERBAL COMMUNICATION

Appearance

type of clothing

hairstyle

strong perfume (cologne)

posture

Facial Expressions

Eyes

small pupils = concentraion

large pupils = tuning out

narrow eyes = intensity or anger

wide eyes = astonishment

eye contact = interest

Mouth

tight lips = anger

open mouth = wonder

crooked smile = doubt

smile = happiness

frown = sad

Body Motion

Head

tilted = caring

chin to chest = aggressiveness

Hands/Arms

open = warmth

fist = aggressiveness, anger

hand to chin = concentration

pointed finger = threatening

finger to mouth = perplexed

hands on hips = authority

Shoulders and Trunk

slouch = tired, weary

shouders back = confidence

leaning forward = interest

leaning away = disinterest

Space between sender and receiver

Voice

pitch

loudeness

speed

quality — pleasant, warm, gentle, dull, rich, unpleasant, strong, nervous

Touch

Non-Verbal Exercises, Participant A

Exercise #1

Communicate disapproval with:

a) your eyes (15 seconds)

b) your face (15 seconds)

c) your body (15 seconds)

Exercise#2

Record your observations. Avoid interpreting the message, just record what you see. (Physical characteristics)

Exercise #3

Tell your partner about something you accomplished in the last month of which you are proud. Be as detailed as you like. It's important that you communicate your pride in this accomplishment. You have 1 minute to verbalize your enthusiasm.

Exercise #4

Communicate a silent challenge. Point your finger and think to yourself "I'll get you!"

Exercise #5

Record your observations and feelings.

Exercise #6

With big smile on your face, and your hands and arms open, verbally tell your partner, "If you are late one more time, I'll fire you."

Non-Verbal Exercise, Participant B

Exercise #1

Record your observations. Avoid interpreting the message, just record what you see. (Physical characteristics)

Exercise #2

Communicate warmth with:

a) your eyes (15 seconds)

b) your face (15 seconds)

c) your body (15 seconds)

Exercise #3

For the first 20 seconds, listen intently to what your partner says. Maintain good eye contact, lean forward and open your arms and hands. For the next 20 seconds start to lose interest. Lean back and take an occasional glance around the room and yawn if you like. Assure your partner that you're listening.

Exercise #4

Non-verbally communicate caring and warmth.

Exercise #5

Lean back, frown a little, cross your arms, and verbally tell your partner, "If you ever need any help, just let me know. I'll be only too happy to make the job easier."

Exercise #6

Record your observations and feelings.

Listening Test

Directions: Read the questions listed below and rate yourself on each of the listening characteristics using the following scale:

Always = 4 points

Almost Always = 3 points

Rarely = 2 points

Never = 1 point

Listening Characteristics	Responses
1. Do I allow the speaker to express his or her complete thoughts without interrupting?	4 3 2 1
2. Do I listen between the lines, especially when conversing with individuals who frequently use hidden meanings?	4 3 2 1
3. Do I actively try to develop retention ability to remember important facts?	4 3 2 1
4. Do I write down the most important details of a message?	4 3 2 1
5. In recording a message, do I concentrate on writing the major facts and key phrases?	4 3 2 1
6. Do I read essential details back to the speaker before the conversation ends to ensure correct understanding?	4 3 2 1

Listening Characteristics Responses

7. Do I refrain from turning off the speaker because the message is dull or boring, or because I do not personally know or like the speaker? 4 3 2 1

8. Do I avoid becoming hostile or excited when a speaker's views differ from my own? 4 3 2 1

9. Do I ignore distractions when listening? 4 3 2 1

10. Do I express a genuine interest in the other individual's conversation? 4 3 2 1

Listening Test - Scoring

32 points or more = excellent listener

27-31 points = better than average listener

22-26 points = you need to consciously practice listening

Under 21 points = messages you receive are garble, not likely to be transmitted effectively

Flip Chart 3

Active and Effective Listening Guidelines Listening and responding in a way that makes it clear that the listener appreciates both the meaning and the feelings behind what is said.

1. Stop talking;

2. Put talker at ease;

3. Look and act interested;
4. Remove distractions;
5. Empathize with talker;
6. Be patient;
7. Hold your temper;
8. Go easy on argument and criticism;
9. Ask questions;
10. Respond to what the person is actually saying;
11. Acknowledge talker's feelings;
12. Avoid judgments - be aware of your personal bias.

Listening Exercise Directions

Listen very carefully to my instructions, I am only going to say it once.

✓ In Box A, put a dot on the small i;
✓ In Box B, print the word spaces in the spaces;
✓ In Box C, spell out two words using the letters in Box C (but not the letter C);
✓ In Box D, answer: Is it legal for a widow's husband to marry her

A	B
I	______________
SOTOWRWD C	YES NO D WHY

sister and why or why not?

Scoring: (1) average;(2) good;(3) very good;(4) you're a trained, active listener.

Flip Chart 4 — Customer (Client) Service

- Communicate clearly

- Be sensitive to their concerns

- Be flexible

- Follow-up

- Impact - Appearance

- Job knowledge

- Use judgment in what you say/do

Telephone Courtesy

- Answer the telephone promptly.

- Identify yourself or the person's phone you are answering (Mr. Hecker's Office).

- If the person is not in or cannot take the call, explain to the caller that they are not in or are on another call and ask to take a message.

- If you do take a message, make sure it is clear. Ask the caller to repeat something if you are unsure of what was said. Make sure you spell names correctly and take down telephone numbers correctly.

- Express a willingness to help. Ask if anyone else can help the caller.

- Avoid slang.

- Terminate the call pleasantly.

Flip Chart 5 - Coping with Stress

- Take care of yourself physically - proper rest, nutrition

- Ask for clarification of assignments and priorities

- Concentrate on your task

- Try to anticipate what is going to happen (know the cases you are working on!)

Flip Chart 6 - Team Concepts

- Have common goal

- Each member contributes a skill

- Each member has a role

- Member's support and get along with each other

- Understand its role in relation to firm

EVALUATION FORM

Please take a moment to fill out this evaluation form.

Pace of Program
1 2 3 4 5
Too Slow Too Fast

Length of Program
1 2 3 4 5
Too Short Too Long

Difficulty of Material

1 2 3 4 5

Easy Difficult

Overall Content

1 2 3 4 5

Not Helpful Very Helpful

Trainer

1 2 3 4 5

Not So Helpful Very Helpful

Comments:

B

ACHIEVING CUSTOMER SERVICE EXCELLENCE

Written By:
Kristen M. Braughler
Pamela M. Kennedy
Mary Anne M. Kowalick

BACKGROUND

During the 1980s, the corporate drive for perfection focused on improving the product. Today, the pursuit of a competitive edge has shifted to enhancing the caliber of customer care and service. It is now time for U.S. companies to raise their service level aspirations and for U.S. executives to declare war on mediocre service and set their sights on consistently excellent service. This goal is within reach if managers will provide the necessary leadership and remember that the sole judge of service quality is the customer.

The confidence that is instilled by an organization that is ready to respond to its customers' needs, inquiries, and complaints will keep customers coming back. Listening closely to customers is one way to anticipate what they want and to go beyond their expectations.

This workshop will teach proven techniques that can be

used every day to help a company stay on top by using the techniques of good customer service. In today's competitive marketplace, customers are looking to companies for better service and this workshop will show companies how to meet these expectations. This program will help you to understand and implement service strategies that will dramatically improve the performance and profitability of your organization.

WHO SHOULD ATTEND

Front-Line Service Providers - Whether you have telephone or fact-to-face customer contact.

Customer Service Managers - Learn the latest techniques to help your people be their best.

Salespeople - Develop unshakable customer loyalty - and easier repeat business.

General Managers - Get an inside look at why exceptional service is the key to growth today - and how to dramatically improve yours.

GAIN SKILLS THAT PLEASE YOUR CUSTOMERS AND PROFIT YOUR COMPANY

- ☐ Learn from the Leaders - Examples of customer service programs that are working.
- ☐ Improving Listening Skills - How to listen to your customers more effectively and review techniques which will result in your customers listening more effectively to you.
- ☐ Empowering and involving your employees in order to provide exceptional service - How to empower employees with the authority to respond and guide employees in the skills to act for customers.
- ☐ Training your Employees - One of the most vital components of your successful customer service program.
- ☐ Measuring your Customer Service Level - This workshop will

help you to determine your service level quality, including a discussion of the importance of customer feedback and how to measure customer service in the organization.

PROGRAM OUTLINE

TITLE	METHOD	TIME
I. Openers		
Role Play	Dramatization	15
Participant Survey (Optional)	Questionnaire	15
II. Introduction		
Introduce Trainers	Introduction	5
Critique Role Play	Discussion	15
III. Overview		
Facts About Customer Service	Discussion	20
Battleground of the 1990s	Discussion	10
Three Levels of Product	Illustration	10
Differentiation	Discussion	15

IV. Skill Development

A. Listening

Listening Exercise	Group Activity	10
Listening Skill Development	Discussion	20

B. Empowerment

Defining Empowerment	Illustration	10
Benefits of Empowerment	Discussion	20
Empowerment Visualization	Guided Imagery	10

C. Training

Assessing Training	Group Activity	20
Importance of Training	Illustration	15
Training Excellence	Discussion	20

D. Measurement

Service Measurement	Discussion	20
Measurement Benefits	Illustration	15

Measurement Assessment	Questionnaire	20

V. Wrap Up

Overview of Main Points Covered	Discussion	15
Integrating What Has Been Learned	Group Activity	20
	TOTAL:	5 hrs. 30 mins.

PROGRAM DIRECTIONS

I. OPENER - ROLE PLAY

A. The instructors conduct a role play involving personnel at an automotive service center and a customer inquiring about the status of a repair.

B. The customer is treated discourteously, transferred to various departments, and made to repeat information numerous times. The conversation ends with the customer feeling frustrated and dissatisfied with the service.

II. INTRODUCTION

A. Introduce the cast of characters and their backgrounds in customer service.

B. Participants are asked to critique what they have seen and to relate similar experiences. This feed back will be recorded on flip charts to initiate discussion on customer service issues.

III. OVERVIEW

A. Discussion of these issues will lead into presentation of some "Facts about customer service". These facts will include the following:

- ✓ Most customers choose a company or service by asking friends or relatives for referrals.
- ✓ A customer who had a bad experience with a company will tell more than 10 people - and 13% will tell over 20 people.
- ✓ For every person who complains, there are more than 25 dissatisfied customers who never let their complaints be known.
- ✓ Perceived-service firms can charge 10% more for their products.
- ✓ Of customers who don't complain, 65%-90% will never use that company's service again.
- ✓ Over 50% of the customers who complain will do business with the company again if their problems are solved. If the consumer feels the problem was solved quickly, the figure reaches as high as 95%.
- ✓ Customers who complain and have their problems resolved will tell an average of five people about their favorable experience.
- ✓ Customer indifference costs the company between 15-30% of gross sales.

The purpose of these facts is to heighten the audiences' awareness of the impact of poor service in the organization.

B. From this point, the instructor will explain to the class that customer service is the battleground of the nineties. Instructor will stress that companies can not survive by conducting business in the manner depicted in the earlier role play. In today's business environment, competition is fierce and although companies strive to differentiate their products through advertising, product design, technology and competitive pricing — more is needed. "More" is adding people to the product or service, and utilizing customer service as a strategic marketing tool in your business.

C. Next, the instructor will turn to a previously drawn flip-chart diagram that illustrates the three levels of product:

The Generic Product - the physical product, based on price.

The Enhanced Product - what is expected, sold on quality.

The Potential Product - where companies want to be, sold on the customer relationship.

The instructor will explain an example of each level in a commonly known industry. Then the instructor will ask the participants to volunteer examples of other industries which display this pattern. The examples the instructor may use include:

A Dry Cleaners:

Generic - professionally cleans clothes.

Enhanced - performs service within 48 hours.

Potential - same day service, drive through window for customer convenience, greets customers by name.

Automotive Tire Shop:

Generic - repairs tires.

Enhanced - tire warranty, timely service.

Potential - Loaner cars for customers, waiting room with current magazines, fresh coffee and television, guarantees all service for life.

Gas Station:

Generic - sell gas at competitive price.

Enhanced - pumps gas, check oil, cleans from windshield

Potential - hand-vacuum car interior, check oil and other fluids, clean front and back windshields inside and out, and offer a free cup of coffee and USA Today.

Group Activity - the instructor will ask participants to get into groups of four and put the above discussed concept "to work". Participants will be asked to brainstorm and think of ways to "add people to the product" in their own organizations. After a reasonable amount of time, the groups will be asked to share their thoughts and ideas with the class. This feedback will be listed on a flipchart and the instructor will emphasize that achieving this "level three" product is what keeps customers with your company.

IV. SKILL DEVELOPMENT

A. Improved listening skills

1. Group Activity - the instructor will tell the class a short story to test the participants' listening skills. The activity is designed to illustrate the complexity involved in developing effective listening skills.

2. Upon completion of this exercise, the instructor will turn to the flipchart that contains important points on how to improve listening skills. The points listed below will each be discussed in brief detail with the participants.

- ☐ Listen - Silent
- ☐ Listen Naively
- ☐ If the customer is on the telephone, picture the person as if they were present in front of you.
- ☐ If the customer is irate, let him speak - Do not interrupt unless you detect a pause.
- ☐ Customers are the most important type of feedback - 80% of technological innovations come from customers.
- ☐ Listen to your customers, suppliers, employees, and competitors.

B. Empowering and Involving Employees

1. Instructor will turn to a flipchart showing the big "E Word" of the 90s - Empowerment. Flipchart will display the definition of Empowerment - "Giving people at all levels the authority and responsibility to solve problems and provide exceptional service."

2. After instructor defines empowerment, several points regarding empowering employees will be discussed. These points include:

- ☐ The paradox of empowerment - in order to gain power you must give some of it away.
- ☐ Good managers recognize that empowerment is not a substitute for leadership or a reduction of their authority.
- ☐ The more people are empowered, the more they need leaders who can set goals and define a vision .
- ☐ The Empowerment Payoff - satisfied customers, motivated employees, increased company profits.

3. After going over these points, instructor will ask participants to relax and close their eyes. They will be asked to imagine a workplace where people at all levels of the organization assume full responsibility for the quality, productivity, and creativity of their work...an environment in which every worker feels involved and committed to the success of the business. Participants will open their eyes and instructor will

inform the class that they have just seen a vision of the successful corporation of the 90s. This activity will lead into a discussion about the transition from authoritarian management practices of the past to participatory management.

C. Importance of Training Employees

1. Group Activity - This skill area will be introduced by the instructor asking the participants to pair off. Instructor will tell the class to discuss with one another their most recent training experience, either as a trainer or trainee. Discussion should include length of training program, format of training, and their assessment of the training. After this activity, instructor will solicit unique training experiences and a group discussion will follow.

2. Upon completion of the group discussion, the instructor will turn to a flipchart on the importance of training. Points will include:

- ☐ Training and development - providing the tools to get the job done.
- ☐ Emphasize teamwork as a principal factor in delivering excellent service.
- ☐ If employees are unsure of how to deliver excellent service, this will not be accomplished.
- ☐ Invest in training - and see results.

3. At this time the instructor will inform the class about several companies' training programs. Companies with excellent training programs such as Walt Disney Corp., British Airways, American Express, and UPS will be included.

D. Measuring your Customer Service Level

1. As a final skill area, service measurement will be discussed. Instructor will focus the discussion around the following questions:

a - How well do you collect, quantify and act on "subjective" customer opinions?

b - How many meetings do you have that focus on the customer and service issues compared to meetings regarding budget, operations, or productivity?

c - To what degree are service measurements consistently fed back to all levels in your organization?

2. Following this discussion, instructor will access a flip chart on measurement including:

- ✓ What gets measured, gets done!
- ✓ Anticipating customer needs vs. reacting to customer complaints.
- ✓ Measuring satisfaction sends a strong signal - satisfied customers are the reason we exist.
- ✓ Company's perception of quality vs. customer's perception of quality.
- ✓ Can you afford not to measure customer satisfaction?

3. A questionnaire will be given to assist participants in assessing their company's service quality measurements.

V. Wrap Up

1. Instructor will spent time recycling the major points covered in the program.

2. As a closing exercise, the instructor will ask participants

to assess how their organizations are doing in regard to service quality. The participants are asked to share their thoughts.

Finally, participants are asked to list solutions or action items that can be completed in the immediate future. Each participant will be asked to state three action items he/she will accomplish during the following week.

C

OCCUPATIONAL STRESS: JOB BURNOUT

LEARN HOW TO BECOME A STRESS-BUSTER.
RECOGNIZE AND PREVENT THE SPREAD OF JOB BURNOUT IN YOURSELF AND YOUR ORGANIZATION.

By:
Patricia Robson

ABOUT THE PROGRAM

Virtually everyone is subject to stress. Stress is a physical and psychological condition that results from an individual's attempt to deal with his/her environment. It is a normal part of everyday life. However, sometimes stress can become overwhelming and even harmful to an individual. In fact, most people suffer to some degree from the effects of stress. According to some doctors, 60 to 80% of all patients have stress-related health problems. Stress can actually make a person ill. It affects all areas of an individual's life on both a personal and a professional level. In the work setting, stress manifests itself in higher health care costs due to an increase of stress induced illness claims. Stress can also cause a decrease in productivity, an increase in tardiness, an increase in absenteeism, and even the abuse of drugs or alcohol. Stress is actually robbing the organization of its employees' services. On a personal level, stress can cause people to become withdrawn, listless, hostile, depressed, and even gain or lose weight. Thus, the ability to manage stress is important to the success, health and happiness of an individual.

Every individual should learn how to avoid stress whenever possible and/or how to cope with stress when it is unavoidable. Although it seems like an impossible task, it can be accomplished. The purpose of this seminar is to make participants more aware of the stressors in their lives and provide them with some techniques on how to avoid the negative effects of stress.

KEY BENEFITS OF ATTENDANCE

By attending this workshop, participants will be able to develop a personalized strategy for dealing with stress. The goal of this program is to make participants more knowledgeable on the subject of occupational stress. Awareness and knowledge are the first steps in combating any problem. Other key benefits are the following:

- ☐ Identification Of Mental & Physical Signs Of Stress.
- ☐ Development Of Personalized Techniques To Deal With Stress.
- ☐ Identification Of Stress Producing Work Environments.
- ☐ Awareness Of Occupational Stress and Job Burnout.

PROGRAM OUTLINE

TIME	TITLE	METHOD	FORM
BREAKFAST			
I. Opener			
5	Introduction	Discussion	
20	Stress In Your Life	Illustration Group Activity	

TIME	TITLE	METHOD	FORM
II. What Is Stress?			
5	What Is Stress	Discussion	
5	The Productivity Zone	Discussion	1
5	Individual Differences	Discussion	2
15	Physical & Mental Signs	Discussion Individual Activity Group Share	3
15	Diagram Of Stressors	Group Activity Discussion	4
III. What Is Job Burnout			
10	Self-Diagnosis Quiz	Individual Activity Group Share	8
5	What Is Job Burnout	Discussion	5
5	Primary Risk Factors	Discussion	6
10	Burnout Symptom Cycle	Discussion	7
COFFEE BREAK (15 Minutes)			
IV. Who Suffers From Job Burnout?			
10	Is Your Stress Job Stress	Individual Activity Group Share	9
20	What Jobs Are Related To Stress	Group Activity Discussion	10
5	High Achievers	Discussion	11

TIME	TITLE	METHOD	FORM
10	Type A Personalities	Discussion Individual Activity	12
10	What Makes A Manager Burnout	Discussion Individual Activity	13
10	Work Stress Checklist	Discussion Individual Activity Group Share	14

LUNCH (One Hour)

V. Tips To Beat Stress: Personal

TIME	TITLE	METHOD	FORM
20	Recognizing Job Burnout	Group Activity	
10	Intrapersonal Coping	Discussion	15
5	Insights On Stress	Discussion	16
20	Relaxation Response	Group Activity	17
5	Exercise Precautions	Discussion	18
5	Selye's Tips	Discussion	19
10	12 Point Prevention	Discussion	20

COFFEE BREAK

TIME	TITLE	METHOD	FORM
VI. Tips To Beat Stress: Work			
20	Hopes & Expectations Discussion	Group Activity	22
10	Work Environment	Discussion	23
5	High Participation	Discussion	25
	Effective Listening		
10	Importance	Discussion	
10	Listening Quiz	Individual Activity	26
10	10 Keys	Discussion	27
5	Kinesthetic		28
15	Job Demands	Discussion Group Activity	29
10	Social Support	Discussion Individual Activity	30
VII. Closing			
10	Summary Of The Program	Discussion	
5	National Burnout Survey	Discussion	32
20	Stress Prescription	Individual Activity Group Share Discussion	31
10	The Rest Of The Packet & Thank You	Discussion	

PROGRAM DIRECTIONS

Prior to attending the seminar, a letter well be sent to each participant. The letter well provide information on the following items:

1) Length Of The Program: Approximately 8 hours

2) Dress: Casual, Comfortable Clothing

3) Breakfast, Morning Break, Lunch, Afternoon Break

4) Location Of The Program: The Workshop Will Be Held In A Conference Room Away From The Normal Work Flow

5) Materials Needed: None. All Materials Will Be Provided By The Trainer

6) Short Overview Of The Program

7) Information About The Trainer

Breakfast items will be set up before participants arrive. When participants arrive, they will be encouraged to get something to eat and to socialize for a short period of time.

I. OPENER

Introduction: Participants will be asked to take their seats. The Trainer will welcome everyone to the program. The Trainer will tell them about the workshop format. Participants will be told that questions will be encouraged.

Stress In Your Life: Participants will be asked to introduce themselves and state what stressors exist in their lives. The

Trainer will begin by giving examples of his/her stressors. Responses from the participants will be recorded on newsprint. (This exercise is designed to be an ice breaker. If done properly, it should allow participants to realize that everyone suffers from stress.)

Throughout the group activity, the Trainer will be monitoring the amount of "good" and "bad" stress responses. The Trainer will ask the question "Can good events cause stress?"

(Answers from this group activity will be used throughout the program.)

WHAT IS STRESS?

What Is Stress?: The Trainer will discuss the current definitions of stress.

The Productivity Zone: The Trainer will show on an overhead the continuum of stress. This diagram will provide participants with a visual representation of the degrees of stress. The Trainer will discuss the relationship between productivity and stress.

Individual Threshold Of Stress: The Trainer will discuss differences in individual responses to stress. An overhead of stress thresholds will be shown to the participants.

Physical & Mental Signs Of Stress: The Trainer will ask participants the question "How would you know if you were suffering from stress?" Participants will volunteer information which will be recorded on newsprint. The Trainer will try to encourage participants to respond to this question with examples of physical, emotional, and behavioral signs of stress. The Trainer will then bring participant's attention to the physical and mental signs of stress checklist which can be found in their packets. The Trainer will read the items and participants will be asked to think how many, if any, of the signs apply to themselves.

Work & Personal Stressors Diagram: The Trainer will refer back to the original group activity to have the group determine which stressors were work related and which were personal in nature. The Trainer will compare this list with the diagram in their packets. The Trainer will discuss the results stress (i.e. medical costs).

WHAT IS JOB BURNOUT?

Self Diagnosis Quiz: Participants will be told to take a few minutes to complete this quiz. This instrument should provide participants with a rough estimate of the amount of job burnout they are suffering from. The Trainer will go over the list quiz and try to find similarities with the original group list.

What Is Burnout: The Trainer will discuss what burnout is. The Trainer will also discuss the differences between stress and burnout. The Trainer will refer participants to the diagram of job burnout.

The Primary Risk Factors Of Job Burnout: The Trainer will discuss the primary risk factors of job burnout found in literature.

Burnout Symptom Cycle: The Trainer will discuss the burnout symptom cycle. The Trainer will provide examples of each stage of the cycle.

Participants will be given a 15 minute coffee break.

WHO SUFFERS FROM JOB BURNOUT

Quiz: The participants will be asked to complete the quiz to determine their job stress index.

Jobs Correlated With Stress : The Trainer will ask participants what is the most stressful job and why. The Trainer will discuss the link between your job and stress. The Trainer will refer participants to a diagram in their packets. This diagram will depict which jobs are correlated with stress. The Trainer will compare it with the group answers.

The Trainer will discuss the connection between high achievers and stress.

Type A Personalities:The Trainer will discuss the connection between Type A Personalities and stress. Participants will be asked to complete a quiz on Type A Behavior. This inventory will provide participants with a rough estimate of their individual level of Type A personality traits.

What Makes A Manager Burnout:The Trainer will discuss the Type A manager. The Trainer will provide stereotypical examples of such a manager.

Work-Stress Checklist: The participants will be asked to complete the work-stress checklist in their packets. The Trainer will go over the stress inventory with the participants.

Participants will be given a one hour lunch break. Lunch will be provided by the Trainer.

TIPS TO BEAT STRESS: PERSONAL

Recognizing Job Burnout:The Trainer will ask for volunteer to "play act" prewritten scenarios of people suffering from stress. The participants will break up into smaller groups to come up with solutions to the different scenarios. The groups will present their solutions.

Intrapersonal Coping Strategies: The Trainer will discuss the coping grid found in their packets. The Trainer will relate this grid to the participant's solutions to the role play above.

Stress Reduction Insights: The Trainer will discuss a summary of common sense stress reduction tips.

Relaxation Response: The Trainer will discuss the use of relaxation in combating stress. The participants will go through a relaxation exercise.

Exercise & Precautions: The Trainer will discuss the importance of exercise in fighting stress. The Trainer will tell participants to review the precautions checklist in their packet before beginning an exercise program.

Seyle's Tips: The Trainer will quickly review Selye's tips in stress reduction .

Points of Burnout Prevention: The Trainer will review the recommended points of burnout prevention. The Trainer will try to relate this list to the list of solutions participants developed earlier in the session.

TIPS TO BEAT STRESS: WORK

Hopes & Expectations: Participants will be asked to discuss their hopes and expectations of their jobs. The Trainer will write their answers on newsprint. The Trainer will compare the group's answers with the results from past training sessions.

Work Environments Correlated To Burnout: The Trainer will discuss the aspects of work environments that have been correlated with stress (i.e. psychological, physical, social, and organizational features).

High Participation Diagram: The Trainer will discuss the

importance of high employee participation in the work place.

Effective Listening Skills:

Importance of Listening: The Trainer will discuss the importance of listening and communication in dealing with stress.

Listening Skill Quiz: Participants will be asked to complete the listening skill quiz. This quiz measures bad listening skills. It should give participants a rough estimate of their listening skills. However, a more accurate measure would be to find someone who knows the participant to complete the quiz for them.

Keys To Better Listening: The Trainer will review the differences between a bad listener and a good listener.

Kinesthetic: The Trainer will discuss how the words participants use can be perceived differently by people based on their processing skills. The Trainer will discuss the difference between kinesthetic, visual, and auditory listeners.

Demands vs. Job Descriptions: Participants will be encouraged to complete the exercise in their training packets on perceived job demands. The Trainer will provide an example during the session. (This exercise should encourage participants to think about the self-imposed demands they place on themselves.)

The Importance Of Social Support Functions: The Trainer will discuss the importance of a social support network in combatting stress. Participants will complete a social support quiz to determine if they have the social support they need in their lives. (This exercise is designed to remind participants not to neglect their social support systems.)

CLOSING

Summary: The Trainer will recap the activities of the day by using the newsprints from the past group activities.

The National Burnout Survey: The participants will be encouraged to complete the National Burnout Survey in their packets.

Stress Prescription: Participants will be asked to write their own prescriptions for the stress they face. They will be encouraged to find a solution to the stress they mentioned in the first group activity.

Thank participants for attending the stress workshop. The Trainer will also discuss the stress workbook found in their packets.

D

CLOSING THE DEAL

By:

John Matlaga

I. OPENER

A. IMPROPER SALES TECHNIQUE (ROLE PLAY)

1. The seminar begins with one of the participants playing the role of a potential customer in his office. The salesperson (seminar leader) is trying to sell a pen to the prospect. The salesperson fails to ask the prospect any questions about what his/her needs might be regarding a pen, but instead focuses on the features of the pen itself. This continues for a minute or so, when the prospect tells the salesperson that he is no longer interested in purchasing a pen and tells the salesperson that he must end this meeting to attend another engagement. The salesperson leaves the sales call wondering what went wrong.

2. The seminar leader now stands up and asks the group "How many times have you been called at home or at work by a salesperson trying to sell you something? Think back to what that call was like. What is anything like the call you just heard? Did you buy from that person?

II. SKILL DEVELOPMENT

A. Prospecting

1. Pre-Call Planning. (Guided Imagery)

a. Ask the group to imagine themselves making a telephone call to a prospect in order to make an appointment for a sales call. Have them imagine a positive response from the person they are calling. What happened? Now have the group imagine the same call but with a negative response from the prospect. What happened differently?

2. Effective Telephone Techniques. (Lecture)

a. Set objectives for your calls and focus on them.

b. Set aside specific times to make your calls and adhere to them. For example, if you are going to prospect on the telephone on Tuesday mornings, set aside every Tuesday morning to make these calls and don't deviate.

c. Use the telephone for setting up appointments only; don't sell over the telephone.

d. Keep your conversation brief and focused. This allows you to maximize your calls.

e. Keep detailed records of your activity in order to identify trends and monitor your progress toward reaching your objectives.

3. Summary and Feedback. (Discussion)

a. Ask the class for questions on the presented materials in order to clarify their understanding.

B. MAKING THE APPOINTMENT (LECTURE)

1. Introduction of yourself and the company.

a. Tell the prospect who you are and the name of the company that you represent. You might also want to ask the prospect if he/she has ever heard of your company before. For example: Good afternoon, Mr. Smith, my name is John Doe with the XYZ Company. Have you ever heard of our company before?

2. Ask permission to continue. If the prospect is busy and you fail to ask him for his time, he may view your call as an unnecessary intrusion and turn you away abruptly. Example: Can I have a few minutes of your time?

3. General Benefits Statement. State the reason why the prospect should continue to listen to you. (Review by example)

4. Build credibility by using testimonials/referrals. (Review by example)

5. Keep conversation focused on your agenda, not theirs. (Review by example)

6. Ask for the appointment using close-end questioning techniques. For example: Which day would be better for you Mr. Jones, Thursday morning or Friday afternoon?

7. Practicing Making The Appointment: (Group Activity)

a. Divide the class into groups of three; one person to play the role of the salesperson, one to play the role of the prospect, and one to be the observer. Have the group role play setting up the appointment from the provided materials.

C. CONDUCTING THE INITIAL INTERVIEW (GUIDED IMAGERY/LECTURE)

1. Ask the group to imagine themselves going on the initial appointment at the prospect's office. How do they imagine themselves? What do they look like? Are they nervous or relaxed?

2. Establishing Rapport.

a. Use proper eye contact by looking into the customer's eyes as much as possible. This keeps the customer attentive and is an indication of your interest in what he/she has to say.

b. Adapt to the prospect's speaking patterns, gestures and manner. For example: If the customer tends to speak at a rapid pace, you may want to have a conversation with him using the same rate of speech as the prospect.

c. Identify common interests. Few things establish trust better than knowing that you are dealing with someone like yourself. Prospects will enter their comfort zone much faster when you discuss common interests.

d. Discuss the prospect's business. The information that you gain about his business will often define the direction you will take in the sales call.

e. Keep your rapport building focused on your objectives. Remember, you are there to sell your product, not to socialize.

3. Reinforce the reason why you are there by restating the General Benefits Statement.

a. State the purpose of your being there.

b. The potential benefit of your product to the

prospect.

c. Check to be sure that the customer is in agreement.

4. Effective Questioning Techniques.

a. Ask permission to take notes. If agreed, take detailed notes of your conversation.

b. Initially, use open-ended questions (probes) to encourage the prospect to think and become involved in the conversation. Once you have asked the question, stay quiet until you have a response.

c. Encourage the prospect's response through active listening techniques. For example: You may want to nod your head up and down, in agreement, to encourage the prospect to continue speaking.

d. Confirm you understanding of his response. For example: "If I understand you correctly, Mr. Smith, you're saying that you're looking for a product that can do the following?"

e. Use close-ended questions to eliminate any areas for misunderstanding. Example: "If I can do this, Mr. Jones, would you be willing to do this?"

5. Making The Follow-up Appointment.

a. Summarize your conversation.

b. Ask for further input from the prospect.

c. Identify action items going forward and gain prospect's agreement.

d. Trial close. Example: "If our company can do for you what we discussed today, are we in a position to do business with your organization?"

e. Agree on a date for a follow-up appointment.

6. Practicing The Initial Interview. (Group Activity)

a. Break the class up into groups of three; one person to be a salesperson, one to be the prospect, and one an observer. Hand out role plays illustrating effective interviewing techniques and have each group play out the scenario. Participants in the group should rotate the roles that they play with each role play. For example, if one person was the observer during the last role play, they should not be the observer in the next role play.

7. Summary and Feedback. (Discussion)

a. Ask the participants in the role play what was effective for them and why? Discuss feedback with the group.

D. Developing the Proposal (Lecture)

1. Organize your notes and categorize your prospect's needs according to priority.

2. Identify your company's strengths and match them with the prospect's needs.

3. State the benefits of your proposal to the prospect. Be certain to present your proposal in terms of benefits to the prospect and not just the features of your products or services. Features of a product or service are thephysical attributes of your product; benefits are how that feature can help the prospect. For example, a feature of an automobile may be that it has an air bag; the benefit of that air bag to the owner of the automobile is that it can save his/her life. People generally shop for features, but they buy benefits.

4. Identify costs.

5. Reinforce your company's qualifications in the industry

and state your interest in their business. For example, "As we discussed, Mr. Smith, our company has been providing high quality products to your industry for the last 50 years. We would be interested in doing business with your organization, as well.

6. Physical Appearance of Proposal.

a. Image is everything; make sure your proposal is professionally done using high quality paper and dark, noticeable ink.

b. Use originals; no copies.

c. Proof read for proper grammar and spelling.

d. Avoid wordy proposals. Make your point in a clear and concise manner.

e. Protect the contents of your proposal with a folder or binder.

7. Summary and Feedback. (Discussion)

E. Presenting The Solution. (Guided Imagery/Lecture)

1. Pre-appointment planning.

a. Participants are asked to close their eyes, relax, and envision themselves going on the appointment to present their proposal. What do they say? Where do they physically position themselves in regard to the prospect?

2. Presentation of the Proposal.

a. Position yourself, physically, next to the prospect instead of directly across from his/her desk. This posture removes the desk as a barrier and helps to develop a more personal relationship. One note: Be sure to ask for permission to do this first.

b. Maintain eye contact with the prospect during the presentation and keep the proposal in your possession. This allows you to maintain control of the presentation.

c. Present the benefits of your proposal to the prospect and ask for agreement along the way.

d. Ask for questions.

3. Practicing Presenting the Solution. (Role Play)

a. Facilitator breaks up the class into groups of three; one person to act as salesperson, one as prospect, and one as observer. Groups should consist of the same members as in prior role plays. Role play scripts are handed out and the groups act out the content.

4. Summary/Feedback. (Discussion)

F. Closing The Sale. (Guided Imagery/Lecture)

1. Envisioning closing the sale. (Guided Imagery)

a. Facilitator asks the class to close their eyes, relax and envision themselves closing the sale. What do they say? How does the prospect respond? How do you answer his objections?

2. Trial Close.

3. If the prospect does not have any objections to your proposal, ask for the order and explain the implementation process. For example: "Mr. Smith, all I need to get the process started is to complete this credit application and order form. Upon the approval of this information, we will contact you in

approximately two days in order to arrange for the installation of your new stamping machine."

4. Overcoming Objections.

If the prospect has objections to your proposal, you will need to address them. The following are three categories of objections and the techniques used to overcome them.

a. Misconception/Misunderstanding.

The salesperson should first clarify where the misunderstanding exists by asking close-ended questioning techniques. For example: "If I understand you correctly, Mr. Smith, what you are saying is that you don't like the fact that our printer is a dot matrix instead of laser, is that correct?"

Ask to make sure that the prospect now understands your explanation. Example: "As I indicated previously, Mr. Smith, our printer is capable of using dot matrix and laser techniques. Do you recall?"

Get agreement and ask for the order. For example: "You can see now, Mr. Smith, how our product can benefit your firm, correct? Do you agree that this would be of value to your firm? Terrific, would you like delivery on Thursday or Friday?"

b. Skepticism.

This objection occurs when your prospect is not, convinced that your product will do what you claim. To overcome this objection, offer proof via testimonials, statistics, or referrals.

c. Real Drawback.

This objection is based on your product having a shortcoming in its design. In order to overcome this objection, first acknowledge the shortcoming, then explain how the positive attributes of your product outweigh the shortcomings. Check to make sure the customer is satisfied with your response.

5. Practicing Overcoming Objections and Closing the Sale. (Group Activity)

a. Ask the class to break up into their groups once again, with one assuming the role of salesperson, one assuming the role of prospect, and one as observer. Hand out role plays and have group role play.

6. Questions and Answer Period.

7. Conclusion (Role Play)

The two facilitators re-enact the role play started in the beginning of the seminar, only this time they incorporate the sales techniques outlined in the seminar. Probing skills are demonstrated, proposal presentation, and closing techniques. At the end of the role play, the salesperson makes the sale and the prospect's needs are satisfied.

E

CUSTOMER SERVICE AND SALESMANSHIP IN THE RETAIL ENVIRONMENT

by
Wendy McKeon

Increase sales and develop loyal, repeat customers by providing outstanding customer service.

ABOUT THE TRAINING PROGRAM

The average business never hears from 96% of it's dissatisfied customers! In addition, for every one complaint, 26 customers have a problem with a product or service received.

We often forget that serving the customer is the most important job that we do. Without the customer, there is no business and there will be no paycheck to take home. The basic customer service skills are relatively simple and easy to learn. What's needed is a firm commitment to place the customer ahead of all other corporate priorities. By increasing levels of customer service and improving selling skills, employee morale will improve and turnover will slow. This workshop is for the salespeople and sales managers alike. Participants will learn the basics of selling and how to instill these skills in the store staff. Learn how to deal with difficult people and turn them into repeat customers. Learn how effective customer service skills can improve efficiency of daily operations.

KEY BENEFITS OF ATTENDANCE

- ✓ Identify your customers - their wants and needs.
- ✓ Establish a customer service priority in your company.
- ✓ Increase customer base and store sales.
- ✓ Enhance the reputation of your store.
- ✓ Improve operational efficiency.
- ✓ Enhance employee morale by making work more interesting.

PROGRAM OUTLINE

TIME	TITLE	
	A. OPENERS	
10	Some Alarming Statistics	Group Discussion
10	Survey	Group Activity
15	Introduce Group	Group Discussion
	B. OVERVIEW	
15	Why We Shop Where We Do	Guided Imagery
20	Unpleasant Experiences	Group Activity
15	Rewards of Customer Service	Discussion
20	Customer Service Basics	Discussion
	BREAK 15 MINUTES	
	C. PRACTICUM	
15	Approach Techniques	Guided Imagery
15	Some Helpful Hints	Discussion
30	Working Together	Group Activity
20	Role of the Manager	Discussion

LUNCH 45 MINUTES

D. SKILL DEVELOPMENT

40	Put Yourself in the Customer's Shoes	Group Activity
15	Customer Service in Action	Group Activity Discussion

E. SKILL APPLICATION

20	Always Room for Improvement	Group Discussion
15	How to Begin	Group Discussion

F. CONCLUSION

10	What's in it for You?	Group Discussion
10	Get Started	Group Discussion

PROGRAM DIRECTIONS

A. OPENERS

1. SOME ALARMING STATISTICS (GROUP DISCUSSION)

a. Begin by presenting a series of customer service statistics. By presenting the statistics in a question format, invite participants to render a guess at the percentage being discussed. For example, "To how many people do you think an unhappy customer relays their experience?"

b. Introduce yourself and describe your retail background as well as the various customer service policies you have personally experienced.

c. Discuss the current retail environment and the increasing importance of customer service in a successful business. Place emphasis on the increased competition from catalogs and outlet stores.

2. INTRODUCE GROUP (ACTIVITY, GROUP DISCUSSION)

a. Administer the Customer Commitment Survey. This will give each participant an idea of the emphasis their company currently places on the value of customer service.

b. Go around the room and have each person introduce himself or herself. Each person should also discuss his or her score on the Customer Commitment Survey as well as any surprising results of the exercise.

c. Discuss the participant's motivations for attending the program as well as individual expectations. Note the different motivations between salespeople and managers. List these expectations on a flip chart for a later discussion.

B. OVERVIEW

1. WHY WE SHOP WHERE WE DO (GUIDED IMAGERY)

a. Begin by describing a favorite store and the things about that store that keep you coming back. Ask participants to talk about a favorite store, restaurant, service, etc.

b. Based on each person's description, have other members of the group identify characteristics which they feel are motivating this person to continue to patronize the establishment.

c. Repeat the process by eliciting several responses and listing on a flip chart the characteristics which are service oriented characteristics when tallying the responses.

2. UNPLEASANT EXPERIENCES (GROUP ACTIVITY)

a. Have the group pair off and have one partner relate an unpleasant shopping experience, one which left her upset or angry.

b. The "listening" partner should jot down particular things which made the experience especially unpleasant for their partner.

c. Return to the group and have the listening partner briefly describe the unpleasant experience and the main reasons or characteristics which made it so. List these items on a flip chart. Also note the action taken (if any) by the person having the unpleasant experience.

3. REWARDS OF CUSTOMER SERVICE (DISCUSSION)

a. Compare the immediate, as well as long term, effects of both good and bad customer service.

4. CUSTOMER SERVICE BASICS (DISCUSSION)

a. Once the group is aware of the effects and importance of customer service, review the basics of good customer service. These are: Be Courteous; Be Concerned; and Be Prepared.

b. Distribute the handout on Customer Service Basics as well as displaying on the flip chart. Ask for input as to additional ideas under each heading.

c. Compile a list of specific examples under each heading. For example, Be Courteous: Recognize customers promptly, be enthusiastic, smile, be attentive, etc.

d. Stress the various ways that these customer service basics can be applied to all types of stores or services.

C. PRACTICUM

1. APPROACH TECHNIQUES (GROUP DISCUSSION)

a. Discuss the various customer approach techniques, i.e. the Friendly approach, the Service approach, and the Merchandise approach.

b. Invite participants to demonstrate what they believe to be an example of each approach.

c. Discuss situations when each of the approaches would be most effective. Stress that the correct approach is half the battle in providing good customer service.

d. Describe how the approach learned ties into the basic of customer service described previously.

2. HELPFUL HINTS (DISCUSSION)

a. Distribute handout on helpful hints on providing good customer service.

b. Remind participants that although these tips may seem obvious, they are good to use as a tool when training a staff. The list would be terrific to hang at the lunch table or in the back stockroom. Encourage the store staff to try a different hint every day.

3. WORKING TOGETHER (GROUP ACTIVITY)

a. Describe situations when both the manager and the salesperson have done things that have hindered optimum customer service. For example, managers may establish unreasonable time frames for the completion of a task (perhaps checking in new stock) thereby rendering salespeople "too busy" to effectively serve customers. Likewise, salespeople regard customers as an interruption to their day.

b. Divide the group into managers and salespeople

(if the group does not contain both managers and salespeople, have each half of the class assume one of the roles). Have each group write a "wish list" to the other group containing suggestions that would help them to be better able to provide good customer service. For example, the managers may include "I wish the salespeople wouldn't gather in a group to talk and ignore the customers." Salespeople may include "I wish the management would provide better training so that we are fully knowledgeable about the products we sell."

c. Have each group present their top five "wishes". Have the opposite group provide suggestions or ideas to make the "wishes" come true.

d. Discuss ways each group could compromise to provide mutual satisfaction.

4. THE ROLE OF THE MANAGER (DISCUSSION)

a. Stress the importance of establishing customer service priorities from the top of the corporate structure. Distribute Form E (Manager Makes the Difference).

b. Discuss how to define performance expectations and establish as well as maintain high standards for customer service.

c. Explain how to incorporate customer service training into the overall training program.

d. Discuss ways to provide effective feedback and coaching.

D. SKILL DEVELOPMENT

1. PUT YOURSELF IN THE CUSTOMER'S SHOES (GROUP ACTIVITY)

a. Break the group into groups of four. Each group of four will contain two customers, one salesperson, and one manager.

b. Provide each group with a different role playing scenario. Participants will be provided with a description of their role and they should NOT share this information with other members of their subgroup. Give the participants a few minutes to contemplate their role.

c. Remind participants that they are to follow the roles given. They may adapt slightly to improve realism as long as the basic content and emotions stay the same.

d. Allow each group to present their role-play to the class. Observers of each role-play should jot down notes as to what could have been done to improve customer service in the situation at hand. These suggestions will be the topic of the next section.

E. SKILL APPLICATION

1. CUSTOMER SERVICE IN ACTION (GROUP ACTIVITY/DISCUSSION)

a. Invite discussion after each role-play as to how better customer service could have been provided. Certain scenarios will not be obvious, for example when outwardly good service is provided, what could have been the next step to further increase sales. Be sure to refer back to the lists compiled earlier of characteristics of good and bad customer service.

b. Provide the groups of four with open ended scenarios. Only the role of the customer will be provided, those acting as the salesperson and the manager should act as they see fit. The person playing the customer will be provided with the limits to their role.

c. Have the groups perform the new scenarios. This time, however, the customer must be satisfied by the salespeople (the customer's role will state minimum satisfaction levels).

d. When role plays are complete, ask for observations from the group. Discuss the effects of customer service on both short term and long term business, using the role-plays as examples.

2. ALWAYS ROOM FOR IMPROVEMENT (GROUP DISCUSSION)

a. Return to the list of customer service "gripes" that was derived earlier. Using the techniques learned, ask for ways that these customer service problems could be corrected.

b. Next refer to the chart of "favorite stores". Discuss ways that even "favorite" stores can become even more profitable by improving service or adding to an already successful approach.

3. HOW TO BEGIN (GROUP DISCUSSION)

a. Discuss ways to develop a customer service awareness and total approach within an individual company.

b. Ask the group for anticipated barriers to developing a customer service program. Talk about ways to overcome or lessen the effect of these barriers. Emphasize the profitable results of adopting an effective service policy and stress the long term benefits to a company.

c. Stress the importance of tailoring each customer service philosophy to best serve a store's customer base.

F. WRAP UP

1. WHAT'S IN IT FOR YOU? (GROUP DISCUSSION)

a. Ask participants how their jobs would change if an extensive customer service program were to be instituted in their workplace.

b. Describe ways to make daily service tasks more interesting by improving customer service techniques.

c. Describe how improving customer service and selling skills can improve employee morale and contribute to a better sense of self worth. This in turn will lead to a more happy and productive staff.

2. GET STARTED (DISCUSSION)

a. Ask for feedback from the group as to the most important aspects of customer service. Have participants discuss how they plan to use their new knowledge and service techniques in the workplace.

b. Compare discussion results with original program expectations, especially noting differences between the managers and salespeople in the group.

c. Ask for any further comments or concerns. Thank the group for their participation and wish them luck in improving customer service in their companies.

d. Have the group complete a program review form. For those who are interested, have information available regarding further training in the area of customer service.

CUSTOMER SERVICE BASICS

✓ BE COURTEOUS

✓ RECOGNIZE CUSTOMERS PROMPTLY

No one likes to think they are being ignored for any reason. Customers like to feel their presence is known and appreciated. Prompt attention is a form of flattery.

✓ BE ENTHUSIASTIC

You may have seen dozens of customers, but the next customer who walks into your store will only see you once. Welcome this customer with as much energy and enthusiasm as you did when you greeted your first customer of the day. Put yourself in the proper frame of mind before greeting your customer.

✓ SMILE

It's contagious! A friendly smile puts everyone in a much better frame of mind—and a more receptive mood.

✓ BE ATTENTIVE

Give customers your undivided attention. Never make the customer feel they might be interrupting your work. We are not doing them a favor by serving them—they're doing us a favor by giving us their business.

✓ BE CONCERNED

✓ LISTEN

Listening is the only way you can be responsive. It's the only way you can be in the position to ask intelligent questions. Listening also demonstrates to your customers that you consider what they are saying is important.

✓ ASK QUESTIONS

Ask open questions that cannot be answered with a "yes or no". Let your customer do most of the talking. When you ask questions, your customers will feel you have their best interests at heart. Questions will help you confirm what you already know and help you gain new information.

✓ MAKE AN EXTRA EFFORT

Go out of your way to satisfy the customer's needs. Search for the needed items. Call the customer when the merchandise arrives. By demonstrating your willingness to go out of your way to help customers, you're showing them that you appreciate their business and want them to be happy.

✓ HANDLE THE PURCHASE WITH RESPECT

Fold and wrap purchases carefully. Remember, the customer now owns the merchandise. By handling the merchandise with pride and respect, you will build respect in the customer's mind as well.

✓ BE PREPARED

✓ KNOW YOUR MERCHANDISE

Asking the customer to wait because you are unfamiliar with your stock uses up your valuable time and frustrates your customer. Don't be afraid to admit you don't know, but be prepared to find out.

✓ BE WELL INFORMED

Read the care labels on merchandise. Handle the clothes, try thing on. Customers will often go from store to store trying to make a decision. It is the people who are prepared with product knowledge who will eventually get the sale.

✓ PROBLEM SOLVE

After you have identified what it is your customer needs, be ready to offer some alternatives. Many customers rely heavily on salespeople for information and advice, especially when shopping for unfamiliar products. By having a thorough knowledge of the merchandise being sold, you're in a position to help your customer make the best possible buying decision.

✓ BUILD CUSTOMER CONFIDENCE

Speak with confidence about your product. Present your merchandise in a positive manner. The confidence and trust you build when you are able to handle the many questions asked of you about your merchandise will go a long way toward building permanent customers.

APPROACH TECHNIQUES

1) FRIENDLY APPROACH

A verbal approach such as "Hi!" or "How are you today?" or "It's beautiful weather we're having isn't it?" along with a smile and eye contact. This greeting helps establish a friendly, warm atmosphere in your store.

2) SERVICE APPROACH

A verbal approach offering your service to help a customer.

"Let me show you where our ________ are."

"I'll leave you to make your decision and be back in a moment to answer any questions." "May I help you?" is NOT an appropriate service approach because it easily allows the customer a chance to say "NO".

The service approach indicates to the customer that you want to and are willing to help her find the merchandise she is looking for. This greeting can be used when a customer is not looking at a particular item, but needs to be acknowledged.

Your approach should be friendly and sincere; you should be willing to help your customer.

3) MERCHANDISE APPROACH

A verbal comment which states a fact, or in some way gives information about merchandise a customer is looking at or indicating interest in.

"I see you are looking at our cotton cardigans. They are all $10 off the ticketed price today."

"Did you know that particular style is made from pure lambs wool? It really is a terrific value."

A merchandise approach should be used when a customer is looking at a specific item. Focus your attention on what they are looking at and comment on it.

HELPFUL HINTS FOR IMPROVING CUSTOMER SERVICE

1) DO UNTO CUSTOMERS AS YOU WOULD HAVE THEM DO UNTO YOU.

2) GREET CUSTOMERS AS GUESTS WHEN THEY ARRIVE IN YOUR STORE.

3) LEARN TO BE A GOOD LISTENER.

4) LEARN ALL YOU CAN ABOUT THE MERCHANDISE YOU SELL.

5) HANDLE ALL OF YOUR MERCHANDISE WITH PRIDE AND RESPECT.

6) NEVER BE AFRAID TO ADMIT YOU DON'T KNOW, BUT BE PREPARED TO FIND OUT.

7) LET YOUR CUSTOMERS KNOW THAT THEY ARE TOP PRIORITY.

8) IF YOU LEARN YOUR CUSTOMER'S NAME, USE IT.

9) OFFER TO CONSOLIDATE PACKAGES FOR YOUR CUSTOMER.

10) KEEP YOUR MERCHANDISE ORGANIZED AND DISPLAYED NEATLY.

11) LEARN WHERE OTHER AREAS ARE — RESTROOMS, TELEPHONES, RESTAURANTS, ETC.

12) SMILE!!

13) WELCOME CUSTOMERS PROMPTLY.

14) BE PROUD OF WHERE YOU WORK. LEARN ALL YOU CAN ABOUT THE HISTORY OF THE COMPANY, THE PEOPLE INVOLVED, AND THE PHILOSOPHY BY WHICH YOUR STORE OPERATES.

15) RING UP MERCHANDISE QUICKLY AND ACCURATELY.

16) DEMONSTRATE A POSITIVE, ENTHUSIASTIC ATTITUDE AT ALL TIMES.

17) ALWAYS RECOGNIZE HOW IMPORTANT EACH AND EVERYONE OF YOUR CUSTOMERS ARE TO YOU AND YOUR STORE.

THE MANAGER MAKES THE DIFFERENCE

DEFINE PERFORMANCE EXPECTATIONS

Set sales goals each day for each salesperson.

Define expectations related to courtesy, friendliness, and selling skills.

ESTABLISH AND MAINTAIN HIGH STANDARDS FOR CUSTOMER SERVICE

Develop a clear idea about the standard you want and how to best establish and maintain them among your staff.

Just as you are accountable for your business, make sure that your employees know what they're accountable for.

Set a good example at all times to reinforce your standards.

SET ASIDE TIME TO TRAIN AND DEVELOP YOUR STAFF IN CUSTOMER SERVICE SKILLS

Make customer service training as important as any other operational training.

Do not assume that your staff knows what to do in a given situation.

Have refresher courses often - do not let anyone become stale.

PROVIDE FEEDBACK AND COACHING

Provide objective feedback.

Identify causes of poor performance.

Encourage open discussion from sales staff regarding opinions about individual performance.

Provide in-store recognition (salesperson of the week, etc.).

F

Making Your Firm's EAP Work

EAP's And the Role of Supervisors

By
Jennifer L. Johnson

EAP'S AND THE ROLE OF THE SUPERVISORS

Maximize productivity by training your supervisors to know how to identify and refer troubled employees to their EAP. Watch as turnover, absenteeism, tardiness, and accidents decrease. You'll be amazed.

BACKGROUND ON THE PROGRAM

Employee's Assistance Programs were first implemented in corporations as a means of treating alcohol and substance abuse among workers. Although contemporary EAP's still treat these problems, they have expanded to include treatment for a number of other personal problems such as marital discord, finance management, stress, smoking cessation, and relationship difficulties. The costs to a corporation of having an EAP are far outweighed by the benefits of increased productivity. An EAP can facilitate maximum productivity by eliminating the problems affecting performance. This results in decreased absenteeism, tardiness, accidents, and irrational behavior.

However, in order for an EAP to work effectively, the supervisors of a corporation must be responsible for both identifying potentially troubled employees, and referring them to the company's EAP. Unfortunately, this task sounds simpler than it actually is. Most supervisors do not know the signs to look for, or are unsure how to confront the problem once it is apparent. Many supervisors fall into the trap of "diagnosing" their employees. The EAP often does not train the supervisors properly to handle this responsibility. This workshop deals with how a supervisor should handle this responsibility. It uses a series of group activities and discussions to sensitize the supervisors to the issues and skills surrounding a troubled employee and his/her referral. The supervisors will learn how to identify the warning signs, focus on job performance parameters, and conduct a referral interview. They will also learn how their behavior can enable the employee's problem to exacerbate, as well as how to conquer their own facilitating behavior. Help your supervisors learn how to properly assess their employees' behavior, as well as their own!

REASONS TO ATTEND:

✓ Become familiar with the warning signs
✓ Learn how to identify troubled employees
✓ Focus on job performance parameters
✓ Conquer enabling behaviors
✓ Break down the barriers to effective referrals
✓ Improve the referral interview

PROGRAM OUTLINE

TIME	TITLE	METHOD	FORM
	A. OPENERS		
15	Defining Troubled Employees	Discussion	
10	Troubled Employees and Your Firm	Illustration	

B. OVERVIEW: EAP'S AND THE SUPERVISOR:

20	Defining EAP's	Illustration	#1
15	Responsibility of Identification	Group Activity	
20	Problems in Identification	Guided Imagery	
15	Supervisors as Enablers	Illustration	#2

BREAK 10

C. PRACTICUM

30	Assessing Performance	Guided Imagery	#3
20	Knowing the Warning Signs	Group Activity	
TIME	TITLE	METHOD	FORM
30	Categorizing the Situations	Group Activity	#4

LUNCH 50

D. SKILL DEVELOPMENT

20	Documenting Job Performance	Illustration	#5
20	Conquering the Enabler	Illustration	
30	Barriers to Referrals	Group Activity	
20	Conducting the Interview	Discussion	#6

E. SKILL APPLICATION

30	The Identification Process	Group Activity	#7,#8
30	Making It All Work	Group Discussion	

F. WRAP UP

20	Reinforcing Skill Acquisition	Group Discussion	#9

PROGRAM DIRECTIONS

A. OPENERS

1. DEFINING TROUBLED EMPLOYEES (DISCUSSION)

a. Ask the group to think of possible problems an employee may have, then have them share their responses by going around the room in a "whip" fashion.

b. Write the responses down on a flip chart.

c. Comment on non-drug and alcohol related problems. If they have not been mentioned, probe for them from the audience.

2. TROUBLED EMPLOYEES AND YOUR FIRM (ILLUSTRATION)

a. Ask the audience how many of them have directly come in contact with employees with personal problems that have affected their work? Allow enough time with their hands still raised to look around the room and see the commonality of this situation.

b. Comment on the magnitude and frequency of these problems and take the opportunity to introduce yourself, providing a brief background on your experience(s) with EAP's.

c. Have each participant now introduce themselves to the group. Since this workshop is conducted for individual organizations (i.e., not public), only have the participants give their names and departments. It is important that titles are not given, so status does not have as much of an adverse effect on group dynamics.

d. Welcome them to the workshop and highlight the skills you are going to cover, and what the expected outcomes are for them as an audience.

B. OVERVIEW: EAP's

1. DEFINING EAP's (ILLUSTRATION)

a. Provide and discuss the background/history of employee assistance programs.

b. Discuss and highlight the costs of troubled employees to performance and productivity by referring to Form #1 which details associated statistics. This helps establish the credibility and need for EAP's as a source of improving productivity.

2. RESPONSIBILITY OF IDENTIFICATION (GROUP ACTIVITY)

a. Hand each participant a blank 3x5 card. Ask the audience to write down a problem they have had in identifying a troubled employee. Instruct them not to write their names on the cards.

b. Collect the anonymous cards and write the responses on a flip chart.

3. PROBLEMS IN IDENTIFICATION (GUIDED IMAGERY)

a. Divide the audience into groups of three or four.

b. Assign the responses from the flip chart to the groups and have them discuss the consequences of these problems to the identification process.

c. Have a team spokesperson report back to the audience relating the problems they discussed and what implications they thought they would have. Solicit audience feedback and discussion after each team shares their dissertation.

4. SUPERVISOR'S AS ENABLERS (ILLUSTRATION)

a. Discuss the tendency of supervisors to be ruled by their emotions and become "enablers" of their employee's detrimental behavior(s).

b. Refer the audience to Form #2 which is a brief article to read detailing a particular supervisor's path to becoming an enabler.

c. Using this article as background, ask the audience to share their impressions of the situation and how they thought the fictitious supervisor handled the situation. Comment on the dangers of becoming an enabler.

5. FOCUS ON PERFORMANCE (DISCUSSION)

a. Talk about the importance on focusing on job performance to increase the effectiveness of identifying troubled employees.

b. Divide the audience into groups of three or four and have them relate specific job performance behaviors they observed that indicated to them that an employee of theirs had a problem.

c. Have the groups report back to the class and solicit discussion. Comment on the variety of job performance indicators.

C. PRACTICUM

1. ASSESSING PERFORMANCE (GUIDED IMAGERY)

a. Discuss the supervisor's role in focusing on job performance parameters. Explain that they should not try to diagnose their employees; it is the EAP representative's job to refer them to the proper counseling.

b. Refer them to Form #3 which lists a number of fictitious statements iterated by supervisors. Have the participants carefully read these statements and decide individually whether they were diagnoses or job performance indicators.

c. Have the audience discuss each of the statements in this light. Using a flip chart, write down the diagnoses and job performance parameters resulting from the discussion. Keep the pace moving!

2. KNOWING THE WARNING SIGNS (GROUP ACTIVITY)

a. Divide the audience into groups of three or four.

b. Using the job performance parameters indicated from the above exercise, instruct the groups to discuss the parameters in terms of being warning signs of a troubled employee.

3. CATEGORIZING THE SITUATIONS (GROUP ACTIVITY)

a. Keeping the audience in their groups, have them turn to Form #4 which is a problem categorization exercise.

b. Instruct the groups to categorize the listed situations per the instructions as personal problems, warning signs, or performance problems.

c. Review the answers with the audience. Encourage questions and discussion about the categorizations.

D. SKILL DEVELOPMENT

1. DOCUMENTING JOB PERFORMANCE (ILLUSTRATION)

a. Instruct the audience to refer to Form #5 which is a series of performance indicators for a particular employee.

b. On an individual basis, have each person in the audience formally document the performance behaviors in a chronological fashion. This helps stress the importance of documentation for the referral and interview stages.

c. Upon completion by the audience, review the correct documentation and solicit any feedback.

2. CONQUERING THE ENABLER (ILLUSTRATION)

a. Discuss the process of becoming an enabler through the denial/cover-up cycle.

b. Show a film called "Need for Decision" which is approximately 10 minutes long. This film demonstrates how a supervisor deals with a performance problem of an employee who may be an alcoholic.

3. BARRIERS TO REFERRALS (GROUP ACTIVITY)

a. Refer to the film just shown and ask the audience to write down on a Post-It-Note a barrier the supervisor ran into in referring his/her employee to the EAP.

b. Instruct the audience to attach the Post-It-Note on the person's forehead to their left. Randomly divide them into pairs and have them take turns talking to their partner about the barrier they have on their forehead.

c. Discuss with the audience some of the barriers a supervisor encounters to effective referral systems. Solicit feedback as to how their partners helped them resolve their particular barrier.

4. CONDUCTING THE INTERVIEW (DEMONSTRATION)

a. Discuss the referral interview, mentioning confidentiality, employee choice of action, and the need to focus on job performance. Warn the audience that techniques may vary, but no diagnoses should be made.

b. Ask the audience for volunteers to be participants in a referral interview. Four different interviews will be acted out, requiring 7 participants. The interviews to be acted out are listed on Form #6.

c. After the role playing, solicit discussion regarding the supervisor's initial comments and the different reactions of the employees. Reiterate that the most important thing is to emphasize job performance, confidentiality, and an employee choice of action.

E. SKILL APPLICATION

1. THE IDENTIFICATION PROCESS (GROUP ACTIVITY)

a. Instruct the audience to turn to Form #7 which is an exercise to be done in groups of three or four.

b. Explain that this exercise involves ranking the items listed in the order in which they should have occurred. This list includes employee behaviors as well as the supervisor's reactions. This will allow the participants to practice the skills of identifying behaviors, documenting a case for an EAP referral, and conducting a referral interview.

c. Mention that Form #8 can be used as a guideline of problem types and signs.

2. MAKING IT ALL WORK (GROUP DISCUSSION)

a. Review the correct sequence for this exercise.

b. Ask the teams to volunteer for a role-play of the exercise, including the behavior problems, performance deterioration, supervisor turmoil, and referral interview. One or two teams can do the role-play, depending on time constraints.

F. WRAP UP

1. REINFORCING SKILL ACQUISITION (GROUP DISCUSSION)

a. Refer back to the expected outcomes discussed in the beginning of the workshop.

b. Ask the group to comment on the appropriateness o f these outcomes to their working atmosphere.

c. Solicit any remaining questions from the audience.

d. Administer the evaluation questionnaire which is Form #9.

Note: All Forms used in this workshop are attached in the appendices. Credit is given where appropriate.

APPENDICES

FORM #1

What do troubled employees cost productivity?

- ☐ Substance Abuse costs American industry over $100 billion annually, and this cost is increasing!
- ☐ At any given time, approximately 25% of all employees in the workforce are troubled by a personal problem serious enough to impact job performance.
- ☐ Related accidents cost U.S. industry over $32 billion annually in disability payments, worker's compensation, lost productivity, and poor morale.
- ☐ The total U.S. industry had to pay in 1990 for related medical benefits was more than $40 billion.
- ☐ Employees who use alcohol and drugs:
    - ✓ file compensation claims 5 times more often
    - ✓ have 4 times as many on-the-job accidents
    - ✓ are 16 times more likely to be absent
    - ✓ use 3 times as many medical benefits
    - ✓ are late to work 3 times more often than NON-ABUSERS

Do EAP's really help cut costs?

- ☐ Currently, there are between 2,500 to 8,000 EAP's providing services to 12% to 15% of the American workforce.
- ☐ The return on investment of EAP's ranges from 2:1 to 20:1. These savings come from increased worker attendance,

reduced health plan utilization, and increased job productivity.
- ☐ EAP's have cut work-related accidents by 70%.
- ☐ The results of a 5-year Dupont study indicate that the average annual benefit to a company from an alcoholism program alone was more than $400,000.

Sources:
Psychology Today, "Help on the Job", August 1987, p. 48.
US Healthcare *DIRECTIONS*, "Fact Sheet", July 1990.
American Psychologist , "EAP's", December 1989, p. 1488.

Form #2

Jim Raymond has been a foreman of the warehousing and distribution facility for five years. His employees do a variety of jobs including receiving, picking and packing, and shipping of automotive parts. One of Jim's best employees was Marge Finney. However, lately Jim had been noticing a decline in her performance. A number of other employees had been complaining that Marge wasn't pulling her weight and they had to pick up the slack. Jim found this hard to believe, so he assumed Marge was having family problems and it would pass. He told Joe Ryan, another employee, to pitch in for Marge.

A couple of weeks later, Jim was reviewing his attendance records and noticed that Marge had missed 3 days work the last month, all of which were Fridays. Upon closer review, Jim noticed that Marge had also been late 2 days+, and left early on the past few days. Jim mulled this over, but figured the other foremen hadn't had any problems with Marge, so he wouldn't make waves. He called in Joe Ryan and told him to continue to pick up the slack for Marge. He agreed hastily, and stormed out. Jim begins to question his decision. A few days latter, Jim was informed by the general foreman, Jack Fox, that Marge had been caught drinking in the ladies bathroom. Jack said to Jim that surely Jim had noticed a change in Marge's behavior. Apparently, Marge admitted she had been drinking on the job for months. Jack asked Jim why he hadn't done anything.

FORM #3

Supervisors' Comments Regarding their Employees:

1. Harry seems to be acting a bit odd lately. Perhaps he and his wife are having problems.

2. Susan has been coming in late for the past three weeks.

3. George has be overreacting to trivial problems at work.

4. Betsy is repeatedly absent on Mondays.

5. Fred's been looking a bit washed out; he must be hitting the bottle again.

6. Yvette has been taking long breaks frequently during the day.

7. John hasn't been meeting his deadlines for months.

8. Jan must be having problems with her kids again. She seems preoccupied.

9. Joe and Irene used to make such a great team, but now Irene won't pull her weight in the assigned tasks.

10. Allie's moods have been widely fluctuating. I'll bet she's having problems paying her bills since she is always dressed so raggedly.

11. Dan is taking advantage of my department's occasional leniency in starting time. He's been 20 minutes late every day this month.

12. Eileen calls out sick once every week. She is probably still trying to cope with her husband's suicide.

13. I was going to promote Helen, but lately she hasn't

made any of the staff meetings. She hasn't even made any excuses.

14. Dave has been acting belligerent to his co-workers for no apparent reason. He used to be so pleasant.

15. Hank has been in three work-related accidents over the last four weeks.

16. Terrie has seemed so tired lately. She probably has anemia.

17. Don has been turning in less and less work.

18. I have seen Shirley drink at parties. I'll bet she has become an alcoholic and that's why her performance is slipping.

FORM #4

Problem Categorization Exercise

DEFINITIONS:

PERSONAL PROBLEMS - Those problems, disorders, or illnesses which have an effect on the health and behavior of an individual. Responsibility for resolving personal problems rests with the individual. Employees experiencing only these types of problems are not subject to disciplinary action.

WARNING SIGNS - Circumstantial or behavior indicators that the employee may be experiencing a serious problem. Employees exhibiting just warning signs are seldom, if ever, subject to disciplinary action.

PERFORMANCE PROBLEMS - Those work-related behaviors which are unsatisfactory to the corporation. These documentable, quantifiable, and objective problems are the legitimate concern of the corporation. Employees exhibiting such behavior can be subject to disciplinary action.

PROBLEM CATEGORIZATION EXERCISE

Using the above definitions, categorize the following situations. Note that some may fit more than one category

Place a 1) beside personal problems, a 2) beside warning signs, and a 3) beside performance problems.

__personality changes
__missed deadlines
__large number of grievances
__marital discord
__drinking problems
__tardiness
__attitude change
__medical problems
__compulsive gambling
__accidents
__emotional problems
__behavioral changes

__wage garnishments
__use of other's time
__financial problems

__changes in appearance
__drug abuse
__large number of disciplines
__family problems
__excessive absenteeism
__poor work quality
__legal problems
__poor productivity

Source: *HEALTH AND SAFETY*; EAP, UAW-GM Human Resource Center, 1989.

FORM #5

Formal Documentation of Performance

Calendar for Carl:

SUN	MON	TUE	WED	THUR	FRI	SAT
	1	2*	3	4	5	6
7	8	9	10	11	12	13
14	15	16	17*	18	19	20
21	22	23	24	25	26	27
28	29	30				

*Deadlines for Carl.

- ✓ Absent 5th, 12th, 19th, 22nd
- ✓ Late 2nd, 17th, 31st
- ✓ Deadlines not met 2nd, 17th
- ✓ Doctors notes for absence on the 5th
- ✓ No vacation or sick time left as of the 12th
- ✓ Outburst to co-worker over switching breaks
- ✓ Left shift on 1st, 9th, 18th, 26th for no reason
- ✓ Went to lunch on 30th and didn't return
- ✓ Ignored supervisor's directives on 25, 4th

You are Carl's supervisor. You request his time sheets from human resources, and you speak with his co-workers. You suspect Carl may be having some problem that is adversely affecting his job performance. Prepare formal documentation below, in chronological order, so that a possible referral would be made based upon observable performance indicators.

FORM #6

Conducting the Referral Interview

Scenario 1:

The supervisor should have, on the desk, a written list of specific job performance inadequacies to be discussed.

SUPERVISOR: "I wanted to let you know two things. First, your job performance is unsatisfactory. I will not continue to accept the kind of work you are doing."

(Referring to paper on desk) "You have been absent 16 days so far this year - four days more than the total sick leave allowed - and nine of them have been on a Monday. On five occasions during the last two months, I have been unable to locate you during times when you were supposed to be at your desk. You have missed three consecutive deadlines - on the Conway, Small, and Williams jobs."

"Your performance must improve or I will have to take action. That is the first thing I wanted to tell you."

"The second thing is this: As I look at your job performance today, I don't see the same person I was seeing two or three years ago. It occurs to me that some personal or medical problem may be causing this poor job performance." If that's the case, it's none of my business, and I don't want to know about it. But I want you to know that our company now has an employee assistance program which operates on a confidential basis and which can probably provide whatever help you may need to deal with your problem."

"If you want to go to the EAP office and talk with Joe Paragon, who runs the program, and if you are willing to follow whatever course of action he recommends, then I don't think you and I will have any further difficulty."

VARIOUS REACTIONS

Scenario 2:

EMPLOYEE: "Are you trying to tell me that I have some sort of problem and that I need to see a counselor? What are you trying to say? Are you trying to tell me that I have a drinking problem? Well let me tell you, I'm no alcoholic, and no one can call me that!"

SUPERVISOR: "Whether or not you have a personal problem is something for you and Joe Paragon to determine, if you decide to see him. All I'm saying is that you have a job performance problem which must be corrected. If you have a personal problem, you are entitled to get help for it. If your poor performance is deliberate, then we have no choice but to invoke the discipline. But we must offer you this choice. It's a matter of management policy."

Scenario 3:

EMPLOYEE: "So you want me to go see Joe Paragon, is that it?"

SUPERVISOR: "It's not what I want that's important. It's what you want. All I want is for your performance to improve, which has not happened. Whether you go to the EAP for help is entirely up to you."

Scenario 4:

EMPLOYEE: "So you're going to terminate me if I don't go. Is that it?"

SUPERVISOR: "I don't think you understand what I've been saying. At this point, your poor job performance has earned you a termination. However, according to company policy, you're entitled to one more chance. We are offering you confidential help in an effort to help save your job. If you insist on termination, that is your privilege and we will oblige you. But the decision to terminate will not be ours, it will be yours!"

SOURCE:
The EAP Manual, William S. Dunkin, National Council on Alcoholism, 1982.

FORM #7

The following is a list of employee behaviors, employee job performance attributes, supervisor responses, and supervisor techniques. List the order in which these events theoretically should have occurred. For this exercise, the employee is Roberta Fleck, and the supervisor is Tom Matthews. Note: Some items on this list could occur concurrently.

_____ Tom thinks Roberta could never be a bad performer.

_____ Roberta verbally abuses her co-workers.

_____ Roberta begins taking extended breaks.

_____ Tom assigns Roberta's work to another employee.

_____ Roberta calls out sick more often.

_____ Tom asks Roberta if there's a problem.

_____ Tom begins to document Roberta's performance.

_____ Roberta overreacts to co-worker's requests.

_____ Tom begins to wonder about Roberta's work.

_____ Tom receives complaints about Roberta's work.

_____ Roberta complains about constant fatigue.

_____ Roberta is caught daydreaming off and on.

_____ Roberta is involved in 4 work-related accidents.

_____ Tom excuses Roberta's missed deadline.

_____ Roberta becomes reclusive and mistrusts others.

_____ Tom begins to be angry with himself.

_____ Tom sets up a referral interview with Roberta.

_____ Roberta only completes 1/3 of her work.

_____ Roberta appears tense and anxious.

_____ Tom feels betrayed by Roberta.

_____ Tom recommends the EAP to Roberta.

_____ Roberta explodes at the interview.

_____ Roberta seeks help through the company's EAP.

_____ Roberta's productivity begins to improve.

FORM #9

SIGNS OF TROUBLED EMPLOYEES

✓ PHYSICAL SIGNS
- ☐ Tension headaches
- ☐ Fatigue
- ☐ Indigestion
- ☐ Interrupted sleep

✓ PSYCHOLOGICAL SIGNS
- ☐ Nervousness
- ☐ Anxiousness
- ☐ Irritability
- ☐ Depression
- ☐ Anger
- ☐ Withdrawal
- ☐ Reduced Motivation
- ☐ Daydreaming
- ☐ Loss of memory
- ☐ Loss of sense of humor

✓ BEHAVIORAL SIGNS
- ☐ Reduced work quality
- ☐ Reduced productivity
- ☐ Mistrust of others
- ☐ Outbursts of temper
- ☐ Missing deadlines
- ☐ Absenteeism
- ☐ Increased accidents
- ☐ Indecisiveness

FORM #9

EAP Workshop Evaluation Form

Rate the following on a range of 1 to 5 based on whether you agree (5) or disagree (1) with each of the statements:

_____1. New skills were learned or sharpened.

_____2. Participation was dispersed among the group.

_____3. Group activities were useful in the practice and transfer of skills.

_____4. The trainer was objective.

_____5. There was ample opportunity for questions and feedback.

_____6. The skills learned can be used on the job.

_____7. The presentation of content and skill was thought-provoking.

_____8. The trainer was credible.

_____9. The group dynamics fostered trust and openness.

_____10. The group seemed to grow together as the workshop progressed.

_____11. Additional workshops on this topic would be useful.

_____12. The information was presented understandably and at a reasonable pace.

_____OVERALL SCORE

G

"SO YOU'RE INTERESTED IN FRANCHISING...."

By:
Brian Bitner Holt

OWN YOUR OWN BUSINESS

There is no doubt that franchising is one of the most popular ways for entrepreneurs to start their own business.

ABOUT THE TRAINING PROGRAM

Franchising now accounts for more than one third of all retail sales, and offers employment opportunities to over 6 million people. The number of franchised units in operation expands at a rate of 6% annually. And as more and more franchising opportunities arise, the growth of franchising will continue well into the future.

This program will introduce you to the franchising concept, help you assess if franchising is an appropriate choice for you, and offer suggestions on how to choose and evaluate a franchise.

THE KEY BENEFITS OF ATTENDANCE

- ✓ Gain a full understanding of what franchising is and how it works
- ✓ Learn the advantages and disadvantages of franchising
- ✓ Determine if you are a good candidate for franchising
- ✓ Assess an industry for future growth
- ✓ Select a franchise of interest to you
- ✓ Learn how to investigate a franchisor

PROGRAM OUTLINE

Time	Title	Method
	A. OPENERS	
20	Obstacles to Starting Your Own Business	Sub-Group Discussion
	B. AN INTRODUCTION TO FRANCHISING	
10	Franchising Defined	Case Study
20	Advantages and Disadvantages of Franchising	Sub-Group Discussion
10	Determine If You're a Good Candidate for Franchising	Self-Test
	BREAK 10	
	C. THE PROCESS OF SELECTING A FRANCHISE	
20	Selecting an Industry and a Franchise	Panel Discussion

D. EVALUATING A FRANCHISE

10	Comparison Shopping	Discussion
10	Investigate the Franchisor	Discussion
20	Seeking Professional Help	Sub-Group Discussion

PROGRAM DIRECTIONS

At the time of registration for the seminar, each participant will be asked to fill out a brief questionnaire. Give participants a name tag to place on their clothing when they enter the room. All supplemental materials mentioned in the workshop (the registration form, case study, self test, and an example of a franchise comparison table) are included in the Workshop Resources and Instructor's Materials section at the back of this packet.

A. OPENERS

1. OBSTACLES TO STARTING YOUR OWN BUSINESS (SUB-GROUP DISCUSSION)

a. Welcome everyone by making the statement "Many people dream of opening their own business, but their dream may be restrained by obstacles."

b. Instruct participants to break into discussion groups of five to seven people. These discussion groups will re-form throughout the seminar to discuss various subjects. The first group assignment will be to develop a listing of obstacles that keep a person from starting a business.

c. After about ten minutes, have each group report its list and consolidate responses on a flip chart in the front of the room.

d. Introduce yourself and describe your experience as a seminar leader and group facilitator for this particular topic.

e. Discuss, in general, how franchising could overcome the list of obstacles. Introduce the idea that although franchising can help overcome certain obstacles, and has a higher success rate than non-franchised businesses, it is not the right choice for everyone and is no guarantee to the success of a business.

f. Take a moment to explain to participants that this program will introduce them to the franchising concept, help them assess if franchising is an appropriate choice for them, and offer them suggestions on how to choose and evaluate a franchise.

g. Also explain that by the end of this program, they will have gained a full understanding of what franchising is and how it works, and learned the advantages and disadvantages of franchising. They will also be able to: determine if they are a good candidate for franchising, assess an industry for future growth, select a franchise of interest to them, and sufficiently investigate a franchisor.

B. AN INTRODUCTION TO FRANCHISING

1. FRANCHISING DEFINED (CASE STUDY)

a. Participants read the case.

2. ADVANTAGES AND DISADVANTAGES OF FRANCHISING (SUB-GROUP DISCUSSION)

a. Have participants re-assemble into the same discussion groups as before. Instruct half of the groups to compile a list of advantages of franchising with McDonald's based on the case study they just read.

b. Solicit the groups' response and write them on a flip chart.

c. Make sure the following points are covered and discussed.

1) Advantages

- ☐ Recognized name
- ☐ Established reputation
- ☐ Proven marketing concept and expertise
- ☐ Training
- ☐ Detailed operating manual
- ☐ On site start-up assistance
- ☐ Benefits of continuing market/product research

2) Disadvantages:

- ☐ Need to conform to standard operating procedures
- ☐ The inability to make changes readily
- ☐ The contractual obligation to pay ongoing royalty

3. DETERMINING IF YOU'RE A GOOD CANDIDATE FOR FRANCHISING (SELF-TEST)

a. Hand out the self-evaluation test and have participants complete the test.

b. After five minutes, review the test answers and open the floor for questions.

C. THE PROCESS OF SELECTING A FRANCHISE

1. SELECTING AN INDUSTRY AND A FRANCHISE (PANEL DISCUSSION)

a. Explain to the participants that they must first select an industry that interests them before selecting a specific franchise to open. An industry is a general business field such as the printing industry, fast food industry . . .

b. From the registration forms, pre-select five participants who can act as panelists representing different industries that have franchise opportunities in them. Have panelists give an assessment of their industry's growth potential and any pertinent comments on franchises that they have investigated. Open the discussion to questions from the floor.

D. EVALUATING A FRANCHISE

1. FRANCHISE COMPARISON SHEET (DISCUSSION)

a. Solicit from the participants what data they feel is important in evaluating a franchise opportunity. Be sure the list includes:

The number of years in business

The number of years franchising

The number of franchised units

The number of company-owned units

Franchise and start-up costs

b. Solicit from the participants where they feel this data may be obtained. Be sure to include:

Company franchise kit

Better Business Bureau

Magazines such as Entrepreneur

c. With the help of the group, create a franchise comparison table on a flip chart (see example in Workshop Resources section at the back of this packet).

2. INVESTIGATE THE FRANCHISOR (DISCUSSION)

a. Solicit from participants ways to investigate franchisors. Write responses on a flip chart. Make sure the discussion includes:

Obtaining and reading disclosure, financial statements, and the franchise agreement

Obtaining from the franchisor information on the experience of personnel, turnover, rate of failure among franchisees, and franchisee terminations.

Consumer litigation, financial statements of company-owned units, and the states in which franchisor is registered to sell franchises.

A list of current franchisees you may contact to ask the following questions:

Assessment of franchisor's disclosure document

Critical analysis of franchisor's financial projections

Detailed history of problems with franchisor

Assessment of training and ongoing help

Information on any special "deals" that have been made with other franchisees.

3. SEEKING PROFESSIONAL HELP (SUB-GROUP DISCUSSION)

a. Re-assemble discussion groups. Assign half the groups to list questions and points to be covered with an attorney, and the other half of the groups will list points and questions to be covered with an accountant.

b. Re-assemble and list group findings on a flip chart. Make sure the lists include:

For an attorney:

- ☐ Do you know franchising laws, state laws, and bankruptcy laws?
- ☐ Could you advise me on organizing my company if necessary?
- ☐ Could you outline the advantages of incorporating, being a sole proprietorship or a partner?

For an accountant:

- ☐ Can I afford to buy the franchise?
- ☐ Please work out a pro forma showing the costs involved in buying and operating the franchise.
- ☐ Project sales and expense projection.
- ☐ Design a cash flow projection and operating budget
- ☐ Discuss various financing options

WORKSHOP RESOURCES AND INSTRUCTOR'S MATERIALS

FRANCHISING WORKSHOP INFORMATION FORM

Name: ____

Most Recent Work Experience:

____

Have you ever been in business for yourself?

_____Yes _____No

Have you ever owned a franchise?

_____Yes _____No

Would you share your experience with the group?

_____Yes _____No

What are the three (3) most important points you want to get out of this workshop?

1. ______________________________________
2. ______________________________________
3. ______________________________________

CASE STUDY McDONALD'S

Dick and Maurice McDonald started their business careers when they decided to buy a small movie theater in Glendora, California in 1931. Dick remembers that running that theater was the struggle of their lives. "With the Depression, small businesses were up against the wall." They noticed there was one place in town making a lot of money, and it was a hot dog stand.

They held on to the theater, saved up the money, and opened a small drive-in in Arcadia, California in 1937. The first McDonald's, a tiny drive-in that sold hot dogs, not hamburgers, did well, and the McDonald brothers decided the time had come to open another location.

Because the Arcadia location experienced a slow down in sales during the non-racing season, the brothers decided to sell if they found a better location. Finally, in 1940, they opened a much grander drive-in complete with car hops. In 1948, they decided some changes had to be made. They had trouble finding efficient car hops. There were problems with drunken dishwashers. So they got rid of all the dishes, glassware and silverware, and used paper plates and plastic utensils. They decided to start a self-service eating spot. Instead of the large menu they used to have, they decided to just serve hamburgers, drinks, and french fries. Some of their customers told them they were losing their minds and they would never patronize McDonald's if they had to wait on themselves — especially if they were only going to be served hamburgers.

But the restaurant's lightening-fast service caught on as did the low prices. The brothers had achieved their goal: their clientele changed from teenagers to working-class families. "Women, in particular, began coming to their restaurant and they brought their children with them. They became the backbone of the business." In 1951, the McDonald brothers made a trial run in the franchise field, and the rest is history.

As the McDonald franchise system grew, protected areas were sold, service and distribution centers were established, standardized menus were developed, and McDonald's "Hamburger University" was formed to train franchisees in the hands-on management of the business. McDonald's continues to stay in tune with the changing eating habits of a more health-conscious America by introducing pre-packaged salads and low-fat hamburgers.

The McDonald's story shows that through franchising, a person with little or no experience in the fast food industry can buy an established business format and operate the restaurant in a protected territory.

Besides the training at "Hamburger University", McDonald's provides franchisees with detailed operating manuals, a site selection analysis, start-up assistance, and a detailed explanation of expected start-up costs. For simplicity, the menu, building design, equipment layout, marketing programs, and operational practices are standardized with no variations allowed. McDonald's charges a franchising fee and an ongoing royalty. Franchising with McDonald's means that you are in business for yourself, but not by yourself.

DETERMINING IF YOU'RE A GOOD CANDIDATE FOR FRANCHISING

1. Will I follow directions, even when I disagree with the franchisor?

2. Am I self motivated?

3. Am I willing to work hard?

4. Will I be an "on the job" worker in the franchise?

5. Do I have the experience to go into business?

6. Am I adaptable and trainable?

7. Can I afford to get into franchising?

Workshop Leader's Guide

1. Will I follow directions, even when I disagree with the franchisor?

If you're the type of person who likes to tinker with things, constantly experiment and make changes, don't go into franchising.

2. Am I self motivated?

People who succeed in franchising have the discipline to get the job done outside the structure of 9 to 5 and even when they're discouraged.

3. Am I willing to work hard?

Your franchise name helps bring business to you, but you have to work hard to keep it.

4. Will I work in the franchise?

The absentee owner does not have a good record in franchising.

5. Do I have the experience to go into business?

People go with a franchise because they don't have specific business experience and they need to use and build on someone else's business experience.

6. Am I adaptable and trainable?

If you're not experienced in business but you're willing to learn, can you learn" ? Ask friends, family and advisors "am I adaptable" and "can I learn?".

7. Can I afford to get into franchising?

Get a professional opinion. Consult with an accountant, your local bank, or the Small Business Administration.

H

DESIGNING PUBLICATIONS WITH IMPACT

By:
Gregory M. Yesko & Associates

INCREASE THE COMMUNICATION VALUE OF PUBLICATIONS AND DOCUMENTS BY APPLYING FUNDAMENTAL PRINCIPLES OF LAYOUT, DESIGN, AND DESKTOP PUBLISHING.

About the Training Program

Written communication is a basic element of business. Often the content of the written message is detracted from by publication "noise" such as poor layout, design, or typography. The resulting lack of readability and focus leads to many important external publications being discarded at a significant cost to the firm. There is also a similar cost with internal written communication such as reports, proposals, internal information publications, etc.

The design and layout of important publications and documents either enhances the message or detracts from it. An old cliché states that "How you say something is as important as what you say." This is true with written communication,. The style of the presentation within the document is also sending an important message.

There has been a proliferation of computer hardware and software that has grown with the desktop publishing industry. Laser printers, optical scanners, and high speed computer systems have all become more available as competition within the industry has reduced prices. Most firms have an internal capability today to produce publications and documents of the highest quality. But the hardware and software components alone do not create high quality documents no more than a canvas and a palate of paints create good art without a skilled artist. This workshop will provide you with the skill to create documents and publications with impact. Learn how to maximize the content of the written communication by applying the fundamental principles of layout and design. Learn how to increase readability and document focus by applying the tools of desktop publishing.

Key Benefits of Attendance

- ✓ Improve the impact and effectiveness of written communication
- ✓ Reduce distracters by following functional design "rules"
- ✓ Increase the quality of documents and publications
- ✓ Learn to apply the tools of desktop publishing to accentuate content
- ✓ Critique layouts of sample documents for improvement content
- ✓ Apply the learned concepts through a hands-on practicum

PROGRAM OUTLINE

TIME	TITLE	METHOD	FORM
A. OPENERS			
15	"I know bad art when I see it!"	Guided Imagery	

10	Who is in the group and why	Discussion	

B. Overview: Designing Publications with Impact

10	The message and the messenger	Illustration	
10	Understanding the need for quality	Discussion	
15	Design: Help or Hindrance	Discussion	
10	Definition of Desktop Publishing	Illustration	

Break 10

C. The Components of Desktop Publishing

15	Computer Components /Capabilities	Discussion	A
15	Software Capabilities/ Limitations	Discussion	B
15	Identify the Tools of Design	Illustration	C

D. Understanding Typefaces

15	Identify the families of typefaces	Illustration	D
15	Understanding effects of selection	Discussion	E
15	The purpose of typeface elements	Illustration	

Lunch for 1 Hour

E. Understanding Graphic Elements of Design/Newsletter Components

10	Use of the impact of photos and line art	Illustration	
10	The use of lines and spot color	Illustration	
7	The elements of a newsletter	Illustration	

8	The flow of thc reader's perception	Discussion	
10	Identify key areas from samples	Discussion	

F. The "Rules" of Functional Design

5	Avoidance of clutter	Illustration	F
5	Understanding balance and imbalance	Illustration	G
5	Consistency	Illustration	
10	Review of examples	Discussion	
20	Critiques of sample layouts	Group Activity	

G. Practical Exercise in Design of a Publication Front Page

5	Introduction of the exercise	Illustration	
30	Practicum i nvolving	Group Activity	H, I

1. Placement of key components on the page
2. Place photos and line art on the layout
3. Place the body test, select typefaces
4. Complete the layout

10	Critique sample layouts	Discussion

H. Review of Training/Solicitation of Feedback

10	Review highlights	Discussion	
10	Distribute course critique	Discussion	J

Program Directions

A. Openers

1. "I know bad art when I see it!" (Guided Imagery)

a. Begin with a guided imagery scene. Have the participants envision themselves as the CEO of a major multinational corporation and they are about to receive a briefing on a major proposal regarding expansion into new markets. Several members of the board of directors are in attendance at the briefing. The importance of this briefing cannot be understated.

b. Put on the overhead a sample of a proposal paper that violates many of the rules of layout and design. The sample is cramped, hardly readable and has little focus. Have the participants share their impressions. Write one word adjectives on the blackboard or on a flip chart.

c. Now put on the overhead a sample that is sharply designed and follows the fundamentals of layout principles.

d. Have the participants share the differences in their perceptions of the two proposals and their perceptions about the preparer.

2. Who is in the group and why? (Group Activity)

a. Introduce yourself and describe your experience as a seminar leader and group facilitator for this topic.

b. Have each participant introduce themselves and discuss their reason for being at the training today.

c. Probe the reasons of those who seem highly motivated as well as those who may be assigned to the program by their firm. List this on a flip chart.

d. Solicit program expectations and list them on the flip chart as well as for use during the program wrap-up.

B. Overview: Designing Publications with Impact

1. The Message and the Messenger (Illustration)

a. Describe the nature of nonverbal communication as it relates to the perception of a person receiving a message.

b. Give 2 or 3 examples of nonverbal gestures that are opposed to or detract from the message being given. Have participants offer examples.

c. Draw the parallel between verbal and written communication.

d. Explain how design style and presentation send a message as well as the content.

2. Understanding the Need for Quality (Discussion)

a. Ask participants to describe an important document or publication they were responsible for.

b. Have the participants describe the various pressures for the highest quality possible. What are the sources of these pressures?

c. Try to solicit examples of both external and internal publications.

d. Explain the importance of quality in terms of individual professionalism and in terms of corporate culture and image.

3. Design: Help or Hindrance (Discussion)

a. Ask participants to describe a publication or document in which they felt the design really augmented the message. In what ways did it do this?

b. Ask participants to describe a publication or document in which they felt the design hindered the message content and why?

c. Explain how design considerations can impair or augment the content of the written communication.

Give some blatant examples. Compare the *Wall Street Journal* with *USA Today*.

4. Definition of Desktop Publishing (Illustration)

a. Describe the definition of desktop publishing as the combination of typestyles, images, art, color, photo and textual content to create documents or publications using computer assets.

b. Give a brief overview of the development of the desktop publishing industry.

C. The Components of Desktop Publishing

1. Computer Components/Capabilities (Discussion)

a. Have the participants describe some of the computer systems that they work with.

b. Have them describe the capabilities and limitations of these systems.

c. Describe the industry standard desktop publishing system components and the capabilities and limitations.

2. Software Capabilities/Limitations (Discussion)

a. Have the participants describe the software they are using for desktop publishing.

b. Have them describe the capabilities and limitations of the software.

c. Describe the industry standard software with the capabilities and limitations.

3. Identify the Tools of Design (Illustration)

a. Discuss the components of desktop publishing as tools of design.

b. Show examples on the overhead of how various tools can be used.

D. Understanding Typefaces

1. Identify the Families of Typefaces (Illustration)

a. Show examples of the major families of typefaces on the overhead. Distribute handout D.

b. "Zoom in" and show the distinction between serified and sans serif fonts.

c. Describe what the major typefaces are normally used for.

2. Understanding Effects of Selection (Discussion)

a. Show an example of a page layout on the overhead.

b. Show the same layout with a drastically different typeface.

c. Have the participants share their impressions about the effect of the typeface change. Show both slides again.

d. Explain how typefaces have an "image" and how they create an effect on the page.

3. The Purpose of Typeface Elements (Illustration)

a. Explain the use of headlines, cutlines, captions, and the reasons for multiple typefaces on the page.

b. Show samples on the overhead of multiple typefaces and their use.

E. Understanding Graphic Element of Design/Newsletter Components

1. Use of the Impact of Photos and Line Art (Illustration)

a. Show samples on the overhead of layouts that were greatly augmented by photos and line art.

b. Have participants describe the visual impact.

c. Show layout samples that could have used art but did not.

Compare and contrast the difference.

2. The Use of Lines and Spot Color (Illustration)

a. Show sample layouts which effectively used lines and spot color.

b. Show examples of layouts where lines and spot color could have improved the impact.

3. The Elements of a Newsletter (Illustration)

a. Show an overhead of a sample newsletter front page.

b. Identify the various components, i.e. masthead, flag, etc.

c. Describe the purpose of the various components.

4. The Flow of the Reader's Perception (Discussion)

a. Show a sample layout and have participants describe where their attention went first on the page.

b. Describe the natural flow of the reader's perception based on the research model (i.e. primary optical area, terminal area, etc.).

5. Identify Key Areas from Samples (Discussion)

a. Show samples on the overhead.

b. Have participants point out the key areas of the newsletter and the "attention getters".

F. The Rules of Functional Design

1. Avoidance of Clutter (Illustration)

a. Show examples of clutter in various designs.

b. Have participants describe contributors to clutter.

2. Understanding Balance and Imbalance (Illustration)

a. Show an example of an imbalance design (Poor).

b. Show the same design with balance.

c. Show an example of dynamic imbalance (Intentional) that is effective. Describe its use as a design tool.

3. Consistency (Illustration)

a. Show a layout with consistency problems.

b. Show the same layout with the corrected problems.

c. Compare and contrast.

4. Review of Examples (Illustration)

a. Show a number of samples on the overhead.

b. Have participants critique the samples.

c. Solicit feedback and discussion.

5. Group Critiques (Group Activity)

a. Break the group up into groups of 5.

b. Distribute samples of flawed layouts.

c. Have the groups come up with corrections to improve the layouts.

d. Have a group spokesman/spokeswoman present their solutions.

G. Practicum in the Design of a Publication Front Page

1. Introduction of the Exercise (Illustration)

a. Distribute the handout materials.

b. Describe the goals and procedure for the exercise.

2. Practicum (Group Activity)

a. In the same groups as before, have each group design a layout from scratch, given the components of the finished product on a separate sheet and a blank layout grid.

b. Groups must place the following key components: photos, line art, body test, headlines, lines, boxes, and captions.

c. Groups must select various typefaces.

3. Critique Group Layouts (Discussion)

a. Have groups present their layouts.

b. Solicit feedback.

H. Review of Training/Solicitation of Feedback

1. Review Highlights (Discussion)

a. Review the highlights of the training.

2. Distribute Course Critique/Solicit Feedback (Discussion)

a. Distribute course critique form and solicit feedback from the group.

b. Compare feedback against expectations given at the beginning of the training.

c. Collect the feedback forms.

d. Wish everyone the best of luck and offer continued assistance if anyone would like it.

Notes on Forms:

Form A Fact Sheet on Computer Components

Form B Fact Sheet on Desktop Publishing Software

Form C Fact Sheet on Design Tools

Form D Sample Typefaces

Form E Sample Layouts with Various Typefaces

Form F Sample Cluttered Layouts

Form G Samples of Balance/Imbalance

Form H Components of Practicum Exercise

Form I Blank Layout Grid

Form J Feedback Critique Form

I

HUMOR: THE NEW MANAGERIAL TOOL

By:
Pamela Lieb

Humor, like a feather in the wind, will sail gently earthward. Just when we think its life is exhausted, it will float lightly up and away, propelled by an unexpected breath of air, changing everything. Unpredictable humor can ease our embarrassment, calm our anger, and relax our tensions.

Is there a correlation between laughter and productivity? As an effective stress reliever, laughter improves both physical health and the body's immunological ability. People with a good sense of humor are better at solving problems, dealing with people, and generally are better workers.

Fun relieves tension and improves concentration, it counteracts boredom and reduces personal conflicts. The enjoyable interaction with co-workers reduces the need to get social support outside the work place. A group of employees that enjoys and supports each other is more productive. So that putting a measure of fun and humor into the work place can increase employee loyalty, productivity, and enthusiasm for the job, which in turn can help a company deal with increasing competition and demands for productivity. A recent Carnegie-Mellon University study finds that employees don't trust management - layoffs and takeovers have "shredded the implicit social contract between employer and employee". If management is to re-create the bond and mold the competitive work forces they need, they'll have to shred some antiquated notions. One of them is that camaraderie and hearty guffaws have no place in the workplace. Humor has emerged as a management tool for the new age manager, in contrast to the industrial era's tool of control and intimidation.

The potential of employees can best be utilized in an atmosphere of open communication. Companies that use a management-by-fun strategy do not believe that levity translates into unproductive time. On the contrary, periodic 2-5 minute "joy breaks" not only inhibit burnout, they also increase energy, and improve mental health. Humor appears to stimulate the right hemisphere of the brain, allowing people to think more broadly and to see complex and otherwise elusive relationships. Humor relaxes people, therefore, training and/or negotiations can proceed much more smoothly when people are relaxed. People respond better to criticism when they are in a good mood. It may be one of the most powerful tools managers have for motivating staff, stimulating creativity, and improving job performance.

Studies have shown that employees who have fun at work were less likely to be late or absent. Job turnover was lower and motivation and productivity were higher. Realizing this, many managers are attempting to instill fun in the workplace and are learning how to relax and enjoy their employees.

The aim of the humor consultants is not to convert workers to comics, but to present humor as a way of coping with the many problems of life and the stress of constant change. Workshops and seminars have been developed to instruct people how to use humor productively.

Most people can't tell a joke to save their lives, but everyone can learn to use humor more effectively. The secret is to develop a style and take the time to practice. Managers can build upon an existing set of skills by cultivating a sense of humor and employing it in the workplace.

Here are several suggestions to developing humor: The first step is to build a comedy collection. It is best to find 25 jokes, asides, or stories that are funny and jot them down in a notebook. After looking at them to see if there are more stories than jokes, adapt a few to a comfortable speech pattern and develop a tone that is natural. It is recommended to look for material from daily experiences but not needle anyone in particular. Know and understand the punch line. Keep the material short, tell it slowly, and always wait for others to laugh first. When attempting humor, managers must remain within their comfort level to be effective. They can utilize analogies to introduce humor, and poking fun at competitors often is effective. When injecting humor, managers should always consider questions of mood, taste, and context. Humor should be used within the context of the corporation and tied to company concerns. Making organizations fun may actually make them stronger.

The critical elements that lead to experiencing fun at work are: 1. people's personal intentions; 2. the organization's culture; and 3. management behaviors. Creating a workplace that if fun begins with a commitment from management to make the organization a more enjoyable place to be. Studies show that company sponsored events can create an atmosphere of fun, particularly ones that offer food. Sports, parties, lunches, and dinners send a message to employees that they are cared about and valued.

Many managers use humor to form a connection with their workers. They can humanize themselves with self-deprecating humor; it comforts the employees to know that the manager shares their faults and weaknesses. Ways that humor can be used in the workplace include: 1. to illustrate points and create the emotional responses that help increase interest, learning and retention of key idea; 2. to help individuals view themselves and others more objectively; 3. to increase spontaneity and flexibility of thinking; 4. to illuminate the positive aspects of undesired changes and help employees tolerate the ambiguity and uncertainty that accompanies change; and 5. to help build rapport, trust, and acceptance of diversity among team members.

Humor can be used successfully even if a person does not know how to "tell a joke". People should take their work seriously without taking themselves so seriously. Humor does not have to be spontaneous to be funny. Good humor is memorable and when the humor arises from the teaching point, trainees recall the message. A manager must be careful when using humor, civil litigation can arise due to joking behavior with racist, sexist, or other overtones. Arbitrators usually support disciplinary action taken against the perpetrators of horseplay when it causes a disruption in the workplace, damages property, poses a safety hazard, or represents malicious intent. Using humor may be scary at first, but it pays off in the long run. People generally like people who can make them laugh. They feel more at ease with them and they are more likely to work with them. If it is true that there are fewer quality people coming along, it is a sure bet they'll wind up working where the smiles are.

Workshop Components

OVERVIEW: CORPORATE CULTURES

- ☐ Identifying types of cultures
- ☐ Examining relationships between supervisory and subordinate personnel
- ☐ Enhancing production through the use of laughter

COMMUNICATION PROBLEMS

- ☐ Employee concerns on new training
- ☐ Barriers to effective listening
- ☐ Extending length of retention times

COMMUNICATION SKILLS

- ☐ Providing methods of effective feedback
- ☐ Using non-verbal behavior

BUILDING HUMOR SKILLS

- ☐ Becoming flexible and confident
- ☐ Process for material development
- ☐ Developing a style
- ☐ Identifying a comfort level

RESULTING FACTORS

- ☐ Emphasizing strengths through style
- ☐ Developing loyalties
- ☐ Building team effort
- ☐ Maintaining balance - Humor/Org. culture
- ☐

WORKSHOP FORMAT

This program is designed to examine the use of humor as a Managerial Tool in a tense or competitive environment. The workshop will allow Managers to discover what type of humor is natural and comfortable for them to use within their Corporate setting. They will be able to utilize these skills to bring out the best in their employees and to work towards improving employee relations. Concepts and skills will be reinforced by way of role plays, group exercises, and style assessment profiles.

BIBLIOGRAPHY

Bardwick, J. *Danger In The Comfort Zone* . AMACOM, New York:1991 .

Bazerman, M. *Managerial Decision Making* . John Wiley & Sons, Inc., New York: 1990.

Batten, J. *Tough Minded Leadership* . AMACOM, New York:1989.

Blake, R., Mouton, J., & Allen, R. *Spectacular Teamwork,* John Wiley & Sons, Inc., New York, 1987.

Brinkerhoff, R. & Gill, S. "Managing the Total Quality of Training", *Human Resource Development Quarterly* , Vol 3, Summer, 1992.

Caffarella, R. *Program Development And Evaluation Resource Book For Trainers.* John WIley & Sons, Inc., New York: 1989.

Cannie, J. K. *Keeping Customers For Life* . AMACOM, New York: 1991.

Capellupo, J. and Chernick, L. *The Defense Industrial Base in a Peacetime Environment.* Panel discussion presented at the

Naval Reserve Supply Corps Readiness Workshop, May 30-31, 1992. St. Louis , Missouri.

Davidson, J.P. 1993 Presidential Award for Quality. Command response memorandum dated January 26, 1993, The Aviation Supply Office, Phila. , PA.

Dobyns, L. "Ed Deming Wants Big Changes, and He Wants Them Fast." *Smithsonian* , August, 1990.

Drucker, P. F. *Managing For The Future* . Butterworth-Heinimann, Oxford,England: 1992.

Galagan, P. "How To Take On Top Management and Win", *Training and Development* , ASTD, June, 1992.

Galagan, P. "Training Keep the CUtting Edge Sharp for the Anderson Companies." *Training and Development* , January, 1993.

Gilbert, M. *Churchill, A Life*. Henry Holt and Company, New York: 1992.

Houston, P. "Timmberrr! *Business Month* , December, 1989.

Hunt, V.D. *Quality In America* . Business ONE Irwin, Homewood, Illinois: 1992

Joward, J. D. "TQL Forum: The Only Way Ahead", *Proceedings* , The Naval Institute Press, June, 1992.

Kanter, D. & Mirvis, P. *The Cynical Americans,* Josey-Bass, San Francisco: 1989.

Kearns, D. "Leadership Through Quality." *Executive* , May, 1990.

Kreps, G. *Organizational Communication.* Longman, 1990: New York.

Mali, P. *Managing By Objectives.* John WIley & Sons, Inc., 1972: New York.

McCormack, S. "TQM: Getting It Right the First Time", *Training and Development* , ASTD, June, 1992.

Mintzberg, H. "The Manager's Job: Folklore and Fact." *Harvard Business Review* , March/April, 1990.

Napier, R. & Gershenfeld, M., *Making Groups Work* , Houghton Mifflin, Boston: 1983.

Niehouse, O. L. "Job Satisfaction: How to Motivate Today's Workers." *Supervisory Management* , February, 1986.

Oliver, D. "Persona". *Proceedings* , January, 1993.

Packard, D. The President's Blue Ribbon Commission on Defense Management- "A Quest for Excellence". Government Printing Office, Washington, D.C: June, 1986.

Peters, T. &Waterman, R. *in Search Of Excellence* . Warner books, New York: 1982.

Provus, M. *Discrepancy Evaluation.* McCutchan, Berkely, California: 1971.

Reid, P. "How Harley Beat Back the Japanese." *Fortune* , September 25, 1989.

Rosen, N. *Teamwork And The Bottom Line* . Lawrence Erlbaum, Publishers, Hillsdale, New Jersey:1989.

Sayer, R. "How I Learned to Let My Workers Lead." *Harvard Business Review* , November/December, 1990.

Shays, E.M. "Cleaning Up Waste in Decision-making." *Business Quarterly* , Winter, 1982.

Senge, P. *The Fifth Discipline* . Doubleday Currency, New York:1987 .

Silberman, M. *Active Training* . Lexington Press, San Diego: 1990.

Taylor, A. "Can GM Remodel Itself?" *Fortune* , January 13, 1992.

Taylor, D. and Ramsey, R. "Empowering Employees to 'Just Do It". *Training and Development* , May 1993.

Treece, J. "The Plants that GM will Probably Padlock". *Business Week* . December 14, 1992.

Wexley, K. & Latham, G. *Developing And Training Human Resources In Organziations* , Scott, Foresman, Glenview, ILL:1981.

Womack, J.P. et al. *The Machine That Changed The World* . MacMillan Publishing Company, New York: 1990.

Index

A

C

D

E

F

G

H

I

L

M

N

O

P

Q

R

S

T

V

W

ADDITIONAL BOOKS OF INTEREST FROM INTERNATIONAL INFORMATION ASSOCIATES, INC.

- The Rising Sun on Main Street: Working with the Japanese
  ISBN 0–945510-11-X
  Second Edition 267 pages, 1992, $12.95
  by Alison R. Lanier
  "...Recommended reading list."
  —ALA Booklist

- The Business-Education Partnership
  ISBN 0-945510-10-1 251pages, 1992, $12.95
  by Arthur G. Sharp & Elizabeth O. Sharp
  "Every educator in the country should have a copy of this book and be required to read it."
  —V. Sink, The Tribune (OK)
  "...[this team] is uniquely qualified to write their book."
  —D. Williamson, The Rocky Hill Post

- How to Select Top-Performing Mutual Fund Investments
  ISBN 0-945510-14-4 177 pages, 1993, $15.95
  by Aaron H. Coleman and David H. Coleman
  Tired of earning only 2 or 3% interest on your money? If so, mutual funds may be for you. The authors, private investment counselors show you how to make 10, 20, even 30% or more!

- Taming the Dragon Part 1: Working with Taiwan
  ISBN 0-945510-16-0, $16.95, Dec. 1993
  by Craig T. Santy

- Taming the Dragon Part 2: Working with China
  ISBN 0-945510-17-9, $16.95, Dec. 1993

- Lessons from the Best Managers
  ISBN 0-945510-07-1 123 pages, 1991 $12.95
  by Paul B. Thornton
  "...explains management principles so that they can be used and practiced."
  — Stew Leonard, President, Stew Leonard's Dairy
  "If you're a new manager, [Lessons] will save you a lot of blood, sweat and tears...even if you've been around the block...a little refresher course may just what you need to renew the faith."
  — Personal Selling Power Magazine

- Corporate Downsizing
  ISBN 0-945510-01-2 295 pages, 1989, $19.95
  by Arthur G. Sharp
  "...the human side of downsizing."
  — The Hartford Courant
  "No punches pulled here...Sharp is sharp."
  —The Bookreader Magazine

Call 1-800-645-6973 to order any book, or for a free catalog. Use your VISA or MasterCard!

If your prefer you may send a check or money order to:

International Information Associates, Inc.
P.O. Box 773
Morrisville, PA 19067-0773 USA

There is a shipping & handling charge that will be invoiced with each order. Call for current price.

Pennsylvania residents add sales tax.

Library, bookseller, and corporate discounts available.

Our books are distributed to the trade *exclusively* by:

In the United States:
Irwin Professional Publishers
a division of the Richard D. Irwin Company

In Europe:
Gazelle Book Services, Ltd. (UK)

In Singapore
Cybertech Productions, Ltd.